THE REAL ONES

THE REAL ONES

How to Disrupt the Hidden Ways
Racism Makes Us Less Authentic

MAYA RUPERT

DUTTON

DUTTON
An imprint of Penguin Random House LLC
1745 Broadway, New York, NY 10019
penguinrandomhouse.com

Copyright © 2026 by Maya Rupert

Penguin Random House values and supports copyright. Copyright fuels creativity, encourages diverse voices, promotes free speech, and creates a vibrant culture. Thank you for buying an authorized edition of this book and for complying with copyright laws by not reproducing, scanning, or distributing any part of it in any form without permission. You are supporting writers and allowing Penguin Random House to continue to publish books for every reader. Please note that no part of this book may be used or reproduced in any manner for the purpose of training artificial intelligence technologies or systems.

Some names and identifying details of certain people mentioned have been changed.

DUTTON and the D colophon are registered trademarks of Penguin Random House LLC.

BOOK DESIGN BY ALISON CNOCKAERT

LIBRARY OF CONGRESS CATALOGING-IN-PUBLICATION DATA
has been applied for.

ISBN 9780593475973 (hardcover)
ISBN 9780593475980 (ebook)

Printed in the United States of America
1st Printing

The authorized representative in the EU for product safety and compliance is Penguin Random House Ireland, Morrison Chambers, 32 Nassau Street, Dublin D02 YH68, Ireland, https://eu-contact.penguin.ie.

To Imani, who always let me be exactly who I am, even—
and especially—when I didn't know who that was

CONTENTS

1
THE OBSERVATION EFFECT
1

2
UNREAL
22

3
THE AUTHENTICITY PARADOX
42

4
CODE-SWITCHED
60

5
LISA VERSUS JESSIE
75

6
CANDACE AND ME
96

7
BLACK GIRL NEXT DOOR
114

8
GOLDILOCKS
130

9
FOR THE FUTURE
147

10
FOR THE CULTURE
169

11
JUST, ONLY, TOO
188

12
COME AS YOU AREN'T
205

Conclusion
WHO I THINK I AM
217

Acknowledgments
229

Notes
231

THE
REAL
ONES

1

THE OBSERVATION EFFECT

I decided I wanted to write this book roughly at the same moment I realized I needed to read this book.

It was 2020, and the Democratic primary race had begun with one of the most energized and racially diverse fields of candidates we've ever seen. And I was proud to be the campaign manager for Julián Castro, the former secretary of the Department of Housing and Urban Development. He was running in a field that included Kamala Harris, Cory Booker, Tulsi Gabbard, Wayne Messam, Deval Patrick, and Andrew Yang.

Our campaign turned a lot of heads and accomplished so much in shifting the national conversation and highlighting crucial issues. Still, competition was fierce; and in the end, the field was getting narrower, and the time came to suspend Julián's presidential primary campaign. It was during this awkward time, when I knew I was going to join Elizabeth Warren's campaign as a senior adviser but it wasn't public knowledge, that I was being hounded by reporters who wanted to talk about the race as if I were unaffiliated with any campaign.

This time, it was a reporter who wanted to talk on background for a piece he was considering writing about the racial dynamics

THE REAL ONES

in the election. It was an issue that had been touched on often during the cycle but hadn't been explored adequately as far as I was concerned. At this point, Cory Booker had just suspended his campaign, following closely after our campaign had done the same earlier that month. Andrew Yang remained the sole candidate of color still in the race that initially began with an impressively diverse field. There had been a number of ways that race had impacted that cycle, and I was eager to talk about the unconscious biases and double standards that candidates of color had faced that were underreported. The reporter didn't know what he wanted his piece to be yet, so we had a wide-ranging discussion. We talked about how race impacted fundraising. Media coverage. Representation in polling. Perception of electability. And one issue that had kept coming up for me during our campaign, but I had never known how to frame it: authenticity.

"What exactly do you mean?" he prompted me. "Like, the candidates of color were considered too authentic?"

"No," I explained. "I think the candidates of color struggle with being viewed as authentic."

"And why is that?"

"Well, a lot of reasons. But I think it's harder for candidates of color to feel comfortable speaking unscripted and that makes them seem stiff or fake."

"But . . . that sounds like you're saying they *are* less authentic," he noted.

I paused. It did sound like I was saying that. "I guess I don't think that should be the measure of authenticity," I tried again. "Because of how people of color are held to a higher standard, being off the cuff comes with more risk. So they're going to be more cautious with what they say and how they say it."

"But does that mean we can't expect candidates of color to be as candid and straightforward with voters?"

"No. Of course not," I assured him with more confidence than I

THE OBSERVATION EFFECT

felt. I was confusing myself. "I guess I just think we have to be thoughtful about what we're asking of candidates of color. Though . . . not to say we shouldn't expect authenticity from candidates of color . . ." I trailed off and he kindly let me. I was flailing. And that was uncommon for me.

I don't typically have a difficult time talking about race and inequality and the ways that these dynamics can play out. It's something I've gotten pretty good at over the course of my career, from my time as a lawyer and a movement leader in Washington to my time in electoral politics. While I spent most of my career in social justice movement politics, in 2020, I became only the third Black woman in history to manage a presidential campaign. This means I have had to talk about these issues a lot, both in spaces where I could fairly assume people agreed with me and also in spaces where I could fairly assume no one agreed with me. But for some reason, on this idea, I was stuck.

I was describing something I knew to be true. I watched authenticity get weaponized against our campaign and the campaigns for the other candidates of color. I was convinced that the demands around authenticity were a factor in why the candidates of color were struggling in this cycle. And yet, I had never heard this argument made—and couldn't really formulate it myself. Authenticity was good. Voters like authenticity. And yet, authenticity was creating a barrier to equality in the Democratic primary race. And I needed to articulate why.

The more I thought about it, the more I realized it wasn't unique to politics. This was a dynamic I had seen before. It was one of the reasons I ashamedly hated talking about authenticity. Every time it came up, I looked for an opportunity to change the subject. I couldn't put my finger on why, but it just felt like a trap.

Whenever I heard progressives criticize a candidate of color for not using the same rhetoric as a white candidate, I was baffled. As a progressive, I, too, wanted candidates to be unabashed in the

THE REAL ONES

views I shared with them, but I confessed I wasn't surprised that the most radical-sounding rhetoric was often harder for the candidates of color to espouse. "She obviously can't say *that*," I'd say of a position I found to be perfectly reasonable. "No one will take her seriously."

Outside of politics, I noticed the same dynamic when these issues came up. Whenever people would talk about having "courageous conversations" with colleagues, when conflict arose, I would listen earnestly. And then I would roll my eyes while silently acknowledging that I would never be able to broach a conversation around a racial microaggression in one of those discussions. Whenever people talked about finding their "authentic self," I would treat it as a thought experiment, like if someone told me to imagine an alien colony. *What authentic self?* I would wonder almost laughingly. And then the realization slowly washed over me like warm water that turned suddenly cold: *Wait. Don't we all do that? Aren't we all . . . lying?*

> *"They'll think we're all like that."*
>
> *"You have to prove them wrong."*
>
> *"You have to be twice as good to get half as much."*

Learning as an adult that other parents of color recited these mantras to their kids as often as mine did was like learning the comfort food you thought you invented is a regional variation and actually a lot of other people enjoy sugar on grits, too. Our first memories of discovering who we were, for a lot of us, are inextricably linked to being told who we needed to be. Many of us grew up hearing routine advice about the white people who were always watching us.

Now, some might think that living a life while being observed—and judged—might affect your ability to live authentically. But the

THE OBSERVATION EFFECT

most important thing to understand about authenticity is that it doesn't exist. Really. In fact, there's an experiment in quantum physics that proves it. It's not just me. *It's science.*

Physicists didn't put things in those terms, of course. Some had set out to measure the behavior of electrons—or tiny bits of matter. The electrons were capable of behaving as either particles or waves, so the scientists designed an experiment where they would shoot the electrons at a barrier with two slits and, depending on how they got through the barrier, that would determine if they were acting as particles or waves.

If they acted as particles, the electrons would go through only one of the slits in the barrier. If they acted as waves, they would go through both the slits in the barrier, and meet again on the other side. In order to measure the results, the physicists set up an instrument designed to observe the electrons. However, when they were being observed by the instrument, the electrons behaved only as particles. The experiment demonstrated a concept called "the observer effect." In other words, it showed that the act of observation changed the observable reality.

Despite my being, if it's possible, the opposite of a quantum physicist, I find myself thinking about this concept a lot. You know how you don't remember being told about Santa Claus—he was just always *there*? In the same way, kids of color have long known about another unseen but always watching presence: White People. Our parents seemed constantly aware—and made sure we were aware—of the ways that White People were watching us and interpreting the things we did. Our parents stressed that we carried a heightened sense of responsibility because of these unseen observers.

Growing up Black helps us to understand so many social limits long before we have the vocabulary to name them. We didn't have to know what double standards were, only that our parents warned us that even if our friends did something wrong and didn't get in trouble, it didn't mean we would be so lucky. We didn't have to

THE REAL ONES

know what respectability politics were, only what it felt like the first time we were tempted to prove to a white person that we were *one of the good ones.*

There are graduate students studying race and privilege who struggle with articulating the difference between *white* and *whiteness*—one word is a descriptor of individual people, the other is a construct that fuels a system of power and oppression. We may have also struggled with explaining these differences, but as Black kids, we understood. There were people who were white, and there were *White People*. And our parents weren't worried about individual people who were white—our friends, their parents, teachers; people we knew and people we loved. To be clear, our parents didn't warn us about any specific white person, which was almost worse because there was always a vague specter of fear around us. If we failed to be vigilant, to always be the best version of ourselves, any white person—even ones we trusted—could *become* White People.

And some of our most visceral memories involved those transformations.

I watched the Girl Scout troop leader turn into a White Person when she told my mother there wasn't space in the troop for me and my sister. My mother then, despite working the night shift at the post office, somehow found the time to became a troop leader just so my sister and I could be Girl Scouts. Adults who I respected would compliment me, smiling indulgently about how smart and well-behaved I was, then transform into White People, twisting their faces into something ugly while conspiratorially telling me I wasn't "like the other ones." I heard this a lot. My sister and I were often paid the excruciating compliment that we weren't like other Black people—that we "didn't count." It allowed everyone to go about their regularly scheduled racism without having to adjust any stereotypes to account for us. We were simply exempted from some of the worst assumptions about Black people.

THE OBSERVATION EFFECT

Those moments hurt me; but in a way I couldn't explain, I felt like those moments hurt them, too. Those moments would make my parents dislike them. They meant I couldn't trust them anymore. But more fundamentally, they meant that those White People were the bad guys. Now, as an adult, I'm able to make more sophisticated racial analyses, and I have no problem explaining that being racist isn't *good* for anyone. Even if it may seem to benefit some white people in some small ways, racism harms everyone. It harms us materially, as Heather McGhee brilliantly points out in her book *The Sum of Us*, where she explores the economic and political costs that everyone—including white people—bear for their racism. But it also harms us morally and on a deeper, human level. The degradation that racism brings about upon White People isn't abated by any momentary benefit it can confer. But that's a hard concept for a child to understand—or at least understand well. As a child, my mind had been blessed, or cursed, with a preternatural sense of responsibility and duty. So I decided it was my job to save my white people from becoming White People. And I could do that by being very careful about who they saw when they looked at me. Since they were always watching, I couldn't just control what they saw, I had to control who I was.

If I misbehaved in public, it would be confirming White People's worst suspicions about not just me but all Black people. Every achievement was an opportunity to disprove a stereotype that White People already had about us. I needed to be agreeable and almost debilitatingly nice, to give no one a reason to dislike me, to exclude me, to see me as different. Thanks to late '90s pop culture, I was bombarded with images of Blackness that I needed to define myself in opposition to: Black girlhood was defined by criminality and oversexualization, both things that I avoided with painful specificity as I grew older. But no image was as persistent or had as big an impact on me as the angry Black woman.

At this point in my life, I can confidently say my positivity and

THE REAL ONES

upbeat personality feel natural for me, but I'm less confident that I can call myself a *naturally* positive and upbeat person. If I had never been confronted as a child with the angry Black women caricatures, I'm not sure if I would now be so quick to forgive and so slow to show anger. I don't know if those are qualities that form—for lack of a better phrase—the *real me* or if they were ones I'd developed to help me manage how White People saw me.

Sadly, I don't think this experience is unique to me, or even especially uncommon. For many of us, childhood—the period of time when we were supposed to be learning who we were—was a time when we shaped ourselves into something that would be palatable to an external other. That dominant perspective was always watching and had the ability to rob us of something precious: whether it was safety, acceptance, stability, or success. In order to protect ourselves, we let who we were be forever changed by the fact that we were being observed.

In school, whenever we studied Black history, I developed a coping mechanism I call the Only Game, which will be very familiar or very foreign to you depending on whether you've ever been the Only in an elementary school class. The Only person of color. The Only immigrant. The Only person with a disability. If you have ever been the Only one with any identity that gets somehow studied or mentioned in a class or during a special presentation, I'm willing to bet you developed your version of the Only Game.

Whenever it was time for the class to learn about racism, and, only as an extension, Blackness, at some point during the lesson, all my white classmates would turn and stare at me. It was usually during a particularly painful moment—when someone in the movie we were watching said the N-word, or the well-meaning white teacher taught kids to collectively supply the answer "They were slaves" in an almost-singsong chorus to questions like "And why are all the Black people in chains in this picture?" In those moments, every head whipped around and dozens of eyes bore

THE OBSERVATION EFFECT

into me so deeply I was certain they would leave marks. I guess, in some way, they did. I guess that's why we're here.

I've always wondered, in those moments, what my classmates expected to see. Were they checking to see how I would react so that they would know how to react? Did they know those moments were painful and were simply acting on a natural childlike curiosity to see me get upset? Did they also feel the awkwardness and were hoping I would smile or laugh, and somehow make it better? I don't know. What I do know is that in those moments, my skin ran hot—*burning*—with embarrassment and resentment that I was being put in this situation. I felt frustration that I didn't know what to do, when clearly I had some unspoken responsibility in those moments. So, I kept my eyes trained straight ahead, careful not to meet any of the eyes in my peripheral vision. I couldn't smile, but I couldn't look upset, so I settled on looking content—an emotion, by the way, that is impossible to communicate through facial expressions—so I would purse my lips and throw in a few errant nods just to signal I was *listening* and, I don't know, *agreeing*, I guess?

But internally, those moments were hell. And to de-escalate my own emotions at those times I developed various coping mechanisms. I would search the posters at the front of the classroom to see if I could find every letter in the alphabet. I would count the syllables in whatever the teacher was saying. I would think of the two longest words I could spell and figure out how many letters they had in common.

As an adult, I recognize now that these are actually behaviors that can be common manifestations of obsessive-compulsive disorder. Many people with OCD use these types of behaviors—counting syllables and letters or reordering words—to pull themselves away from distressing or intrusive thoughts. I don't make this realization lightly. In fact, when I first made the connection after I understood more about OCD, I wondered if I actually had OCD and had just never been diagnosed. Once I felt satisfied

THE REAL ONES

that that wasn't true for me, I focused on a more sobering fact. Black people—in fact, all people of color—are underdiagnosed for OCD. There are a number of factors to blame for this fact, but I wonder how many kids of color learned to play these Only Games to send their minds somewhere else to deal with the mental and emotional strain of constant otherness. When those same techniques manifested in ways that would have been clocked as "symptoms" to a mental health care professional, the kids simply never reported the behaviors as something out of the ordinary. As a result, those kids were rewarded for their resilience in learning how to deal with the impacts of racism by not getting the mental health support they needed.

I never knew them as compulsions, only as games—my Only Games. And they worked. They distracted my mind for long enough until the hot sensation in my skin subsided, the looks mostly dropped, and I could be less concerned with what I was doing with my face. And that's how I knew the game was over. I had won when everyone else felt comfortable again. It was one of the most enduring lessons I learned in those years—how to, in the face of my extraordinary discomfort, make white people feel comfortable.

If observation can transform our reality, what happens to the kids who are told that people are always watching them to confirm or dismantle stereotypes? What happens to the kids who were stared at uncomfortably by their classmates whenever certain topics came up in class? Did that observation—and the proliferation of stares that lasted the rest of our lives—tell us that while we are capable of behaving as particles or as waves, as *this* or *that*, that we must only behave as one? And if so, is there a version of us that exists that is unconscious of the way a dominant culture views us? Or is *who we are* a product of our own little observation effects?

I'm not talking about code-switching. That's easier, more explainable. Code-switching is how people of color learn to survive a white gaze when we know our authentic self wouldn't be fully accepted. We shave off parts of ourselves depending on who our audience is, and save the rest of ourselves—the fuller, less cautious, more colorful versions—for when we're among folk. To code-switch, it is presupposed that there's an identifiable *real me*, and a *me that's more palatable to white audiences*. What I'm talking about is harder. It's whether I ever developed a real me. If the question "Who am I?" was always being posed alongside the edicts of "who I had to be," I could never know who I would have become without that threat of being othered.

This paradox is too familiar to be profound. I'm not alone in experiencing this; and the more I've asked about this experience out loud, the more people I've met whose experience is both nothing like mine and crushingly identical. I've spoken to friends with disabilities who can't tell if their almost painful ability to brightside any situation is natural positivity or just an extension of the need to be an inspiring—and therefore palatable—disabled person. Women recall being called "bossy" and pretending they couldn't beat the boys at kickball or didn't have the right answers, and they now wonder if their people-pleasing tendencies are natural or were developed in order to be accepted as nice little girls. I hear it from my queer friends whose dark senses of humor may be innate but may be the defense mechanism they cultivated because being in on the joke kept them safe.

Sometimes I wonder if this matters. As adults, aren't we all a collection of our various experiences cobbled together to make us whole? Does it matter if some of us are more conscious of the reasons behind certain pieces of our personality? Being able to tell you why I became a certain kind of person doesn't undermine the fact that I did, in fact, become that person. And maybe this wouldn't matter if we weren't bombarded with relentlessly positive messages about the need to uncover and embody our authentic selves.

Authenticity is supposed to free us, but for some of us, it stands in the way of that freedom. There's tension between a desire to be

THE REAL ONES

authentic and the undeniable reality that, as a Black woman, I have had to contort myself in an effort to be more socially acceptable. This tension puts authenticity in a bind: It must either expose my genuine experience as a Black woman as counterfeit or it must stretch to make room for the ways I've consciously conformed—something that seems to contradict its very definition. This tension is irreconcilable. And unless we name it, our efforts toward antiracism, inclusion, and fostering greater belonging will always fall short, as they will always be missing an essential ingredient. In many ways, authenticity operates as a barrier to inclusion and equality. It sets a bar that some of us were never allowed to reach. And because the distortion happens so early, our later efforts at dismantling structural racism come too late. By the time antiracist interventions could help address the problem, the damage has already been done. And because of that, the problem has become so invisible that it's hard to even name, which makes it impossible to address. The goal of this book is to name it. One of the unintended costs of authenticity is true inclusion and equality. In addition to everything else, racism forces us into a narrow lane of acceptable authenticity. In this way, "authenticity" takes from us our ability to be ourselves.

This is even more true as authenticity becomes a currency in the world. In recent years, as the social internet has transformed all of us into brands, the ability to tell a cohesive and authentic story about ourselves, our lives, and our experiences is necessary for professional and social settings. There is a troubling dissonance between the toxic positivity around the promotion of authenticity and the struggle many marginalized people feel around whether we were even allowed to have an authentic self to begin with.

It's not enough to be a particle if you should have been a wave! they say. But even as they say this, they never stop watching us. So we stay particles.

When we talk about performative authenticity, it's almost al-

THE OBSERVATION EFFECT

ways in conversations about social media, and the judgment around it is subsumed by its self-contradictory name. If authenticity is performative, it's not authentic. If the thing being performed is real, it's not really a performance; it's an illustration. Thus, performative authenticity can only be lobbed as an accusation. It's an effort to knowingly pass off as real something that is undeniably fake.

But what if there were a more excusable form of performative authenticity? Way before Instagram, many of us learned to curate our identity, and we didn't just do it for the cameras. Or rather, we did, but the cameras were always on.

It's understood that it's dangerous to curate and selectively present only certain versions of ourselves for online consumption. The implication being that this type of curation—showing only what we want the camera to see and leaving the messiness, the flaws, the *authenticity* off-screen—is a lie. And the courageous thing to do is pan the camera out and show everything else. Imagine not just the finished glamour shot but the coffee cup–strewn table, the piles of unfinished laundry, the bright lights set up to make your skin glow.

But what if you were assumed to be messy since before you could really remember? Your coffee table wouldn't be cluttered; your laundry would be done and folded. All of your lights would be ring lights, your home bathed in glowing, flattering hues.

In each of these scenarios, the motivation is the same: wanting to present yourself in the best light. But in one, you're consciously curating a shot, whereas in the other, you are curating a *life*.

You're not self-consciously setting up the moment—you're just always posing.

This is more than simply a thought experiment. One of the more frustrating examples I have seen of toxic positivity around authenticity is watching people shame women on social media for posting flattering selfies, wearing makeup, using filters,

THE REAL ONES

or otherwise managing their online images. As if we don't know that women are subjected to relentless criticism and harassment online for the way they look. So now, in order to justifiably take a picture of herself and post it, a woman has to offer an apology: "Felt cute, might delete later."

This is especially hard to watch when the people being shamed don't have the privilege of meeting a conventional standard of beauty. As we began to demand authenticity, it seems particularly cruel that this is demanded of those whose authentic selves have been marginalized. Women of color, fat women, women with disabilities, gender nonconforming people, and transgender women are met with relentless reminders that for any number of reasons, they do not meet the definition of what American culture has deemed "beautiful." These women are then required to twist themselves into a reductive standard that was created without our expansive and diverse beauty in mind.

As our collective fascination with authenticity grew, marginalized women who use tools to craft themselves toward dominant beauty standards have gotten the most criticism. Women who use things like plastic surgery, fake eyelashes and nails, online filters, weaves, and GLP-1 medications for weight loss are then scolded for contributing to unrealistic beauty standards. These critics often miss the point entirely. When authenticity can be used as a cudgel to deny someone access to something that makes them feel more comfortable in their skin, it seems we've lost the plot. For example, how does calling a full glam makeup look or plastic surgery "inauthentic" sound to a trans woman who uses them as tools to look *more* like her authentic self?

Even after gaining the privileges of celebrity, marginalized people can't seem to escape the trap of authenticity. Yes, it's inspiring when celebrities use their positions to push back against certain elements of the beauty industry in the name of being real. But we shouldn't ignore how differently these efforts are received based on

THE OBSERVATION EFFECT

who's doing the pushing. Often straight, white, thin celebrities—people with relatively little to lose by stepping outside conventional beauty norms—can resist those norms and be praised for their authenticity. They're celebrated for being brave, raw, and refreshing. Yet celebrities of color who years ago were told they were "too ethnic," who later have been styled and shaped into superstars, now face critiques that they lack authenticity. I am old enough to remember when Beyoncé was criticized for her curves and fat-shamed for her muscular thighs that somehow didn't fit the trendy waif aesthetic of the time. I'm old enough to remember her getting laughed at in interviews for sounding "country" and "ghetto." So now that she is BEYONCÉ, I understand people think it's fair game to demand that she show us her natural hair (which she did and *still* got criticism), comment on her being too skinny, complain that she never gives interviews, and accuse her of trying to "look white" when she has blond hair. But this all seems a little too "damned if she does, damned if she doesn't." She gave us authenticity and got scrutiny in return.

I know it may seem like I'm about to argue an uncomfortable case in favor of inauthenticity. But that's never been my aim. Authenticity is a perfectly laudable goal. It's a word that encompasses its desirability in its name. Like *body positivity*. Or *self-care*. It's a buzzword that dares you to defy it—who wouldn't want something that on its face is . . . good?

Authenticity, body positivity, and self-care are good ideas that poetically fall victim to their own seeming universality. Body positivity is a lovely framework that does nothing for people who face discrimination and violence because they're fat. No amount of sparkly thinking or "feeling beautiful at any size" combats medical discrimination based on weight, an inability to find clothes that fit at most department stores, or the gap in wages that fat people experience.

"Self-care" began as a necessary intervention to hustle culture

THE REAL ONES

in a capitalist society. But the language around it quickly became about luxury instead of dignity. It became synonymous with consumerism that was only available to people with money and the ability to take time off to pamper themselves in increasingly inaccessible ways. It stopped being a critique of capitalism and became a form of it.

The point is that these ideas lost their power when they went from specific observations to generic platitudes. These ideas aren't one-size-fits-all. And the truth is that authenticity isn't for all of us.

I don't want to demonize authenticity. But I want people to think deeper about what they're asking for when we tell people to be authentic. We need to ask if it really is a goal equally available to all of us. I argue it is not. So we need to acknowledge that asking for authenticity is a bigger request—and is more costly—for people of color, and more broadly, people with any marginalized identities. People need to recognize that when someone isn't showing up authentically, many times it's because they learned that it's dangerous to do so. And if someone wants to change that, they need to focus on making society safer—not making us braver.

The first time I remember someone calling me the N-word, I was nine years old. When the boy on the playground said the word at recess, my skin burned hot.

"You can't call me that," I'd murmured angrily, repeating what my dad told me about that word and what it meant. I hoped it would carry the same power for him as it did for me when my dad had told me "No one can call you that," like this advice had been a protection spell.

"But you are one," the boy had insisted. I fumed and stalked over to the teacher on duty at recess. Close to tears, I recounted what he had said.

I think the teacher hoped her firm advice was comforting, but when she shook her head at me and warned me in a stern voice, her words felt like an admonishment: "Don't you dare cry. Don't get

THE OBSERVATION EFFECT

upset. He doesn't know what that word means, so if you start crying, it'll just make it that much worse."

As soon as I got into my mother's car, I started to cry, and it was all I could do to talk her out of storming back into the office. Instead, she agreed to go home and handle it over the phone. Later that evening, I watched my parents on the phone with various combinations of the boy's parents, the teacher, and my school principal. I watched them giving each other *that look*, rolling their eyes, speaking with venom barely disguised as politeness. And I knew that that teacher and that boy's parents had turned into White People.

"Her mother and I don't expect this kind of thing to go unanswered," my dad said as he closed his call with my school principal later that night. "She's a good kid." It was one of those things that was the exact right thing for him to say and the exact wrong thing for me to hear. Of course, it made sense to appeal to the principal's understanding that a well-behaved child should get the benefit of the doubt. But when I heard that, my young mind heard it as a confirmation that I *was* always being watched and that my behavior affected whether I would be expected to endure racism. It was the wrong lesson for me to learn: If I was a "good kid," it could save me from racism.

Particle or wave? Always a particle. People are watching. Be a particle.

Authenticity is who we are when we aren't concerned about who we are supposed to be. But there was never a moment I can honestly remember when "who I was supposed to be" existed separately from who I was. In that way, authenticity has always struck me as a bit of a paradox, a brain teaser that I alone was trying to solve. How do you separate two things that only exist in relation to each other? How can you pretend that they are independent traits, when one necessarily leads to the other?

Black girls navigate a world not made for us, so how could any

THE REAL ONES

of us define who we are without also being shaped by the social pressures around us? Any conversation around authenticity has to recognize how social pressures impact my sense of self. If someone asked me to imagine a "me" without that social necessity, they are ignoring the stark realities faced by anyone growing up as a person of color.

I think my experience was exacerbated because in addition to growing up in a predominantly white community, I went to schools and came of age professionally in predominantly white spaces. I imagine there are people of color who grew up in more diverse communities who, while still being impacted by the observation effect in a society where the white gaze is ever present, have a very different relationship to it. Likewise, I imagine there are a number of people with underrepresented identities who, for a number of reasons, can describe a different experience with developing their own sense of self and relationship to authenticity. With any of this, your mileage may vary. Which is exactly why I think it's so important to dismantle the deceptively simple idea that authenticity works the same way for all of us.

Authenticity is a privilege. And while I appreciate the movement that tells us it shouldn't be, I'm not speaking normatively; I'm speaking factually. While we all fight to make authenticity a right and not a luxury, we can't ignore the fact that currently it still is a luxury accessible to a select few. And historically, it always has been. Skipping that recognition and uncritically demanding authenticity is not offering freedom—it's simply demanding a different performance. One that still harms people of color. And still reinforces racism. There have been a considerable number of efforts to address racial inequality and bias over the years, and these efforts have sparked an intense amount of backlash from opponents. However, that isn't because these efforts have been resoundingly successful. In fact, despite a number of smart and thoughtful people who are genuinely invested in the issues of privilege and

THE OBSERVATION EFFECT

oppression spending considerable time on these issues, despite a number of good faith efforts in a number of different places and industries, we are still plagued by issues of systemic racism and inequality that belie our efforts toward addressing them. Obviously, structural inequality has no panacea. But this level of effort without sustained and consistent impact points to something being missing.

What we have been missing is how the pressures around authenticity operate as invisible but insidious barriers to equality. Without understanding how authenticity is simultaneously demanded of and stolen from people of color, we will never have real inclusion. Because inclusion that ignores the way marginalization shapes people is not true inclusion.

I grew up in California—and, well, Black—so unsurprisingly winter sports have never played a big role in my life. I eschew the Winter Olympics, and never saw much value in a ski trip beyond hanging around the lodge and sipping a spiked hot chocolate. But in spite of my unblemished record of having never skied in my life, I think an example about skiing is useful here.

When I imagine people skiing, I think of what I always assumed was the typical scene: a ski lift carrying people and their skis up a mountain for them to ski down. However, some people forgo the ski lift in favor of "skinning," or alpine touring—essentially hiking up the mountain to ski down it. It's a way to save money on an expensive ski lift ticket and skip the lines; and apparently, some people find it enjoyable. I don't get it. I'm still back in the lodge.

Skinning requires different equipment than regular alpine skiing—the skier will either wear skis designed to move up the mountain, which will be lighter and have less support, or will attach skins to their regular skis, which will have to be removed and carried down, adding weight to the entire setup. As a result, going downhill, the skinner will usually not perform as well as the skiers who took the ski lift up and are using regular alpine skis.

THE REAL ONES

Imagine trying to address this difference in performance. You would look at the skinners' equipment and note that it is not optimized for downhill skiing. But changing their equipment isn't an option because they would never have gotten up the hill without it. Any efforts that take place once the skinners are already up the hill are too late. The equipment they have is the only reason they got up the hill, but it's also the reason they won't perform as well going down.

Attempting to address inequality without acknowledging and dismantling the pressures created by authenticity is like trying to address the disparities in downhill skiing between the skiers and the skinners without understanding the reason behind it. When what is asked of us coming up the hill is different, it will naturally impact how we perform on the way down.

As I will explore in this book, there is an irony that the very same systems that caused many of us to trade in our authenticity in the first place are now the ones that demand a fabricated version of our authenticity. The entertainment world that erased us now clamors for our stories, our style, our slang. The corporate jobs that told us we just didn't fit with the culture shifted and asked us to lend diversity numbers and credibility to their ranks (at least before these efforts to increase diversity came under attack from President Trump). The politics that never seemed to speak to us or our issues now search for us to run their campaigns and to run for office—to energize their bases, to appeal to a more diverse electorate, to prove they mean what they say.

And every step of the way, the gatekeepers tell us the same thing: We want your authenticity. Only they don't. They want their expectation of what our authenticity might look like, if we had been allowed to fully realize it. But we weren't, and a crude fetishization of our authenticity won't get us any closer to realizing it. Because if observation changes our objective reality, those of us

THE OBSERVATION EFFECT

who learned that someone is always watching were changed at a fundamental level.

I think the ability to discover and embrace our authentic selves is incredibly important and incredibly powerful. Further, if we want to truly target and address systemic racism, we need to allow authenticity. However, I don't think that the only path toward authenticity is to try to discover who we were before all the external forces seeped in. That ignores too much for me. That would be to deny formative experiences that shaped me, and it's why the conversation around authenticity has never quite seemed to fit. This book is not the case against authenticity but rather an argument for a reimagined authenticity that doesn't privilege a version of ourselves that is divorced from all the observation we have been subjected to our whole lives.

I'm less interested in understanding if I would have been someone different had the stares, the hyperawareness, the need to protect white people from becoming White People never gotten to me. I'm more interested in what all those experiences—which are mine and have shaped me *authentically*—mean for me now. I want a conversation about authenticity that doesn't require me to ignore so much that has made me *me*. I want to solve the authenticity paradox once and for all. For all of us.

2

UNREAL

Are you calling me a racist?

That used to be the phrase I most dreaded hearing. It has since been replaced by *Just to play devil's advocate*, or *Actually, my buddy and I just started a podcast about dating.*

But there was a time when the worst thing someone would say to me was that I had made *that* accusation of them.

And so, I trained myself to hear those words—*are you calling me a racist?*—as a deafening alarm signaling that I needed to walk back the implication and reassure the white person in front of me that I meant no harm in acknowledging the way they had just harmed me. And the worst part was how good I was at it.

I was thirty minutes late for a happy hour with some friends. When I walked in, an acquaintance, a white woman who I had only met a handful of times, adopted an absolutely mortifying blaccent.

"Mmm, where you been, girl? You had to get yo hair did?" She whipped her neck back and forth in an imitation of a Black woman I assume she remembered vaguely from a '90s movie, who bore no resemblance to me, especially the code-switched version—the only one she had ever met.

I looked at her curiously. "Was that supposed to be an impression of me?" I asked with an uncertain laugh. "Well, it was . . . uncanny."

"It's a *joke*," she huffed. "*God!* You can tease me about literally anything—I don't get why we can't joke about stuff like that!"

"But—I don't sound like that? So you're not actually teasing *me*, you're teasing . . . other Black women?"

I posed it as a question. It *was* a question. I wasn't stating offense, I was asking permission to be offended. It wasn't granted. She rolled her eyes and shrugged, and I smiled indulgently at the table to let everyone know their silence was more than enough support and they didn't need to feel troubled to offer any more, a pressure that, in truth, they were clearly in no danger of feeling. I ordered a drink, and everyone moved on.

Later, after a couple of drinks, she pulled me aside for an apology.

Her eyes immediately welled with tears. "I was just joking earlier but you, like, looked *offended*."

I paused. "No, it's fine," I reasoned.

"Okay, but you looked *really* offended. Like—like you thought I was being racist or something."

Yes, I thought.

"No," I said.

We looked at each other in silence.

The silence started to eat at me. Yes, it was uncomfortable, but that wasn't all that was bothering me now. *I* was already uncomfortable. *I* had been uncomfortable since she'd made the comment. The silence started to eat at me because I knew it was uncomfortable *for her*.

She looked expectant, and I realized I needed to give her what she had pulled me aside for. An apology.

"I'm sorry, I really wasn't," I offered. "And talking about race in a big group of people is awkward. I totally get why you shut down. And honestly, the fact that you're even addressing it with me, when

THE REAL ONES

it would have been so easy to just let it go, is exactly *why* I know you didn't mean anything by it." I comforted her.

She picked her drink back up and took a sip. "Ugh! You are so good at this!" She wiped her eyes dramatically. "I feel like, I wish everyone had a version of you to talk through race issues. It's like your superpower!"

It's a bird. It's a plane. No. It's bullshit.

Several years ago, Gillian Flynn popularized the concept of the Cool Girl in her novel *Gone Girl*, where she explained the unrealistic expectations that women were supposed to meet in order to be desirable to men—they should love watching sports, inhale junk food, love casual sex and abhor commitment, and above all else they must consistently conform to conventional standards of beauty. And she was supposed to be all of this authentically. That it's "the real you" is the central conceit of the Cool Girl.

This passage resonated with so many women because it gave startling clarity to something many of us had struggled to name. The Cool Girl was such a specific trope, but she was supposed to be effortless in a way that belied that specificity. A Cool Girl couldn't just study up on NFL standings, she had to just know them. She couldn't just be a good sport and watch the Vin Diesel movie—she had to *love* it. It was not just enough to perform; we were supposed to *embody* her and perform without seeming to perform.

For many people of color, that constant pressure felt familiar, and it was interesting watching so many white women have this aha moment around how they had been made to be Cool Girls but not connect this to the ways that they, too, have demanded similar performances.

Black girls have our own version of the Cool Girl. The Cool Black Girl. I first introduced the concept of the Cool Black Girl in a piece I wrote for *Salon*. As I explained then, the Cool Black Girl is urban but not hood. She's down enough to use slang her white friends will want to poach, but won't embarrass them by sounding too

UNREAL

Black. She's willing to date white men but is unbothered when they don't want to date her. She's unflinchingly patient and endlessly supportive of the white women around her. But the core trait of the Cool Black Girl was still apparent authenticity. This performance hinged on the ability to make white people feel like all of this labor was without effort and not anything they needed to feel guilty about. Because above all else, a Cool Black Girl never—ever—makes a white person feel uncomfortable about race.

I know because I used to be the Coolest Black Girl.

She was my product of the observation effect. I don't remember exactly when I developed my Cool Black Girl alter ego. I know she was cobbled together over years of experimenting between religiously never talking about race, self-consciously allowing myself to talk about it, and then realizing my talent for comforting insecure white people through their relationships with race. Somewhere I let her become my identity, my superpower, but also my archvillain. And like any respectable villain, she is impossible to get rid of, and I am sometimes forced to admit that I need her.

I would love to roll my eyes at the happy hour story and the countless other similar examples. Times when I could have attempted an uncomfortable and valuable conversation about race among friends, but in order to keep the relationship, I immediately comforted the white person away from having it. But I can't so easily dismiss those moments as mistakes, because honestly, in those situations, the Cool Black Girl saved me.

Perhaps the hardest thing to admit about the Cool Black Girl is how seductive she is. When I first introduced her in the *Salon* essay, I told a misleadingly linear story about how I became the Cool Black Girl and then had a moment of clarity. After I understood who and what she was, I let her go and was happier. And that's maybe not *untrue* but certainly incomplete. I did have the moment of clarity—I had multiple moments—but I didn't let her go, not completely. I did something a little harder: I recognized why I had relied on her, I chose not to rely on her so heavily, *and* I also admitted to myself that there are times she is better suited for a moment. She has undeniably helped me to be successful.

I came of age professionally as the ideas that formed books like *Lean In* and *#GirlBoss* were being popularized. I was in my late twenties and early thirties during the time people were trying to gaslight young women into thinking gender discrimination and unconscious bias in workplaces could be combated by spunk, pluck, and a girl power mindset. According to this theory, all we had to do was refuse to play into the double standards and they would go away. We were told to negotiate like men, demand our place at the table, and confidently take credit for our work.

In reality, when we held back during salary negotiations, it wasn't out of fear of an openly sexist response. We didn't imagine that if we pushed back, a cartoonish old man would sputter angrily in response, "But—I wouldn't pay you that much—*you're a woman!*" Rather, we feared that we'd be labeled what you could not be in a corporate workplace: a "Problem." Someone that the partners whispered about because they complained too much. Someone who was too moneygrubbing, which was a fascinating thing to be accused of. At our jobs. Where we worked. *For money.* But this was the mid-2000s and we were expected to pretend that we weren't just doing these jobs for the paychecks but rather because we felt genuinely passionate about document review and memo writing.

The hint that you were a Problem never came directly. It was in innocuous-sounding questions being asked. Partners wondered aloud about whether you were "in over your head," whether you "fit in" whether you were "happy here." These were the common euphemisms and, if you squinted, they sounded like kindnesses. But it was concern trolling—the friendly-sounding nature of the questions barely masking that they weren't questions at all. They were accusations.

And in my time in workplace settings, I had also been privy to enough conversations to know that those demands we were encouraged to confidently make often came at a social and professional cost, especially for women with identities that made people think they were already too entitled. As a young, Black woman attorney at a large corporate law firm, I felt some of my colleagues probably assumed that I had gotten into a top law school and into my current position only through affirmative action. In fact, some of them said as much to me about other Black attorneys at rival firms who outranked me. I felt I couldn't complain about anything at work because this would be seen as a lack of gratitude for what I had been *given*. I was allotted a smaller margin of error before I'd become a Problem. This created a double bind for me that would become routine throughout my career. The *Lean In* path to success might work for white women—though I doubted it—but that wouldn't work for me. Black women who are demanding don't get called feminists; we get called aggressive. When Black women take credit for our work, we get told we're not team players. And it costs us.

I remember the advice I received from a white woman partner when I was a junior associate. She insisted to me—and my other white women colleagues on this project—that we needed to smile less. We were coming across as too unserious, not tough enough. I remember trying to clumsily explain to her things were different for me—I *needed* to smile as a Black woman so people wouldn't think I was angry.

"No," she told me shortly. "*All* women have to deal with this. If you smile too much, people won't take you seriously." I didn't want to offend her, so I went out of my way to avoid smiling and look *serious* that day. At the end of the day, a different partner—a white man—swung by my office to ask if I was okay because he had heard from a few people that I was in a bad mood. He said it conspiratorially, a kindness, letting me know that the fact that it was being observed could be a Problem for me. When I met with my team the next day, I wanted to scream, "I told you so! It *is* different

THE REAL ONES

for me! I should have smiled!" But what kind of feminist would that make me?

Well, a Black one. But I didn't say that. I was Cooler than that.

So, what should you do when anti-Black bias makes the white feminist approach untenable? I didn't know. But the Cool Black Girl always seemed to. I lied. I saved the white women from the uncomfortable truth that their own little conscientious objection to patriarchy didn't play out for me the same way. I nodded along with everyone else when someone said it was "freeing" to not have to worry about appearing pleasant while making an argument. And I saved the white man asking me if I was okay from any discomfort by telling him I'd had a headache. I let him wince sympathetically and nod understandingly, both of us relieved I wasn't going to be a Problem.

As a Black woman, I know that my professional title does not mean I'll receive the same respect and deference a white man would receive in the same role. As a result, I learned to seek permission from those I am supposed to lead, and I have had enough experience to know that that expectation is not just in my head. Once, after speaking with a white woman *who worked for me* about how a disrespectful comment she had made about me had gotten back to me, she offered what I think was a genuine attempt at contrition: "I do honestly consider you to be, like . . . my boss." She said it like it was a kindness. I believe I even said "thank you."

The Cool Black Girl is the reason I haven't been slaughtered by moments like this. She is skilled at asking permission from a team she leads to actually lead them, and pretending not to have read the email that was accidentally forwarded her way questioning her right to be there. She has the chameleonlike ability to both apologize to one partner for not smiling and to pretend to another that the whole experiment was a feminist victory. The Cool Black Girl is terrific at validating white tears while biting back her own. She knows how to handle things when the conversation subtly changes from how a microaggression has hurt her to how an *acknowledgment* of that microaggression has hurt a white woman. She is a big part of the reason that I have survived, and even thrived, in professional spaces. I owe a lot of my success to the Cool Black Girl.

Writing this feels like admitting something salacious. Because now, we're being told to bring our whole selves to work. Now that authenticity has become such a ubiquitous and unquestioned goal, the Cool Black Girl's conscious camouflage—her ability to hide, to obscure, to *lie*—feels like the ultimate betrayal. I'm not supposed to rely on her anymore. I'm supposed to loathe that performance and clamor for the spaces where I can be unapologetically and authentically myself. And this is especially the case for Black women. As a Black woman, my authenticity is currently prized. That *currently* deserves time and a half for the work it's doing in that sentence.

We live in a moment where the impact that Black people and especially Black women have had on culture, politics, marketability, fashion, music, and style is being recognized—and monetized. People trust Black women to save the democracy that still constantly fails us. Young Black women and queer folks choreograph viral dances for TikTok that make white influencers famous and determine the *Billboard* status of popular songs. For years, corporations tried to decode Black Twitter to use its power to drive sales and trends. Designers and stylists copy Black women's style so that magazines can feature their creations on white models.

At the core of all of this is some dangerous mythmaking around Black women and authenticity. Now there's a coveted form of Black womanhood that is being elevated from which all these things flow, a paradigm of Black womanhood and aesthetic that is an unlimited fount of style, culture, political awareness, and strength: the Authentic Black Queen.

The Authentic Black Queen is a fully realized, self-actualized paradigm of Black realness. Her style is effortlessly chic: trendsetting, bold, and fearless. She wears outfits that will have white women calling her "brave" before buying a version of it themselves a year later when our style is mass-produced. She wears her hair natural and styled with products that will prompt curly-haired white women to buy them en masse and proudly display them to up their street cred. She has an encyclopedic knowledge of all things Black and an impeccable familiarity with all Black cultural touchstones regardless of regional or generational difference. Her politics are unimpeachable, her racial justice lens unassailable. She can detect racism with a sixth sense: If something is problematic, she will clock it and dispense with the offender with an evisceration that will prompt as many wig-snatching memes as have ever been tweeted. When she speaks, it's a testimony, and white people close their eyes and snap their fingers as she takes them to church with her Black slang and affect that somehow never make anyone whisper about whether she sounds unprofessional. When she speaks, she makes white people understand the problem. When she speaks *to them*, she lets them know that they aren't part of that problem. She is Black perfection. And much like the Cool Black Girl, she isn't real. She's the fabricated facsimile of authenticity that whiteness now demands of me after robbing me of an ability to actually develop authentically.

"You really are our Wonder Woman," a white movement colleague told me reverently, and even though I cringed inwardly, I smiled.

I suppose this was my own fault. In the run-up to the 2017 *Wonder Woman* movie, I wrote a piece about how I always imagined Wonder Woman as a Black woman and how she embodies many struggles that seem to reflect the experience of Black girls and women in this country. I should have anticipated the ensuing comparisons: awkward compliments that I felt guilty accepting and even more guilty rejecting.

At the time, I was working in the reproductive rights movement and navigating its intensely complicated racial politics. The reproductive rights movement has historically been run by and centered the needs of straight, cisgender white women, and it showed. The movement has a notoriously racist history and that has seeped into its present. Planned Parenthood founder Margaret Sanger was a noted eugenicist who argued in favor of abortion in part as a way of stopping certain "unfit" people from having children. The resources and energy in the movement have historically gone to the issues most pressing for rich white women. For a long time, *abortion rights* meant legal access to abortion, but it didn't touch on economic or geographic access or other barriers that poor women and women of color faced. It didn't address the discrimination transgender and gender nonconforming people face seeking access. Issues like surrogacy were viewed through the lens of the families who paid for a surrogate's assistance, rather than the lens of the surrogate who was vulnerable to economic exploitation. Even the framing—*choice*—indicated that as long as the government stays out of the issue, everyone is free to choose.

Obviously, this isn't the experience of most people in this country, and we have seen that illustrated in the years since we lost *Roe v. Wade*. For women with options—the ability to travel freely and at a moment's notice, the means to pay for health care and emergency care when needed, the ability to take time off from work when needed—the realities of the loss of the constitutional right to an abortion can be mitigated. However, for those who are living in states with abortion bans without access to these resources, we have already seen the worst happen.

In 2024, after Georgia passed a draconian six-week abortion ban, Amber Thurman, a young Black woman, was admitted to the hospital after a rare complication arose with her abortion. She had taken medication to terminate a pregnancy, but she had not expelled all of the fetal tissue from her body. The standard of care for this complication is a procedure to remove the tissue—an abortion. But because of confusion at the hospital about whether conducting such an abortion would be legal, she languished in a hospital bed for twenty hours. When doctors finally operated, it was too late. She died of septic shock.

She was a twenty-eight-year-old medical assistant and a mother of a six-year-old son.

This gutting example is sadly not a unique story. Without a constitutional right to abortion, we don't even have a choice movement. We have money or luck.

When Black women founded the reproductive justice movement in 1994, it was to address these types of shortcomings within the reproductive rights movement; and over the years, the reproductive rights movement has come to better understand these critiques.

In policy spaces, some liberal, well-meaning white women, who in roughly equal measure want to do the right thing and are desperately afraid of being called racist, have managed to both over- and underreact to these critiques. While no real power shifting has happened—the majority of resources and funding still goes to historically white-led organizations—this has resulted in a weird microcosm where my identity as a Black woman seemed to give me comically outsized credibility.

One day, I was convening with several organizations from across the movement. I was being asked about a colleague at another organization whose clumsy tweet suggested that the reproductive rights movement could only be allies in racial justice fights, meaning she wasn't thinking about the many people of color already in both the reproductive rights and racial justice movements. Three white women from different organizations came to me in disbelief that this other woman could be "*so* insensitive!"

"It's ridiculous," one fumed. "White women—we are *so* racist!" They looked at me expectantly while I hedged. I knew the woman we were talking about, and I liked her. More than that, I liked the way she had handled the situation. She heard the criticism, apologized, and took the tweet down. No defending what she *really* meant or insisting people had misunderstood. It was exactly the way to handle a misstep like this; and without more evidence that she'd actually meant to be nefarious, I was fine to let this go.

Also, and I cannot stress this enough, this was five years before we would ultimately lose *Roe v. Wade*, the writing was on the wall, and Donald Trump was president. *We had much more important things to talk about.* Besides, I more than suspected that some of the unwillingness to let this die out was other white women being self-congratulatory and relieved over not having been caught making a similar mistake themselves.

"Were you livid?" one asked me with wide eyes.

No, I thought.

"Yes," I said.

Then with a sigh I continued. "This is exactly the problem—white women think of repro as *their* civil rights movement. They fetishize marginalized identities so much that they ignore that they aren't in this movement alone. Reproductive justice *is* racial justice."

The speech wasn't my style, but that didn't matter. They didn't want to hear from me, they wanted to hear from the Authentic Black Queen. The women in front of me nodded so hard I thought they might tip over. Or maybe I was about to tip over—the combination of roles I was playing for them had made my head spin. By agreeing with how racist the tweet was, I was validating their racial justice radar. By making them my confidants, I was absolving them of being the type of white women we were discussing. And I was providing whatever satisfaction white people derive from this kind of performative racial smackdown. I had rendered my ruling and the crowd felt pacified. The Queen had spoken.

THE REAL ONES

And after my little takedown, I was given a whole new superpower. "Thank you so much for your labor on this stuff. You really are our Wonder Woman."

Sigh.

The Authentic Black Queen has the same job as the Cool Black Girl, only they serve different cultural moments depending on whether white people need to be made to think racism isn't a thing or that racism is a thing, just not *their* thing. With the Authentic Black Queen, instead of being celebrated, Black women's supposed authenticity is being fetishized, and the performance we're invited to engage in to showcase this authenticity is no more real than our Cool Black Girls. And there are no conveniently placed telephone booths for us to transform into one or the other—we have to be ready to be both. *Always.*

The Authentic Black Queen is less about equipping Black women with the freedom to describe our own reality and more about presenting a specific—and commodifiable—version of what that reality is. There is a cruel irony to the fact that the forced colorblindness of the 1980s and 1990s gave way to today's demand for Black women to be "unapologetic." We are told to perform authenticity on demand even though we have been vilified and punished for appearing as ourselves at other times. Further, that authenticity itself is judged and required to be something that feels familiar to a broader—and whiter—audience. So even when our authenticity is supposedly prized, that authenticity isn't meant to serve *us*.

This dynamic is further complicated by the fact that I wasn't just performing for a white gaze. Within communities of color, authenticity policing happens and furthers the need for these performances. In this example, in addition to the expectation of the white women who approached me, I was also conforming to an expectation from other women of color. The Authentic Black Queen is beloved by some women of color who cynically took advantage of the outsized credibility that our voices received in these movement spaces simply because of the racist history of the movement. This dynamic created an added pressure for me to perform accordingly or risk looking like I'm refusing to show solidarity among women of color.

This raises another issue that is difficult to discuss, but sometimes the most stringent policing of our authenticity happens from within our own communities. One of the unfortunate impacts of having proscribed certain experiences that we are allowed to authentically claim is that we can start buying into the constraints and policing them for one another. The futility of this is revealed by just how often, in safe spaces, we all confess to these imagined sins and are met with others in our community admitting the same or similar things. I have bonded with so many Black people over these imagined border crossings: certain "white songs" we love, certain Black movies we have never seen, references or slang we don't get. And as we voluntarily give up our Black cards to one another, only to have them returned in acceptance, I'm reminded that apparently a quintessential Black experience is having any number of things that you think would make someone else question your Blackness. Even so, these performances continue to be demanded of us.

The people clamoring for me to be the Queen are also asking me to pretend that my authenticity would have always been met with the same acceptance it is being met with now. Basically, it requires me to admit that my past moments of Cool Black Girl–ness were simply me not having the courage to be who I really am. All this pretending ignores the very real systems that force us to perform at all and reduces the entire problem to our just needing to find our voices. Further, the one-dimensionality of the Authentic Black Queen makes it seem like nuance is a betrayal, and it doesn't allow me to account for my entire self any more than the Cool Black Girl does.

When I was in college, I took a class and learned about a theory where the morality of an action is determined by the outcome it produces. There seemed to be a lot of obvious holes in this theory for me, and I was immediately skeptical. In response to my question, my white TA chose to put me through a thought experiment that should have told me everything I needed to know about who he was. "Maybe slavery had some moral value, because if it weren't for slavery, you'd be living in Africa in poverty and without the freedom or choices you have here."

As an aside, but an important one: There are only a few things I strongly believe with absolutely no real proof. That bigfoot is real. That Bill Laimbeer really did foul Kareem Abdul-Jabbar in Game 6 of the 1988 NBA Finals. And this: If suddenly everyone understood with searing clarity that being controversial doesn't make you interesting, white male enrollment in philosophy graduate programs would drop overnight.

My TA's idiotic thought experiment was as simplistic as it was cruel. But I didn't say that. Instead, I let the Cool Black Girl take over. It stung, but I didn't lash out. Instead, we talked about history and whether or not we can even assume America would look like America, or Africa would look like his caricature of Africa, without the U.S. slave trade. We debated whether I would really be better off if not for slavery and, therefore, whether slavery could be understood to be morally acceptable. Now if this were the end of the story, the Authentic Black Queen could tell it proudly, about how she suffered through racism from a TA, and how she would handle a man like that differently now. She could explain that my discomfort with the question wasn't showing my bias; it was showing his. Because I don't believe he would have put this example to any of my white peers. She could describe how bad it felt in the moment to have to play by his rules and how freeing it is that she would never do something like that now that she is comfortable being her full, authentic self.

So now I want to admit the part that Authentic Black Queens

aren't allowed to admit. Something that I wouldn't admit even then, back when I didn't know how truly disturbing my thoughts were: I could tell that I'd impressed him by not calling foul play on the subject matter, by allowing him this gross display of racism disguised as intellectual curiosity. And impressing him felt good. There was something insidiously satisfying about his approval. I believed that saying it was a racist question would have been *cheating*. It wouldn't have been winning my case on the merits. Instead I let this white man with his "unbiased" worldview be the arbiter of objectivity. And if I could prove my case—my humanity—on the terms he had laid out, I felt like it would mean more than if he had just mercifully chosen a less horrific example to help me understand consequentialism. I've never lost a debate so completely, but I walked away feeling like I won. And this is the difficulty with the Authentic Black Queen: She doesn't let me tell the whole story because she doesn't make room for the Cool Black Girl. She can't—they don't have space for each other because there is nothing natural about this evolution. The Cool Black Girl doesn't grow into the Authentic Black Queen. And that means I can't feel liberated by her authenticity—I feel suffocated by it.

I know the Cool Black Girl pandered and tried too hard to make white people comfortable. But my willingness to forgive good faith missteps, my desire to give grace, and my belief that any path to justice—including racial justice—must have space for people to make mistakes and grow from them, are *real*. But they don't fit the Queen's ethos. Likewise, I know the Authentic Black Queen pretends to have been fully formed with impeccable racial justice politics and is preoccupied with impressing white people. But my confidence and the way I can articulate my racial justice analyses are *real*. But they are also too strident for the Cool Black Girl. To perform one is to deny the other, and since neither feels entirely real *or* entirely false, I'm stuck.

The problem—at least for me, and I suspect for more of us—is a persistent feeling of phoniness. A sense that we are not being real or, more aptly, that there is no real version of us. That we developed a sense of social inauthenticity that allowed us to get through the day-to-day but may have prevented us from getting any further. Moreover, that a desire for safety and success and acceptance urged us to create a number of different versions of ourselves and stopped us from ever developing the real ones. And that lack of realness defines us. It somehow feels like more than being fake: Being fake is self-conscious. It's realized. It's intentional. We are something else. *Unreal.*

Working in politics helped me understand this on a different level because authenticity is an amorphous concept in politics that somehow simultaneously seems to mean everything and nothing. As only the third Black woman to have run a presidential campaign—and the first one who was running a campaign for someone who was also a person of color—I knew I was going to need to walk a tightrope both with how we presented him and with how I led our effort. I would need to run an authentic campaign. Whatever that meant.

Interestingly, political authenticity doesn't seem as connected to genuineness as it perhaps should be. An authentically boring candidate doesn't get credit for being themselves just because it's an honest personality trait. According to accounts from those closest to her, Hillary Clinton is authentically a serious-minded wonk. Her head for the policy minutiae, her studious demeanor, her *nerdiness*—those qualities seemed to form, for lack of a better phrase, *the Real Her.* However, she constantly dealt with criticisms concerning her authenticity, which indicates the value of authenticity may be second to apparent authenticity.

Moreover, it's a pretty ridiculous concept if you really think about it. And I have. A lot. People want authenticity in a politician because we want to believe that who we are seeing is who they really are. So, when the doors are closed and the cameras are off, the version they showed us in public is the same version they will be in private. It's an understandable desire, but the wheels come off the wagon in the execution. Because the only way to prove authenticity is to see them when the doors are closed and the cameras aren't on. So, authenticity becomes measured by who can best publicly present private interactions without letting the knowledge of an audience transform it into performance. Or at least, who *can best convince us* that they are having authentic interactions. The measure of authenticity is how much we believe a performance. And that belief is as much about us as it is about the politician.

I happened to start working in politics during a cultural moment when people of color, who grew up being told not to talk about race, were suddenly in a political ecosystem demanding that we do it with ease and comfort. And we'd have to translate that ease and comfort onto white candidates and candidates of color alike. It was a demand for authenticity that didn't feel like it was asking for anything real. On the Julián Castro campaign, a Mexican American candidate was running during a presidency that had been won in part through vitriol about immigrants. We had to present Castro's case in a way that made Latinos feel seen and white voters feel included. Race was an issue in the election in a way it never had been before, so we would need to talk about it enough, but not too much. We would need to provide education and inspiration to audiences who were asking for very different things, and, above all, we needed to do it in a way that made everyone feel comfortable.

And realizing that is part of what made me think I could run a campaign, despite not having worked in electoral politics before. Because in a weird way, the thing that had best prepared me for that moment was having spent my life and career up to that point searching for a concept of authenticity that felt *authentic*, but instead embracing ones that felt unreal. I was going to have to lead a campaign built by the Authentic Black Queen but run by the Cool Black Girl.

It's tempting to think of the Cool Black Girl and the Authentic Black Queen as opposite poles—the goal being to travel from the confines of one to the enlightenment of the other. But the performance of the Authentic Black Woman, while currently prized in some spaces, is still not about us. And that becomes even more clear as the culture once again shifts, this time toward an "anti-woke" backlash that punishes us for the same race consciousness that was being celebrated just a few years ago. The speed with which the Authentic Black Queen has moved in the eyes of many from "wise" to "fatiguing" is itself proof that the obsession we see with Black women's authenticity is not about us. It's an invitation to perform a pre-understood version of Blackness, one that is cohesive and conscious in a way that actually feels unfamiliar to many of us who are supposed to embody it. For many of us, our authentic selves developed in fits and starts, interrupted by moments where we tried to blend, to bend, and to make others comfortable around us. So our authenticity will not carry the smoothness and consistency that is demanded of the Authentic Black Queen. She is sure-footed where so many of us still stumble. We struggled developing our own lens around racial identity where she seems to be expected to have always had a current and sophisticated understanding of it. She delivers her speeches and wisdom and white people applaud and self-flagellate in equal measure.

This Authentic Black Queen is a performance of authenticity that simply fits into current norms around racial identity. This performance is designed to make white people feel secure in their race politics of the moment, in much the same way the Cool Black Girl's postracialization fit into norms of the past. It makes the two of them sisters of some sort: Even though one is a clumsy racial agnosticism and one is an over-the-top deification of Blackness, the result of both is a cultish racial monotheism that worships white comfort. And neither one is fully real or fully fake. They are simply, beautifully, unreal.

And while that helps me make peace with my two avatars, it leaves me just as stuck as before with respect to understanding my own authenticity. If neither the Cool Black Girl or the Authentic Black Queen is entirely real or entirely fake, neither can be said to embody *me*. And that brought me to the concern that lies at the core of why discussions of authenticity have always troubled me: I feared that I didn't have an authentic version of myself and that this was all because of my identity as a Black woman. If the goal of authenticity is to uncover who I am when I'm not concerned about what I'm supposed to be, but part of who I am is being ever mindful of who I am supposed to be, is authenticity simply beyond my reach?

3

THE AUTHENTICITY PARADOX

I always thought there should be a word for the opposite of a guilty pleasure. If a guilty pleasure is something you love but keep secret for fear of social stigma, what is the proper term for something you hate but pretend to love for fear of the same? A guilty aversion?

The problem is that when I ask for help naming this concept, I'm then forced to confess the universally beloved things I'm only pretending to like. Which is exactly what I'm trying to avoid. But since I'm outing my deep discomfort with the concept of authenticity, now seems as good a time as any to pitch my idea for how we can talk about our guilty aversions.

I call mine my "Okay, Awesome" list. The reference comes from the title of an early episode of one of my favorite shows, *How I Met Your Mother*. In the episode, the characters go out to a popular and exclusive club called Okay, which, when mentioned, repeatedly prompts the response "Okay?! Awesome!" But once at the club, the characters are reminded of all the ways these clubs are actually awful. Overcrowded dance floors. Overpriced bars. Deafening music. Obnoxious people.

THE AUTHENTICITY PARADOX

When Ted, the main character, laments the fact that while he knows he's *supposed* to love places like this, he hates it. His love interest for the episode wisely explains "because all the stuff you're supposed to like usually sucks." The two of them charmingly spend the night listing a number of other things that we're supposed to love (New Year's Eve, parades, cruises) that they actually hate.

That scene spoke to me and became my own little private joke with myself (and thank you to all the *HIMYM* fans who saluted Private Joke with Myself). I would mentally catalog things that it seemed everyone else loved that I just couldn't get on board with, and whenever those things would come up, I would respond with some variation of "Okay, awesome!" and then do my best to find a way to get out of it later.

Through the years, my list changed and grew. Picnics were a staple (sorry to the man who took me on one for a date, and I pretended to love it); tea came off only after *Ted Lasso* made me feel less alone about not seeing the appeal of drinking potable mulch. Trivial Pursuit lost its place to Cards Against Humanity.

But authenticity has been my guiltiest guilty aversion, the very top of the "Okay, Awesome" list. Whenever someone mentioned it, I felt uncomfortable and wasn't able to name why, which was even more troubling because of how seemingly *good* authenticity was supposed to be. What kind of person doesn't want the things that authenticity offers? Over the past several decades, authenticity—and our search to embody our authentic selves—has become a staple of what it means to have a healthy personal and professional life. Not wanting to pursue an authentic life is like eschewing health or stability.

We are encouraged to chase it unapologetically and protect it fiercely. And why wouldn't we? Authenticity is, as Brené Brown succinctly and beautifully put it, "the daily practice of letting go of who we think we're supposed to be and embracing who we are." It is knowing who we "truly are and behaving in a way that aligns with that vision."

Authenticity requires that we are introspective enough to meet our true self and brave enough to listen to her. It's a signal to others that they can trust us. In business, it can win over consumers, be the strongest marketing tool, and make a brand resilient. It has become a theory of leadership. In politics, it's currency and a necessity for getting elected. It's freeing. It's a form of self-care. An act of resistance. It carries an air of moral virtue. And given the role authenticity plays in helping us to unlock inclusivity, feeling discomfort with the former felt like a rejection of the latter. So my discomfort with authenticity did more than confuse me. It shamed me.

Embracing authenticity is a self-guided exploration by its nature. It can only be achieved by discovering who we are when no one is looking and learning how to harness that version of ourselves in all other areas of life. In this journey, we are taught to be wary of the external forces—outside voices and pressures—that urge us away from who we truly are.

This exercise assumes that who we are exists independently of external forces—that our true self developed, and those external forces create detours from that self. But for those of us who learned these concepts together—those of us who collapsed the question of "Who am I?" and "Who do I need to be?" and developed a joint answer to both questions, there are no detours. All exits merged into one path, rocky as the path may be.

Authenticity requires self-awareness, but it despises self-consciousness. Ideas like conformity and desire for social comfort and acceptance are supposed to be anathema to authenticity. Consider an easy example. As a young person, I'm asked to name a favorite color. I love the color orange, but I'm told blue is a much more popular color. Because I want to be trendy, I convince myself to love the color blue; and as I get older, I continue to treat blue as

THE AUTHENTICITY PARADOX

my favorite color. I buy all my favorite outfits, all my accessories, and decorate my home in shades of blue.

Discovering my authentic self allows me to be aware enough of what happened to understand why I chose blue over orange, and allows me to embrace the love of orange I have ignored for years.

As I accept my love for orange, I buy all new clothes, finally allowing myself to wear the bold outfits that I had secretly loved. I redecorate my house and allow my bright accent wall and statement pieces to change the entire feel of my home. As I begin prioritizing my true preferences, as opposed to how I will be perceived, I feel even more confident in my style. The freedom that comes from not having to hide and fully accepting myself shapes how people see me. I feel confident and grounded in my authentic style, and that confidence makes people see that style as trendy. Poetically, the thing that I wanted comes more easily when I am embracing my authentic desires rather than trying to fit in.

This is an attractive scenario, but it doesn't ring true for many of us.

Take the same example. Only this time, imagine that when I was told to name a favorite color, I was only given the option of blue or green. Sure, I saw other people choose orange, and I was initially drawn to it, but I was told *my* choices had to be between blue or green, so I never meaningfully considered orange as an option. Because I don't like green, I chose blue, and blue becomes my favorite color for years.

As I get older, I begin to uncover my authentic self, and I realize I was unfairly told to choose between only two colors, but can actually choose any color I want. When I'm asked why blue is my favorite color, the only answer I have is "I don't like green," which is now a completely irrelevant statement. So arguably, I can now embrace a love of orange. But in this scenario, it's not that I have been secretly loving orange every day but hiding it. In fact, I never think of orange. So adopting it as my new favorite color doesn't seem like

THE REAL ONES

getting closer to my authentic self. Nor does erasing my love for blue because I would also be erasing the reality that for a long time I felt like I had only blue and green to choose from. Even though I now recognize that as a false choice, it still shapes how I see this question, even if I no longer feel trapped by it.

Or imagine this time when I'm told to choose a favorite color, instead of being told that blue is trendier, I secretly discover that we are being sorted according to our favorite colors. Someone has decided that having blue as a favorite color is indicative of success as an adult. So people who choose blue as their favorite color will be put into classes and programs that will funnel them into good colleges and enable them to get well-paying jobs. Choosing orange will result in being sent to an underfunded school with no hope of higher education. So while I like orange, I choose blue to ensure I have more options as an adult.

When I start to uncover my authentic self, I am conscious that I only chose blue because it would afford me a better life. Even if I'm now able to like whatever color I want, I'm understandably going to be wary of making a different choice. And any real discussion of my authenticity would have to make room for the fact that I both know blue isn't technically my favorite color but I also am probably not going to let go of it. And if that tension is read as a failure of authenticity on my part, then authenticity is not going to be a meaningful concept for someone like me.

These two latter scenarios are common experiences for people of color, and they're the reason our conversation around authenticity has never felt accessible for me.

One of the advantages of being a part of a dominant group is that society has an unlimited imagination for what they can authentically be. White people are granted the full spectrum of humanity from which to choose their likes, dislikes, desires, personalities, and dreams, none of which will threaten their identity as an authentic white person. They can pick their favorite color

THE AUTHENTICITY PARADOX

from all the colors in the crayon box. Moreover, they generally don't have to rely on those choices to earn them acceptance or safety or opportunities. That is not to say they don't also experience external forces that may urge them away from their authentic choices, but usually those forces are closer to the voices that say "blue is trendier" not "blue will give you access to the life you want." Thus the process of uncovering their true self and loving orange out loud can feel freeing for them.

For people of color, this process can be more complicated. We are often told—either implicitly or explicitly—that there are a limited range of acceptable choices for who we can authentically be. And we are policed through a number of different ways to stay within that acceptable range. And this policing happens both from inside and outside the community, which shows just how insidiously effective these limitations are. Communities of color often become deputized in gatekeeping the range of acceptable authentic behaviors and identities other people in the community can embody. Expressions like "Oreo," "banana," "coconut," and other similar epithets connote a person of color who acts in some way like a white person (that is, Black on the outside, white on the inside, etc.).

These narrow lanes become self-reinforcing and limit how people of color can authentically show up in the world. Again, this is not unique to a racial dynamic. In fact, this kind of socialization happens across all kinds of underrepresented identities, whenever people are told they can only choose between limited options for who they can be. And those decisions are often impacted by a need to seek acceptance or safety.

Imagine a young queer woman who doesn't feel safe coming out. In an effort to hide her sexual orientation, she adopts a high femme style hoping it will help her pass as straight. Granted, she has plenty of straight girlfriends who feel comfortable in sweats one day and in a dress the next, but she also knows that's not an

THE REAL ONES

option for *her*. In order to effectively camouflage, she feels the need to adhere more closely to gender stereotypes. Whenever she deviates from a stereotypically gender-conforming style of dress, she gets stares that let her know she is raising suspicion about her sexual orientation. The choice for her is implicit, but it's clear: Adopt a consistently femme appearance, or be clocked as a lesbian by people who do not make her feel safe.

Because of this dynamic, while she initially feels more comfortable in jeans and a hoodie, she starts to feel safer in skirts and dresses; her makeup becomes a shield. Soon her aesthetic is as much about how she feels comfortable as it is about hiding her identity. As she gets older and finds a community where she is entirely comfortable coming out, her style doesn't change. At some point, she starts thinking about authenticity and whether she is being authentically herself. While she knows she consciously changed her style in an effort to camouflage, it seems dismissive of who she has become to call her current style inauthentic.

Further, her style is inextricably linked with how she was socialized as a queer woman. It has impacted how she understood her identity—how she moves in queer spaces, the way she presents herself, the ways she has experienced acceptance and objectification. It seems artificial to declare it inauthentic simply because it was a conscious response to external forces, because responding to those types of external forces *is* an authentic experience for her as a queer woman. And because those forces helped shape her, trying to strip them away runs the risk of stripping away pieces of herself.

This is the authenticity paradox. Because of this tension, I always felt like authenticity wasn't for me, and that it wasn't for a lot of us. Our true selves don't exist as static beings to be uncovered—we are dynamic. And that dynamism is central to who we are and to our underrepresented identities, but it is read as a betrayal of our authenticity.

THE AUTHENTICITY PARADOX

It is tempting to think of this as an entirely philosophical discussion, but it has much more practical implications. Our current understanding of authenticity creates untenable pressure that stops us from achieving true equality, inclusion, and belonging. This is more than a thought exercise. It is a prescription for a new approach to authenticity that relieves rather than furthers marginalization and can lead us to equality.

When I attempt to uncover my authentic self, I am met with many traits and values that I both genuinely hold and that came from self-conscious efforts to shape how I may be perceived. I am a genuinely optimistic and positive person, but those were also learned behaviors to distinguish myself from the angry Black woman tropes that proliferated in popular culture when I was a child. I genuinely value diplomacy and empathy and my ability to extend compassion to multiple contradictory positions at once. But I also know I honed these traits because of a need to navigate the feelings of countless white people turned White People who I have been able to manage with these skills. Maybe who I am is the result of external forces, but my authentic experience as a Black woman is as someone who has been shaped by those forces. It seems a massive oversimplification to say my true self existed independent of all of those forces, rather than that my true self has been formed by them.

I need an understanding of authenticity that can allow me to have consciously formed pieces of my identity in response to external forces, and still be read as authentic. I need a vision of authenticity that can accept that maybe blue isn't authentically my favorite color, but my decision to pick blue and the reasons I did are a part of my authentic experience. And for too long, our collective understanding of authenticity required me to simply declare orange as my true favorite color. And that misses too much for me.

THE REAL ONES

If authenticity requires self-awareness but loathes self-consciousness, what has been missing, at least for me, is self-reflection. My own interpretation of who I truly am is too often erased from an understanding of authenticity.

In actuality, our cultural conversation about authenticity is unnecessarily limited. In academia, there is a useful distinction drawn between two understandings of authenticity: essentialist authenticity and existential authenticity. Essentialist authenticity requires the person to enact their core personality characteristics, by first seeing beneath the layers of personality that obfuscate one's true self.

Existentialist authenticity requires the person to enact their core values and beliefs, and set aside personality traits that hinder one's ability to live authentically. A person must choose among their range of dispositions, to create the self out of those dispositions.

Our popular conversations about authenticity generally assume an essentialist understanding of authenticity: Our true selves exist, static, and the pursuit of an authentic life involves peeling back the layers of external pressures. This is simply never going to feel possible for most people with underrepresented identities.

An existentialist understanding of authenticity may be more accessible for people with underrepresented identities. But it still misses a critical point, which is that it still imagines authenticity as an effort to determine *who* we are, rather than to understand and embrace the reasons behind *why* we are.

Self-reflective authenticity is my effort to bridge this gap. I'm crafting this concept as an acknowledgment that for many of us, our true self doesn't exist in spite of the efforts we have made to move away from it. Rather, our true self is an amalgamation of who we were, who we had to be, and who we have become. And just as critical to this understanding of authenticity is the *why*. My understanding of authenticity often isn't about the choice itself but the

THE AUTHENTICITY PARADOX

fact that a choice needs to be made at all: the reason we may have chosen one personality, value, or trait over another. Because the very act of needing to choose is at the core of my understanding of self, of being a Black woman living in a society that wasn't designed for me. Self-reflective authenticity is less concerned with my true favorite color and more concerned that I am able to understand why that is a loaded question for me. Living a self-reflectively authentic life is about understanding, embracing, and forgiving myself for why, at any moment, I am choosing one color over another.

Self-reflective authenticity is how I have learned to make my peace with my unrealness. Essentialist authenticity tells me that since both the Cool Black Girl and the Authentic Black Queen are performances, neither is authentic. This understanding of authenticity asks me to journey back to a time before I was conscious of the forces that helped me create either of these avatars and try to squint my way through the darkness to find whoever I was then. But that person doesn't exist. If I peel away the Cool Black Girl and the Authentic Black Queen, I'm not left with a Mildly Self-Aware Chocolate Princess. There was never a *me* that came before a time when I needed *them*.

If essentialist authenticity is all about ignoring how you're being perceived in favor of your true self, but the experience of being a Black woman in this country is a study in how you're being perceived, then essentialist authenticity can't exist for me. The external forces that I am supposed to ignore on my path to my authentic self actually are the same forces that delineate the path itself. Those forces—for better or worse—helped create me. There hasn't been a moment when I have been conscious of a concept of self that I wasn't also conscious of how that self was being perceived. And responding to those ways I was perceived is part of the experience of being a Black woman. It is an authentic experience that I had *because* I'm a Black woman. Thus defining my authentic self as the person I would be if I *weren't* conscious of those external forces is, in essence, defining my authentic self as someone who is not a Black woman.

Okay. Awesome.

This is why essentialist authenticity felt so alienating to me—because it is literally alienating to me. It is asking me to uncover my true self by engaging in a thought experiment that imagines me as someone else. When I take this thought experiment to its logical conclusion, I disappear.

But freed from an essentialist understanding of authenticity, I can recognize that there is an understanding of authenticity that doesn't assume a static version of myself that has simply been buried under years of performance and focuses instead on the self that has been born from the need to perform.

The challenge, I realized, was not to claw my way from one performance of authenticity to another, but to understand what authenticity means to me, to Black women, and, more broadly, what it means to any of us who have been shaped—at a fundamental level—by a need to lie.

Those lies have, at different times, conferred upon me safety, social acceptance, professional success, and a perverse and hard to name (and even harder to admit to craving) social credit that comes from being the Black person who can help translate race to white people. And for a long time, I have understood that in return, those lies stole from me my ability to ever be wholly authentic. But if part of my process of defining the real me involved these lies—this unrealness—maybe it doesn't undermine the journey but instead paves it.

Maybe in a world that isn't designed for all of us, the messy, disjointed, dishonest, fractured process of creating, uncreating, and re-creating ourselves *is* the authentic experience. The contradictions aren't there to be smoothed out, flattened into an easily understandable trope—they are *me* at my most authentic.

I'm uncomfortable writing this. Authenticity *means* honesty. I

THE AUTHENTICITY PARADOX

feel like I'm cheating when I say my experience performing inauthentic versions of myself was in fact an authentic experience. And yet, this is profoundly true. And I suspect that this experience is not unique to me. Anyone who has had to ask the question "Who do I have to be?" right alongside the question "Who am I?" had to live those contradictions. Cool. Queens. But real.

To be clear, self-reflective authenticity is not only for people of color, or even people with underrepresented identities. In fact, I think it is a much more expansive exploration of who we are that could benefit everyone. However, part of the confusion I am trying to resolve in this book is the challenge of authenticity when society narrows lanes for us, and that is an experience that is unique to people with underrepresented identities. Because of this, the question of "authentic self" is uniquely fraught for minorities in ways that white men without any underrepresented identities are unlikely to have experienced.

These narrow lanes make it even harder to understand our authenticity because they limit the acceptable range of experiences we are credibly allowed to embody. When I was growing up, I was frequently told by White People who thought they were complimenting me that I wasn't "like other Black people." Not only is this simply a gross statement, but this also placed an artificial limit on how they saw me. When I expressed an interest in things they considered to be stereotypically Black, the reaction I got was one of disbelief—that I was being inauthentic. So when I pretended not to like hip-hop or nail art or other things people around me would deem "too ghetto" they read me as authentic, even though I was lying. This dynamic can also play out within Black communities. Having grown up in a predominantly white area and then gone to a predominantly white institution for college in a majority white city, there were a number of interests that I had that are not stereotypically associated with dominant Black culture. On the occasions that this created a dissonance when I was in Black spaces, I'd be accused of inauthentically embracing white interests, and so I was again in an ironic situation where lying allowed me to be read as authentic.

This leads to a further concern that troubles me about essentialist authenticity that self-reflective authenticity helps to solve, which is that there's obviously no yardstick we can use to assess whether we have embraced our authentic selves. Authenticity is treated as an individualized pursuit because it's understood as an internal goal, but that's not entirely true. Embracing my authenticity is only half of the equation—the other half is actually external. For my authenticity to yield the positives associated with it, it has to be perceived by others as authentic as well.

Authentic leaders aren't simply managers who call themselves that. Their teams have to experience them that way. Likewise, politicians aren't asked to self-identify as authentic and then voters take their word for it. The question of whether a candidate is authentic is almost entirely about how voters interpret them.

So the final arbiter of authenticity isn't our own congruence at all, but rather whether we are credibly seen as having reached equilibrium. For something that is supposed to be all about who I am, rather than who others want me to be, the perception of other people seems to count for an awful lot.

This furthers the authenticity paradox for me: If my authentic experience misaligns with others' perceptions, and their perceptions hold sway, is authenticity really even about *me*?

In 2023, the Merriam-Webster dictionary chose *authentic* as the word of the year, reflecting a significant increase in the number of lookups. As they put it, "authentic" was "the term for something we're thinking about, writing about, aspiring to, and judging more than ever."

That description is telling. We aren't just aspiring to authenticity. We are judging it.

When I was brought on to manage Maya Wiley's New York City

THE AUTHENTICITY PARADOX

mayoral campaign, the folks building her team made it clear that they wanted me because I would bring credibility among progressives. She was a first-time candidate, and we had gotten early indications that many of the progressive would-be endorsers wanted further assurance of how she would be running her campaign. One of my first moves when I came on board was setting up meetings with activists and leaders across the city who had expressed skepticism to understand the crux of their concerns.

The meetings weren't very illuminating, largely because no one could really articulate what their concerns were, only that they had them. Once I established a better rapport with some of them, they gave me more insight. I was somehow simultaneously less and more confused.

People didn't doubt her politics, more her demeanor. "She isn't fiery enough," they told me in hushed tones. Even more uselessly, "She doesn't give people *that feeling*." And if we were being compared to master orators I could maybe understand that, but the leading progressive at the time, Scott Stringer, had taken to joking about how boring he was on the campaign trail.

"Does *Scott* give people that feeling?" I asked incredulously. Even though I knew the answer: He didn't have to.

Maya wasn't being compared to Scott, she was being compared to the other woman of color in the race—Dianne Morales—the Afro-Latino candidate who was running a long shot far left campaign. She later ran into staffing problems and many people on her team quit after alleging discrimination and an attempt to stop them from unionizing against the campaign. Dianne apparently did give people *that feeling*, but they still weren't supporting her because she couldn't win.

"But she comes across as authentic," people explained to me. "Maya's missing that authenticity."

Maya is a civil rights attorney who became well-known for her appearances on MSNBC, breaking down legalese to nonexpert viewers and making plain the ways that Donald Trump deserved the impeachment charges against him. She's an academic whose rhetoric is professorial more than it's preachy. Her values are progressive, but her entire demeanor tells people she'll meet them where they are and bring them along. That *is* who she is, but somehow it *read* as inauthentic for a Black woman. And to be clear, most of the people I met with were not Black women themselves. But their read on a Black woman's authenticity credited their own perceptions over her actual experience.

Okay. Awesome.

In politics in particular, I have seen perceptions overtaking facts. In this arena, white male candidates find it much easier to earn political authenticity than other candidates. Women of color candidates are asked to embody a very specific vision of their experience—one that both matches the expectations from a broader audience of what their experience should be and also does not present too much otherness to still be relatable to that broader audience. They are told that we must win the voters in our own community to succeed, but we must also appeal to white voters in order to be taken seriously. We are asked to perform a version of our culture that will make voters in our community feel seen, white voters feel comfortable, and everyone feel like we are being unapologetically ourselves. And if holding all of this at the same time gets too heavy, voters question her authenticity and deem her unelectable.

This same double bind doesn't exist for white male candidates largely because we have so many narratives that they can authentically embody. When it comes to women of color, we have fewer examples. So these candidates are unceremoniously shoved into the few narrow models of candidates we have seen before, and failure to fit within those visions means voters are less likely to find their narratives resonant.

THE AUTHENTICITY PARADOX

If, when you embody your truest self, you are perceived as being authentic, there's no contradiction for you. It's only a paradox when there's inconsistency. When you at your core do not get read as real. And when that happens, the quest for authenticity feels like a fool's errand.

If I can say "this is who I am" and your response can be "I don't believe you," then the authenticity question isn't entirely an internal one. It's not just a matter of how I present, it's whether you believe me. And that has just as much to do with culture, environment, and unconscious bias as anything else.

Essentialist authenticity is particularly susceptible to this because its emphasis on uncovering a true self makes it a more factual inquiry. From this understanding of authenticity, there exists a true self, and the goal is to uncover it. Thus, if I can point out that you used to behave one way and now you behave differently, I at least have an argument that I am actually identifying your true self.

Understood this way, essentialist authenticity is not an individual pursuit at all. It's a hybrid project that, while we can work on as individuals, can only be assessed externally. Authenticity isn't writing a book; it's defending a dissertation. And there is nothing objective about the metric being used to measure us. It's comparative: I'm deemed authentic only in relation to others around me; and as a Black woman, this equation is one that makes me understandably uncomfortable. Our authenticity is simultaneously prized and policed. Our authenticity is demanded, but is then placed under a microscope. And if it doesn't match up with the expectations others may have about what an authentic Black woman's experience looks like, I am deemed to have failed in my quest for authenticity.

Self-reflective authenticity solves this problem by refocusing the inquiry on my own journey toward the real me and how I arrived at that answer. It is an inquiry that only I can undertake for myself, and I am the ultimate—and only—authority on it.

With self-reflective authenticity, if you fail to perceive me as authentic, that does not immediately undermine whether I am actually acting in accordance with my authentic self. The answer to you not seeing me as authentic is not more self-work or actualization for me. Instead, self-reflective authenticity solves this incongruence properly by focusing on social conditions that limit our ability to recognize some people's authentic experiences. That's powerful for those of us who are used to people questioning our experiences when they don't line up with their expectations.

We are used to judging people based on our own perceptions of whether they are being authentic. Instead, we need to focus on creating the conditions where people can feel safe expressing themselves. This is not a mere thought experiment. It is the key to creating and sustaining inclusive spaces.

We need to stop calling ourselves the objective judges of someone else's authenticity. Instead, we should judge their honesty. If we feel someone is being inauthentic because we have seen them express an opposing value or belief, we are questioning their sincerity or their consistency. When we believe they are hiding a vulnerability, we are asking for greater transparency or even expressing a wish they felt more comfortable around us. With this shift, we can assess things that outsiders are more equipped to assess, rather than assessing someone's authenticity, which properly should be left to them. And we can focus on creating spaces where people are comfortable being fully authentic rather than judging them for not being brave enough to show up that way regardless of the cost.

Then we can leave the question of authenticity for individuals to explore in their own journeys. Self-reflective authenticity can give us a new cultural conversation around authenticity, and

THE AUTHENTICITY PARADOX

maybe those of us who have always felt uncomfortable with the concept of authenticity can participate in these conversations with a little less trepidation. And maybe I won't have to fake my enthusiasm and try to figure out a way to get out of it later because it really will be okay. And maybe even awesome.

In fact, I'm willing to try if you are. Ready?

Okay. Awesome.

4

CODE-SWITCHED

As we've discussed, during public conversations about authenticity, people are generally operating under the assumption that there is a single "true self" that all people possess. That understanding often doesn't fit the experiences of people with underrepresented identities, who, even if we don't always have the language for it, have had to be more comfortable with the idea that we don't always present—or can't even identify—a "true self." Perhaps nowhere is this more pronounced than when we discuss the concept of code-switching.

When Vice President Kamala Harris became the Democratic nominee for president in the summer of 2024, some of the first and most pointedly racist criticisms she drew were around code-switching. Immediately following her nomination, there were a number of accusations that she was "debuting a Southern accent" or other ways of euphemistically implying that she employed a blaccent when speaking to predominantly Black crowds. Trump made the attack more directly when he said—to a room full of Black journalists—that Harris had suddenly "happened to turn Black."

The fact that this issue drew such ire is itself telling. In politics,

CODE-SWITCHED

it's not uncommon for candidates to adopt the vocal patterns and mannerisms of the audience they are speaking to, or even to play up memories or interests that make them seem like they're a part of the community. In fact, it's so common it's become a cliché. Donning a flannel shirt rolled up to the elbows, a candidate drops his *g*'s and talks with relish about his childhood spent "helpin' out on the farm" when visiting Midwest states. Touring a factory floor, he adopts a macho swagger and reminisces about "Daddy gettin' laid off from the plant" in the Rust Belt. They pepper "ain't" and "y'all" throughout their speech in the South. They "aw shucks" their way through sampling local delicacies, insisting that each one reminds them of their favorite auntie's recipe.

The kind of pandering that white candidates do toward communities of color is usually done carefully so as not to be offensive. White candidates attend Black churches and visit Black barbershops. They attempt to speak Spanish or at least pronounce Spanish words with an accent. They eat cultural foods and they appear with popular celebrities. But generally they do not change their vocal cadence to appeal to communities of color, especially Black communities.

There is always a bit of pretense on the side of the audience and the candidate. We already knew John Kerry probably didn't eat a lot of cheesesteaks before he committed the sin of ordering one with Swiss cheese instead of Whiz. We also knew George W. Bush wasn't *really* a rancher. But the pretense is allowed because what candidates are really trying to show is that they are just like you. And that kind of pandering is accepted because we recognize that is something natural that voters want to feel even if we intellectually know it's not true. So why did it cause such a commotion when Harris did it?

To me and many others, there was no mystery to solve. Harris was code-switching and speaking with different audiences and supporters in a way that felt natural for her, familiar to them, and

THE REAL ONES

possibly new to onlookers, particularly non-Black ones. We have long been familiar with the idea that there is a version of ourselves that we embody when we're in public and one when we're just among folk. Watching it play out *so* publicly for the vice president was certainly interesting, but it was still unsurprising. Of course Kamala Harris—the Oakland-born, Howard alum, AKA sorority member Black girl who positively cackles with delight at inside jokes with her sister—doesn't always sound like the carefully cultivated image we would see when she was speaking on behalf of the Biden administration.

But this explanation didn't quiet the critique, and, in fact, seemed to spur it. Just as quickly, a conversation developed about whether Harris was in fact code-switching and opponents were either misunderstanding—or pretending to misunderstand—what that entailed and just how common it is, or whether Harris was doing something more cynical. Critics accused Harris of "blatant pandering" to Black voters. The implication seemed to be that code-switching required a naturalness that Harris lacked, that this is not an accent she uses normally and this is, therefore, inauthentic.

The demand that Harris admit to pandering is really a demand to admit that the type of culturally specific Blackness—the casual use of "brothas and sistas," the knowing coo of "girrlll," the assertion that "we gon' win in 2024"—is merely a performance. This betrays a misunderstanding that these critics have about code-switching and authenticity, which is that both the version of herself Harris embodies around predominantly Black audiences and the one she embodies elsewhere are on some level *her*.

It's interesting to see code-switching discussed so publicly today. Twenty years ago, it was an in-community-only conversation. Among Black people, it was something we all did, but we didn't talk about it. And while I imagined other underrepresented communities were having similar conversations, I never expected to

CODE-SWITCHED

know about them *because that was kind of the point*. Now that the term and concept has become so widely used, it is often used in a number of different ways and to refer to a number of different behaviors, and a consistent definition is hard to find. In some ways, that lack of definition makes sense. What's understood doesn't need to be explained, after all, and we knew what we were doing when we code-switched even if it was never explicitly taught to us.

One of my frustrations with how code-switching is sometimes defined now is that in order to make it broadly approachable to a wide audience, it is often reduced in a way that robs it of its usefulness. So to start, I want to provide a definition of code-switching and some related ideas for our purposes.

Code-switching is often simply understood to be the practice of shifting communication style, mannerisms, style of dress, and other external signifiers to fit in more familiarly with a given audience. Understood this way, code-switching is positively unremarkable: I'm code-switching when I text my boss differently than the way I text my sister. When I use internet slang when sending a tweet. When I speak differently when giving an interview than I do when I'm explaining the same concepts to a friend. Understood as simply responding differently and making conscious changes in communication and presentation based on audience, code-switching is a completely unnoteworthy dynamic. This is simply learning how to be an effective communicator and knowing your audience. This is more accurately referred to as "linguistic mirroring" or "the chameleon effect."

This isn't what we in the Black community meant when we talked about code-switching. Before it was a part of the national political discourse, it was just something that we knew at some point we'd do in order to fit into predominantly white spaces. We changed our hairstyles, references, voices, and patterns of speech when we were among mostly white people. We nimbly slipped into

THE REAL ONES

and out of AAVE—African American Vernacular English—(or Ebonics, as I learned it). And we did it because we knew the cultural cues we kept hidden in our spaces—the undeniably Black speech, habits, and behaviors—would be rejected in white spaces. Jobs, schools, any interaction with a stranger where we had to behave "professionally"—we knew white spaces when we saw them and we knew what to do.

Code-switching, as social linguist and educator Sunn m'Cheaux has explained, is more than just altering speech based on the audience. "[I]n order for code-switching to be in effect, there has to be some sort of social context, historical context or a power disparity of some kind." This is important: Code-switching is not merely knowing your audience. It comes from knowing that your culture and presentation will be rejected by the dominant culture. It requires an imbalance of power, and it serves as a correction toward safety and acceptability.

I remember the first time I was conscious of how different my dad sounded at home versus when he went to work. I was about eight years old at the time; and while he was on the phone with his boss, I noticed that he sounded different, but I couldn't put my finger on what it was. *Nice? Polite?* No, he was always polite and there was nothing abnormal about his general kindness. *Formal?* Closer, but not quite. Gone was the slang, the casualness, the inflection of his voice that I knew so well, but it wasn't strictly speaking formally: He was speaking to someone he clearly liked and sounded comfortable with. I realized what tipped me off was his laugh. My dad had a fantastic, contagious laugh that my sister and I loved. When he found something particularly funny, he had a rolling laugh that started as a roar, always accompanied by a clap of his hands, and petered into a snicker he often couldn't stop, which would start the laughter all over again.

But on this phone call, his laugh was warm but measured. There was no clap, only a head nod, but—and this was important—

CODE-SWITCHED

it sounded real. He was finding genuine amusement in whatever was being said, but still dimmed his usual exuberance.

For some reason, that flipped the switch for me. There was something about watching him want to communicate joy and closeness, but in a controlled way, that came to define code-switching for me. As I got more sophisticated and realized what settings prompted code-switching, I understood it more fully, but that moment always stayed with me as a marker. Code-switching was about controlling—not completely changing—who you were. The version of my dad he code-switched into was still him—just not all of him.

As I got older, I developed my own equation for code-switching, which I knew would be different from what I had seen my parents do time and again. My biggest fear about code-switching was that it was a rite of passage for Black people that I wouldn't need. That I was already code-switched. No adjustments needed, I would have more natural cultural comforts in an all-white environment than I would in a Black one.

My parents' preoccupation with how white people would see us seemed odd to me as a child. If they were so concerned about white people being White People, it seems the simple answer was that we could have just . . . lived around Black people. My parents had been the ones to decide, after all, that we would make our home in a small, almost exclusively white town instead of living in nearby cities like Riverside or Redlands where they actually worked and where there would have been greater diversity. Instead, they each commuted over an hour each way to get to and from work for the dubious prize of my sister and me usually being the only Black kids in class. In a town where I remember seeing Confederate flags hung proudly from store and home windows. But they made the choices they did because of the opportunities they thought it would provide us. They had both grown up in Cleveland, Ohio, and were aware of the challenges that we'd face in a similar setting. But

THE REAL ONES

not having experienced them, they didn't know the challenges inherent in having us grow up in a predominantly white community where we were such an extreme minority.

Not having grown up around Black peers always made me a little insecure about how my Blackness was perceived by other Black people. I was actually more conscious of the ways that I needed to shift my behavior on the rare occasions when I was in all-Black settings rather than in the predominantly white ones I was used to. I didn't know if I could credibly sound Black. I tended to speak like the people around me; and growing up, outside of my immediate household, that was overwhelmingly white people. I remember on a trip to Cleveland, where my extended family still lived, a cousin I was meeting for the first time on that trip asked me and my sister pointedly why we "sounded like white girls."

There is this enduring belief—a suburban legend, if you will—that a number of Black people of my generation are haunted by this kind of experience. Black kids who grew up in non-Black dominant spaces were told at some point we talked white, dressed white, acted white . . . *something* white and it permanently shaped us. There is a lot of anti-Blackness at the core of this conversation, so I want to take a moment to discuss it.

I have definitely in my life been told by Black people that my voice, behavior, style, mannerisms, and interests were "white." That I wasn't sufficiently Black in some way. And as a young person, that rejection stung and it confused me, but it was also something I would have been able to work past pretty quickly. Still, anti-Black racism will never miss an opportunity, so the Black kids who were told they were acting white often were told that we should wear it as a badge of honor. Speaking proper English, working hard in school and getting good grades, being respectful—these are the things that were popularly associated with Black-on-Black bullying about acting white. Often this conversation is used as a way to ex-

CODE-SWITCHED

plain continued discomfort that some Black people still feel around other Black people.

To be clear, identity policing absolutely happens within communities of color. I credit the 1980s and 1990s and the thorough job they did of defining Blackness so narrowly for this. But I also admit my own insecurities here. Because of the fear that I wouldn't fit in, I found myself anticipating discomfort when I was in predominantly Black spaces, and that discomfort replicated itself. Moreover, I was likely subconsciously accepting the internalized racism that told me I should feel pride in not being like other Black people—that the rejection meant that I was *better*. My insecurity made me seem uncomfortable and that discomfort made me seem displaced in Black settings. And I believe that displacement was perceived as whiteness. Which I get, because, let's be honest, discomfort and internalized judgment toward Blackness is a pretty central ingredient of whiteness—to be clear, to the *racialized construct* of whiteness, not to all white people.

Interestingly, former first lady Michelle Obama described an almost identical experience in her memoir, *Becoming*. And truthfully, so many Black women have had similar experiences that it no longer carries the shame it once did: that we were somehow left out of a sorority of Black girls. In fact, it's become clear to me that a lot of us had the experience at some point of being told we sounded white. And, funnily enough, I was always clamoring for an authentic Black girl rite of passage; and it turned out, I'd already had it—it just wasn't the way I had expected it.

As I moved into young adulthood, I largely stopped worrying about whether my Blackness matched anyone else's. I felt less insecure about the ways I didn't immediately read as culturally Black to some people with an overly specific understanding of what that meant. And as soon as I felt more confident owning my Blackness, I stopped feeling that cultural displacement.

In addition to simply getting over myself, I also realized that my

THE REAL ONES

fears that I hadn't developed any common Black cultural markers were completely unfounded. Culture works in such an interesting way. You can't always see it; it's just a part of you. Yes, I was influenced by the peers around me, but I was also influenced by the music, media, art, and culture my parents introduced me to and that I was independently drawn to out of a natural desire to see myself reflected. I adopted styles, references, traits, and behaviors from the Black shows I watched, from the movies my parents rented, from the portrayals of Blackness that I sought out.

I was drawn to the music my parents listened to—Motown and old-school soul—which gave way for my love of R & B and hip-hop, which further deepened my love for Black culture. But just as quickly as I recognized those pieces of my identity, as proud as I was to identify them, I was equally aware that they could cost me in certain settings. I knew better than to list hip-hop as one of my favorite types of music in a town where the most popular radio station proudly boasted "all of today's hits—with *no* rap or R & B!" That was, *I kid you not*, the tagline of our top hits radio station.

Law school was where I perfected my style of code-switching. This was where I saw that wearing my hair in braids would be considered "political," especially when coupled with my activist résumé. A Black law firm partner had given me this advice when she came to a career fair at my law school. She whispered it to me as a kindness and a lesson that I just knew she had come about the hard way. I also learned my willingness to talk about race and racism was considered intimidating in work settings. So I went to my corporate law firm job ready to bite my tongue and be performatively diplomatic so that no one could ever call me strident in my beliefs. I remember a white partner coming to me with a complaint about another Black employee, insinuating that he had only been hired because of affirmative action.

"But I'm saying that to *you*, so obviously, it's not about race," he nonsensically said as he talked to me about race.

CODE-SWITCHED

"Of course," I assured him just as nonsensically. I was later told he reported back to some other partners how easy I was to work with.

To be clear, this code-switching is distinct from the unrealness I describe elsewhere in the book specifically because of its self-consciousness. Here, there was no nagging question about whether everything about me was a performance. I knew what was being asked of me at the firm and how I needed to perform. Then I went home, exhaled, and complained about these white folks to my family, my Black friends, and other Black associates. Code-switching never bothered me—it was simply changing outfits based on the weather. Both were me, just styled for different occasions. For me, the difference could be summed up easily. Remember those spinning tops where each side was a different color, but when you spun it fast it gave the illusion it was changing colors? Code-switching is placing the top with the red side forward on a shelf with red toys. Unreal is trying to say what color it is while it's spinning and wondering if it can be said to have a color at all.

I remember once while working at a law firm a partner had accompanied me to the mail room, where a majority of the staff was Black. When I went down there alone, their conversation wouldn't stop, and I would comfortably join in and hang out for a while before heading back upstairs. This time, despite our greeting one another familiarly, the conversation awkwardly came to a halt. We were all pleasant, but it was a much more formal interaction than I had ever had there.

When we went back upstairs, the partner joked to me self-deprecatingly, "I guess I kind of dampened the mood, huh?" He laughed. "No, it's good that you have that kind of camaraderie here," he continued genuinely. "At least when the old white guy's not in the way!" We laughed heartily and I assured him he was fine. It was a kindness that I took as such: He was glad I had a reprieve from the whiteness of the firm. But I thought it was interesting that

THE REAL ONES

he thought that was my only escape. I don't think he knew how often the Black associates and I went into someone's office, closed the door, and did the same thing.

I remember once talking to a white colleague, who had become a close friend, about Dave Chappelle who, at that point, had recently made the decision to walk away from *Chappelle's Show* when he expressed discomfort seeing white people in his audience laughing at some of his race-conscious satirical jokes but not knowing if they were laughing for the right reasons. As an aside, it's so disappointing when someone who seems like a brilliant and insightful critic of power and privilege is actually just expressing frustration that they don't have power and privilege. But I digress.

Talking with my friend, I acknowledged I understood what Chappelle was saying.

"It does feel weird watching white people laugh at the expense of Black people without knowing *why* they're laughing," I explained.

"Huh," he said thoughtfully. And then, completely unaware of the impact this would have, he continued. "I didn't think you were the kind of Black person to worry about things like that."

It was the first time I realized how good I'd gotten at code-switching. My white friends didn't suspect there was another, more racially conscious, political side of me. I had . . . won? I had made my code-switching seamless to my colleagues at work, which I guess had always been the goal. But I was surprised that the people watching me had no cognitive dissonance. They fully believed a professional Black woman could be so comfortable and honest in the white corporate world without hiding away any aspects of her identity.

I tell this story because what I recognize in Kamala Harris is someone who white people believe is more themselves in predominantly white spaces than in Black ones. The accusation is that, when speaking naturally, she does not sound Black. They see her speaking to Black crowds not as her exhaling and shifting into behavior that is just as, if not more, comfortable, but as the same pandering to Black voters that white politicians may do because there is nothing natural about them fitting into this space. They believe that the authentic her is the one they have already seen. That she is code-switched. And being confronted with the truth that she simply has a cultural fluency that they may not have been aware of means they have been tricked.

This is a particularly frustrating criticism because Harris wouldn't be where she is without code-switching. Conservative opponents can clutch their pearls and call it phony if they want to, but the truth is, code-switching remains a necessary tool for Black people who want to succeed in corporate environments. According to research, white people *do* prefer when Black people at work code-switch, making it a necessary skill to develop in order to survive in predominantly white work environments.

The criticism Harris has received mirrored the way people spoke about then-candidate Barack Obama in 2007 when he first began gaining momentum on the national stage. While our collective comfort with discussing race has grown considerably since that time, Obama's style of speech did get some attention, specifically as people noted he didn't tend to speak the way many of them expected him to. Then-senator Biden came under fire for clumsily complimenting him by calling him "articulate." But the implication, which was shared by others, was that he didn't talk Black. In those early days, he rarely used AAVE or any slang. Robin Lakoff, a linguistics professor at the University of California, Berkeley, reported that he employed none of the "Black rhetorical traditions" like rhyming or familiar cadences. Lakoff compares Obama's cadence to other gifted Black orators—Jesse Jackson, Johnnie Cochran, and Martin Luther King Jr. The difference is not in rhetorical talent, but simply that Obama's pattern is not stylistically Black. As Lakoff succinctly put it, "He doesn't sound black unless he deliberately wants to, but that's very seldom."

THE REAL ONES

If we care about progress, then it's important that we ensure that the historic firsts like Obama and Harris aren't considered exceptions. The media and politicians will try to disclaim their successes as outliers and fail to make broader space for more people who look like them. Obama's and Harris's opponents often emphasized their biracial backgrounds; Trump often accused Harris's Black identity as fraudulent—these politicians are all laying groundwork to make it harder for the next Black person to succeed on the ground they have trod, and we have to be diligent that they are not successful in doing this.

Baked into Lakoff's description is the idea that Obama has to be intentional to sound Black, but not to avoid it. The belief that underlies her assumption is that he was at his most authentic when he *doesn't* sound Black. Now almost twenty years later this is almost funny. We have now seen Obama in enough settings around predominantly Black crowds and simply in the more comfortable position of not having any more campaigns to run to see that he sounds like a Black man. And I have never gotten the impression that he is having to be very deliberate in order to do so.

I think something much simpler is going on. According to research, white people are particularly bad at determining when people of color are being authentic. A study at the University of Granada even found that white people couldn't differentiate authentic smiles from fake ones on Black faces, but they could on white faces. Despite code-switching becoming a more commonly understood topic, white people are still simply bad at identifying it when they see it. I imagine this is especially true for Harris who, as a biracial woman, has another underrepresented identity that likely makes her conversant in an entirely different set of cultural signifiers that I, as a non-Indian woman, do not fully appreciate. Seeing her interact in more predominantly Indian spaces will probably make us more attuned to some of the ways she appears different from what we are used to among this community. The impulse to declare something amiss is based on an unnecessarily limited understanding of how cultural signifiers show up and what they mean about someone's identity. She should not have to apologize for an ability to move seamlessly between cultures and comforts as a biracial person. In fact, she should be able to openly celebrate her multicultural identity.

Particularly when someone like Harris or Obama has succeeded in such a predominantly white space, the assumption seems to be that they must be more comfortable in that space, and to the extent they code-switch, it's to seem more Black. Embedded within this assumption is the same essentialist idea of authenticity that we have already rejected: There is no real Kamala Harris and fake Kamala Harris. Code-switched versions of us are still us. Just maybe not *all* of us.

When code-switching went mainstream, and everyone started talking about it, an interesting thing happened. White people started judging it. For public figures, it was in the press. For most of us, it was just among our peer groups. But as white people started becoming aware of code-switching, they began feeling comfortable noting when someone was doing it and whether it was convincing. Essentially, it allowed white people to start publicly commenting and critiquing racial behaviors of people of color without it being considered racist. It was quite a feat. In return, people of color got the ability to be conspicuously inauthentic and not pay a penalty for it. Code-switching matters because it represents the only time we collectively give up the conceit that white people don't know we change our behavior for their comfort and that they would prefer we do so.

The central argument of this book is that people of color are shaped at a fundamental level by the way racism marginalizes us: that our need to style who we are from such a young age to get comfort, safety, and acceptance from the dominant group impacts

THE REAL ONES

our concept of authenticity. But the underlying assumption is that this happens on a subconscious level from people in both the dominant and minority communities. While that is still true, with code-switching we see that not only does it happen consciously as well, but we get proof that the social inauthenticity we employ subconsciously is, in fact, very socially necessary.

5

LISA VERSUS JESSIE

I think my struggle with authenticity began the moment I understood that being a Black girl felt like two separate identities to people around me, when they felt like one to me. I also learned that being a *strong girl*—or what I'd later understand as being a *feminist*—meant lying about one piece of my identity, my Blackness, in order to feel embraced as the other, my girlhood.

In part, I have the shortcomings of 1980s and 1990s public education to thank for this limited understanding. What I learned about Black people in school wasn't in math or reading or art. I learned about their role in history, and it was always through the prism of the Civil Rights Movement and a political fight for equality. This lesson was also always in February. Whenever I heard about gender in school, I'd hear a teacher insist that women could do anything men could do even if we hadn't seen it yet. My formative lessons about my own identities taught them as a struggle—a battle for equal rights that wasn't finished. My identities only existed when we talked about politics, so I didn't have another way of understanding them and they became political identities for me. But I also learned that those identities—*Black* and *girl*—weren't quite the same.

THE REAL ONES

In school, whenever we studied Black history, I played my Only Games. But in the moments when gender came up in class, I didn't have to play the Only Game. That was partly because I was never the Only Girl, but there was another difference between these moments that taught me to understand race and gender differently. While I understood that there were concepts like *sexist* and *the women's movement*, they weren't presented as sources of ongoing pain and shame. We weren't confronted with brutalities that people were subjected to because of their gender. Gender was a difference we talked about openly, not only when something had gone wrong. Occasionally, we were told to line up or placed in groups based on it. When we learned about important women, they were nonchalantly referred to as "the first woman who . . ." without a lot of fanfare, and certainly none of the boys stared uncomfortably at the girls for the rest of the lesson.

Obviously, this was as much a failure in the way we learned about gender as the way we learned about race. There should have been fuller pictures told about both movements—the pain people experienced and the beauty, culture, and triumph. They should have been identities that were trotted out not only during social studies lessons but during art and music and science and at story time, celebrating contributions that people of color and women of all races contribute everywhere. Gender shouldn't have unnecessarily been presented as clean binaries to a bunch of children whose identities could have fallen anywhere on a spectrum.

This particular failing in my education taught me that I had two pieces of my identity—one to be celebrated and one to be mourned. One put me in community, while the other made me feel intensely alone. I wanted to protect that feeling of being in a community for as long as I could. And it transformed my early teenage years into a battlefield in a strange, cold civil war where I was the sole casualty.

My memory of the first time a man whistled at me remains

crystal clear in my head. Despite that, I have two very different stories about it. One that actually happened. One that was, well, a lie.

I was fourteen, and it was a hot, bright day in Palm Springs. I was wearing jeans shorts with embroidered doilies, showing off my long legs and smooth dark brown skin. I wore a green-and-white checkered shirt that was just long enough to cover my stomach, but when I raised my arms it would ride up to show my midriff. I wore my fresh box braids under an oversize black hat, which, while it *totally wasn't the reason I bought it*, I was convinced it made me look exactly like Janet Jackson in *Poetic Justice*.

As I walked through the mall parking lot back to where my mother was parked and waiting for me, a white man in his early twenties slowed down his car, rolled down his window, and looked my body up and down appreciatively. He gave a slow, low whistle.

I saw red. I squared my shoulders and found myself channeling Jessie Spano, the white überfeminist whose passion was usually played for laughs on the sitcom *Saved by the Bell*.

"I don't answer to a whistle," I seethed. He looked up at me, surprised, almost impressed. When I continued to glare at him, my hand on my hip, he looked sheepish and drove away. I rolled my eyes and continued walking to my mother's car.

Almost. That's almost what happened. The real story was different.

What actually happened when he whistled: I was split into two pieces and the civil war that was constantly brewing inside me in these moments threatened to leave its cold equilibrium and run hot. One side—the side who (somewhat) understood feminism, who instinctively recoiled at any compliments directed at my appearance and who genuinely identified with Jessie Spano—was outraged. The other side, the side who knew that girls who looked like me didn't get whistled at by men who looked like him in my small, white town, *wanted* to be outraged as well. But she wasn't.

THE REAL ONES

She identified with Lisa Turtle, the talkative gossip queen and lone Black character from *Saved by the Bell*, and knew she wouldn't have many chances to be considered the pretty girl.

I'm a forgiving person, but there are some people who will forever be on my list. The person who heard the pitch to store flour in a bag and said "10/10. No notes." Whoever decided Crypto.com was an acceptable name for a stadium. And the person responsible for canceling the brilliant, meta, and genuinely hilarious 2020 reboot of *Saved by the Bell* that somehow updated the show with a much more thoughtful and self-referential analysis of gender, race, and class and still retained the nostalgia and wacky humor of the original. You can't pour powder from a bag, stadium names are supposed to make people believe in sports, and the *Saved by the Bell* reboot was gone too soon. Some things are just *true*.

Even so, I feel the need to defend the version of *Saved by the Bell* that raised me, which was nothing if not a celebration of the most one-dimensional tropes.

Jessie Spano was a capital-*F* Feminist, and the 1990s told us that meant strident, strong, and quick to anger. She constantly called out the casual sexism around her, from lesson plans to the antics of boys who put down girls in that special way that was just allowed on sitcoms of the era. But since her feminism was often played as a joke, her lectures invited eye rolls and groans from everyone around her. Those who were critiqued rarely learned a lesson or changed their behavior. Her chief sparring partner was A.C. Slater, the sexist jock who called girls "chicks" and "babes" and lazily mocked the women's movement. And he eventually fell for her. For her part, Jessie learned to laugh off her boyfriend's dismissiveness, proving that opposites attract and love conquers all—including values.

Lisa Turtle, on the other hand, was a rich, superficial Black girl who the writers, in their infinite wisdom, gave a love for shopping instead of a personality. She was an incurable gossip and a boy-

LISA VERSUS JESSIE

obsessed teenage girl stereotype, but for all her talk of dating and boys, she never actually had a boyfriend. She was the unrequited love interest of the obnoxious but lovable goofball Screech and—it seemed—no one else.

The distance between Jessie and Lisa was a fascinating one for me because each had a claim to being my on-screen avatar. Even at a young age, I knew Jessie's politics appealed to me. Her rants about gender equality and workers' rights and the environment made me feel seen and let me know that there were other girls who overthought the politics of things that their friends took for granted. She made me feel more normal. I'm so grateful that young people now have so many other ways to express their activism and to connect with like-minded young people. In my day, we couldn't go to TikTok with its earnest soliloquies on social justice authored by other kids our age. We had Jessie Spano. But out of a combination of affinity and desperation, I always identified with the token Black character in any show I watched, so my allegiance also gravitated toward Lisa.

There was another tension between them that I was never quite able to capture until the show did it for me. In one episode, through an amazing instance of contrivance, the only way to raise money for the new cheerleader uniforms was to have an auction where girls bid on dates with boys. Jessie predictably finds the entire thing sexist, and criticizes Lisa and their other best friend, Kelly Kapowski, for being willing to participate. Ah, Kelly—the quintessential It Girl. She was the gorgeous cheerleading captain who had no problem with the sexism inherent in the boy auction or with getting a date. I loved Kelly Kapowski. But I never once identified with her. But Jessie not only refuses to bid on her boyfriend, Slater, she forbids any of the other girls in the school to do so.

Meanwhile, Lisa, in a rare turn, actually has a love interest in this episode (you could always tell if Lisa will have a romantic storyline because there will be a Black actor guest starring for

THE REAL ONES

precisely one episode). This time, Lisa has fallen for a Smart Boy, which, since I honestly can't remember the character's name, and that's literally his only defining characteristic, will also serve as his name for our purposes. Smart Boy reads for fun and takes French and is, therefore, according to 1990s television rules, a genius. Lisa falls hard, but Smart Boy thinks she's too vapid for him, which crushes her. In order to win Smart Boy's affection, Lisa—who is pretty popular and shouldn't be able to change her entire identity this easily—changes her entire identity. She pretends to be an intellectual in order to impress him, which mostly consists of dressing like a 1950s librarian and making comments about philosophy. At some point, her friends call her out on the fact that Smart Boy isn't falling for *the real her*, and she sadly says that at least this fake Lisa has a boyfriend while the old one didn't.

Ouch.

There it was. Lisa's storyline versus Jessie's. The episode's lesson was an allegiance to authenticity as an end in and of itself, without a real discussion as to why someone like Lisa may not have opted for it in that moment. Jessie's politics stopped her from wanting to bid on Slater, but it didn't stop him from wanting her to. Suddenly, Jessie's feminism seemed very specific to a certain kind of girl. The girl who could shun romantic attention but still receive it. Lisa wasn't that kind of girl. Neither was I.

The episode stuck with me, and I wasn't able to articulate why. It felt unresolved because it seemed like the narrative was faulting Lisa without fully understanding her position. In the end, she shows Smart Boy who she really is, and dumps him for not liking her for her. It was a good lesson, but it felt like an incomplete lesson, and it frustrated me that Jessie never had to answer for an inconsistency. The narrative never got to hear Lisa and, by extension, me. That gap never got resolved. The version of feminism Jessie espoused wouldn't work for Lisa, because if a core tenant of feminism is "reject boys who chase after you for the wrong rea-

LISA VERSUS JESSIE

sons," feminists can only enact this if *the boys are chasing you* in the first place.

Like Lisa, I was also the sole Black girl in most of my social settings; and when we got to an age where we were supposed to notice boys noticing us, I noticed that was missing for me.

I was supposed to complain when boys chased me, or whistled at me, or obviously leered at me, but being expected to complain about it meant that it was supposed to happen. And it didn't. And as the sole Black girl in most of my classes for most of my life, I knew why. The small, white town where I grew up had a lot of quiet racism. My sister and I were both well-liked enough, and we did well in school, so we were often simply exempted from some of the worst assumptions the white people in our community tended to make about Black people. However, that didn't translate to every setting, and I eventually learned that dating was one of them.

When I talked to my white girlfriends, they would admit, in hushed tones as though it blunted the sting, that they could never date a Black person. I knew the white boys in my class had to feel the same way. Once, freshman year, a white guy in my class announced to me, apropos of nothing, that if he dated a Black girl his mother would kill him. I think he was trying to tell me he liked me. I'm still not completely sure. I remember it hurt, but I would never admit that. We had an unspoken deal. I faithfully ignored the ways that racism impacted my life when I was in high school, and in turn, no one talked openly about my race. Except in those rare whispered moments of honesty that reminded me no matter how much we ignored it, it was still there. So instead of acknowledging that racism limited my dating opportunities, I did other things to take myself out of the running. And feminism was a shockingly effective way of doing that.

I became wholly uninterested in dating, treating it as an immaturity that someone as serious and focused as I, a teenager, would

THE REAL ONES

not waste time pursuing. And I was so effective at creating this narrative that even the one boy who did ask me to be his girlfriend in junior high school hardly blinked when I told him I "wasn't ready" to date as though that were an actual answer.

So when more invitations didn't come, I was able to take comfort in the fact that I wasn't being rejected, people were just respecting my wishes. I didn't need that kind of attention or approval anyway, and, in fact, it was offensive. *Because feminism.*

But my body developed the way it developed, and my thick thighs and wide hips filled me out. And while high school beauty is largely based on your ability to look just like everyone else but a little better, outside the four walls of my school, my curves attracted attention. I found myself paying more attention to the outfits I wore to go to the grocery store than I did to what I wore to school, because that was when I would get treated the way girls were supposed to get treated. I got the stares and the comments, but they wouldn't be from boys my age. They were from older men and, to my surprise, often white men, who made comments like the man in the parking lot did.

When I got the chance to feel noticed in that way, I took it. So while it still embarrasses me to admit it, in that moment, in that parking lot, Lisa beat out Jessie. It wasn't even close. Jessie didn't stand a chance. When the white man in his early twenties slowed down and looked my fourteen-year-old body up and down appreciatively and gave a slow, low whistle, I said, "Thank you."

"You're welcome." He grinned lasciviously.

The second his car turned around the corner, I was overcome with a combination of embarrassment and guilt and shame and—honestly—pride. But that pride started the cycle of embarrassment, guilt, and shame all over again. I hated how he looked at me, but I had also wanted someone to look at me like that. And I wanted someone like him to notice me—a white, conventionally

LISA VERSUS JESSIE

attractive man—who I knew to be the arbiter of what was attractive. It felt like acceptance, and that acceptance felt like loss.

When I reached my mother's car, I told her the Jessie Spano–approved version of the story, and by the time I thought about it again later that night, I'd almost forgotten that that wasn't exactly what had happened. When I recounted the story to my friends the next day, I continued to tell my edited version and barely remembered it hadn't been true.

I didn't know that much about what it meant to be a good feminist, but I knew well enough to be ashamed. While my simplistic version of feminism, which I used as much as a shield as I did an ethos, told me to be offended by that attention, I craved it. And then I felt guilty for craving it. I especially felt guilty for knowing that part of what had made that man's attention valuable was his whiteness. Despite growing up in an overwhelmingly white environment, my parents did everything they could to show us positive depictions of Black people and Black love. But dominant cultures are gonna dominate; and even at fourteen years old, I had already learned a few critical lessons: that white men were the romantic default and that their acceptance carried power. And that many white men would never romantically consider Black women.

It wasn't just random comments from classmates that confirmed these lessons for me. Pop culture did a lot of the work of showing me how Black women were viewed. From the John Hughes teenage rom-coms that dominated the 1980s to the Disney movies that I lived for in the 1990s and from *Cheers* to *Friends*, there were rarely non-white characters featured in most popular media of the time; and if they were, they were never the romantic leads. In fact, *Sixteen Candles* actually made a joke of the mere idea of interracial dating, when Randy asks Sam about her dream sweet sixteen birthday and suggests a pink Trans Am as a gift.

"A black one," Sam responds.

THE REAL ONES

"A Black guy?!" Randy gasps incredulously.

"No!" Sam laughs. "A black Trans Am. A pink guy!"

That comment still doesn't come close to the most racist offering of one of the defining movies of my generation. That distinction belongs to the inclusion of Long Duk Dong, an offensive racial caricature of a Chinese foreign exchange student who spoke with a heavy accent and was used wholly for comic relief at his expense.

The point is that most mainstream (read: white) media did not feature prominent roles for people of color. And I quickly noticed that Black people were nonexistent in these shows or movies except for the occasional guest star or random scene. And when Black women were featured, it was often for comic relief, offering a caricature of Black stereotypes that created a clear image of how Black women were seen: loud, aggressive, angry, uneducated. And unattractive to the main characters. That is, unless I was watching something specifically marketed for a Black audience.

Interestingly, in a very real way, I saw more representation of Black people and stories in media when I was a child than I do now, when consciousness about diversity in casting is possibly higher than it has ever been. Compare that with the acknowledgment of the 1980s and 1990s that different communities connected with different stories, and writers simply created what now seems to be a feature of the past: the Black Show.

A Black Show wasn't just a show starring Black people. It was a show written for a Black audience, based on experiences familiar to a Black audience, and trying to connect with a Black audience even if it meant alienating other audiences. It meant that these shows didn't just feature Black people but told Black stories, made Black references, and celebrated Black culture. Some did such a good job of it that they were virtually unheard of outside of the Black community.

While it flies in the face of today's preference toward multiracial casts, I actually preferred this now-outdated method of telling our stories. An ironic result of today's constant hand-wringing about diversity in Hollywood is that it feels like we have actually gotten *less* diverse storytelling. While a modern movie or a show rarely features an all-white cast anymore, no matter how much diversity is added in casting, unless the creators consciously decide to honor their characters of color in the writing of those characters, the result is often a multiracial cast telling overwhelmingly white stories.

What the Black Show did well was showcase Black life, and for someone who both loved television as much as I did and had as few windows into Black life as I did, that was a welcome education. I loved shows like *A Different World*, *Martin*, *Living Single*, and *New York Undercover*. My sister and I still mark the holiday season with a viewing of *A Cool Like That Christmas*, an animated gem I had always hoped would have the same trajectory as *The Simpsons* and become a weekly show after a successful Christmas special. I imagined my life in college and young adulthood mirroring these characters I loved, complete with the romantic storylines I had never seen featured in the white media I consumed.

Now the romantic storylines of the Black shows came with their own baggage; and, while it was empowering to see Black women be the tip of love triangles and the sought-after "will they/won't they" girls, I couldn't ignore that overwhelmingly it was light-skinned Black women who got this romantic attention in the shows I loved. Whitley and Gina and Sandy—I loved them all fiercely, but they fit a very specific and familiar vision of Black beauty—light-skinned with fine hair—that I didn't fit. Another unfortunate trope of the Black show was that many of the light-skinned women had dark-skinned best friends who were—either implicitly or sometimes explicitly—compared unfavorably to them. The most memorable example was on the show *Martin*. Gina, Martin's longtime girlfriend and eventual wife, had a best friend, Pam. Pam was portrayed as inferior to Gina in every way.

While at work, Gina was an executive, Pam was her assistant, whose career advancement was directly tied to Gina's. At home, Gina had Martin, while Pam was perpetually single. And—most notably—Pam was the subject of a constant barrage of over-the-top insults from Martin. And those jokes came at the expense of her dark skin, her masculine features, her nappy hair and the weave she wore to—essentially—capture some of the beauty Gina had naturally. He dehumanized her—literally comparing her to animals—and mocked her for being single. And while Gina would scold him gently and roll her eyes, she let it happen. Obviously, as a practical matter, the entire conceit was unbelievable. Pam—played by the immaculate Tichina Arnold—is beautiful. And in-world, she did occasionally have love interests including Martin's best friend, Tommy, for a period of time. But the narrative of the show let those jokes happen and had the characters react as though, on some level, everyone thought he was right.

On Black shows, I was Pam; on white shows, I was invisible. The message was clear. Within the Black community, Black beauty was narrow. Outside the Black community, it was virtually nonexistent. But white men remained the default. Many of my friends had never heard of the Black shows, but everyone watched the white ones. So I took away a simple lesson: While some Black men may one day find me attractive, white men would be the true judge. So their opinion mattered more.

I became deputized in my own oppression. I wanted to be objectified because that's what I understood it meant to be a woman, but I wanted to abhor objectification because that's what I understood it meant to be a feminist. It became a vicious cycle that swallowed me up, expelled me, and left me both whole and devoured. And while I felt intensely alone, I know that I wasn't.

There are many of us who have chafed against the confines of our burgeoning understanding of womanhood and what it meant to be feminist when the battles we were told we should fight were not always the ones that had been waged against us because of our differ-

LISA VERSUS JESSIE

ent identities. Feminists are still told to reject the male gaze, despite the fact that we all have different relationships with male attention. We are told that relying on partners for financial and logistical needs is dangerous, despite women with different identities having differences in wages, career opportunities, or physical ability.

There are a lot of women who don't fit into conventional beauty standards who still get told that their worth is based on their ability to garner a certain type of attention, but that attention is often still denied them in settings beyond the street. Women of color, femmes, trans women, fat women—we all often get fetishized by the same men who would tell them they could never bring them home to their family. We get hollered at from parked cars, but never asked to a dance. As children we had our curves both appreciated and policed—often by the same people—and got told it was our fault we get sexualized by grown men.

But we're also still told this is what it means to be a girl or a woman. That getting that kind of attention is a rite of passage into this sorority; and for those of us who didn't fit neatly into what beauty standards told us we were supposed to be, we were told we should be grateful for the attention.

And—even if we don't always want to admit it—some of us are. And that reality can hurt as much as the harassment does. The violence of street harassment doesn't start at the moment of the comment or stare or whistle. It starts when we first learn the misogyny and racism that makes us connect the approval of men—especially white men—with acceptance. It's subtle, but the violence is there. And it creeps into our psyche, under our skin; it itches, but we can't pull it out. It reduces us and makes us think we needed it to. It tells us we should be grateful when men make us uncomfortable. It eats us alive. And then it makes us say *thank you*, while it whispers *you're welcome.*

This was one of my first lessons of feminism in white spaces: I had to define things in terms that weren't necessarily familiar to me, but I needed to pretend that they were. So I would pretend that I felt trapped by the confines of princess culture that Disney created when, truly, I felt locked out of it. I had to pretend that I hated how media portrayed women as insurmountably weak, when in truth, I saw Black women portrayed as superhumanly and unfairly strong. But for the sake of an authentic women's experience, I would need to lie. Those lies would keep me in the sisterhood. They would make the white women around me feel like I was one of them. And that was *something*. That was enough. I could fit into this version of being a girl, as long as it would let me.

To that girl, Hillary Clinton and her version of being a First Lady was a salve.

Of course it's almost odd now to think of Hillary Rodham Clinton as a First Lady; she has obviously achieved—and been heartbreakingly denied—many more roles than that one. But that role was my first introduction to her, one that so perfectly encapsulated my first understanding of feminism from one of my first feminist heroes.

I remember the pride I felt when she stood up to the uproar over her remarking that she would not be staying home baking cookies. She was the logical extension of Jessie Spano feminism. Yes, she was married, but she was an intellectual equal to her husband. And while he got to be president first, everyone talked about her running eventually. When she got married, she didn't cease to exist and proudly went by Hillary Rodham Clinton. She wasn't just his wife on the trail—she talked about policy. She was a wife and a mother, but she was a woman. *First.*

Despite my affection for this version of feminism, in truth, it really never had much affection for me. If our feminism is an answer to the way we're taught to be girls and, by extension, women, that version of feminism was answering a question that had never been posed to me.

That version of feminism was based on challenging the stereo-

LISA VERSUS JESSIE

types that the world had about white women. That didn't accomplish much for women of color, particularly Black women, who are often portrayed in ways that are not just different but diametrically opposed to white women.

Hillary couldn't be my balm, not fully. Because she soothed a burn that was different from the one seared into my skin. White women and Black women have historically been seen in fundamentally opposing ways, so what could feel like a subversion of stereotypes for a white woman could just as easily look like a reversion to stereotypes for Black women.

Where white women have faced limitations being reduced solely to physical beauty, Black women long encountered the opposing issue of not being considered objects of romantic desire. Where white women have dealt with stereotypes casting them as weak and helpless, Black women have contended with the stereotype that they possess a preternatural strength and animalistic physical prowess. Where white women are assumed to want to forgo a career for a home life, an unshakable myth about Black female identity has involved being an overextended Black superwoman shouldering the world's burdens without complaint.

But because white womanhood was still culturally treated as the standard, the stereotypes that white women grappled with defined both stereotypical femininity and the feminism that was designed to challenge it. But since I didn't see myself in the limited visions of femininity that existed, it was difficult to see myself in the victory Hillary represented by challenging them.

Then there was Michelle.

In 2007, it occurred to me that the First Lady could be a Black woman before it really resonated that the president would be a Black man. And I allowed myself to be excited about that in a way I never would have when I was a girl. Of course, I was thrilled that Michelle—like Hillary—was her husband's intellectual and professional equal and identified as a feminist. But interestingly, with

THE REAL ONES

her, I happily focused on the aspects of her role as First Lady that I had rejected so many years ago. I was proud when she eschewed taking on a more prominent policy role in favor of prioritizing raising her daughters. I loved that she was a style icon who graced the covers of magazines. I listened to the breathless commentaries on her clothes and cried when I saw the gown she wore at the first inauguration hanging in the Smithsonian National Museum of American History.

I cherished the pictures and whispered stories about how smitten President Obama still seemed about her after all their years together.

She was strong and smart and beautiful and loved. Yet I never once felt like my reaction to Michelle Obama was a departure from the feminism I still proudly embraced. It mattered that her dark skin and unapologetically Black features were seen as beautiful, and her iconic biceps were considered both strong and feminine. It mattered that she forwent bigger policy portfolios to place more focus on raising her own Black daughters, challenging both the unrealistic expectations that are placed on Black women to do everything and the idea that young Black girls are not worthy of that kind of attention and care.

Early in 2007, she was called angry and emasculating. Her parenting was questioned. Her love for the country was denied. Despite how she tried to present herself, she was constantly reminded that while she was a wife, and a mother, she was a Black woman. *First.*

It's easy to forget how limited the cultural imagination was for how Black women could be seen before Michelle Obama spent eight years in the White House expanding that vision. Now we have Kamala Harris. We have Olivia Pope and Beyoncé. We have *Black Panther.* We have a Black Disney princess. And now, Michelle Obama's approval ratings are so high, her ovation at the 2024 DNC was so tear-inducingly long, and her book tour and podcast have

LISA VERSUS JESSIE

been so well received that people forget the recent past. When people wonder if Michelle would ever run for president, I roll my eyes. See, I have never forgotten it wasn't always like this for her. I think a lot of us never will. I know she won't.

There was nothing accidental about how she is currently seen, and Michelle had made huge sacrifices, as she has now discussed at length since leaving the White House. She was under constant pressure to present herself, in many ways, as what would be considered anathema to the ways that Black women had been presented in popular culture, and she did this so masterfully she helped change popular culture. But there was nothing effortless about her seemingly effortless grace. We get to be carefree Black girls because Michelle was the careful Black girl.

Like Hillary before her, Michelle Obama defined a new kind of First Lady—no less feminist but starkly different because her feminism challenged stereotypes of Black women. They each presented such disparate visions of the role, to the point that there was an obvious dissonance. How am I able to simultaneously hold my pride in Hillary as First Lady, who came so close to the presidency herself, and my pride in Michelle as "Mom in Chief"?

Resolving this dissonance is, to some extent, the real answer for me to the question of Lisa versus Jessie. My feminism has had to grow to be wide enough for both of them—to transform from *versus* to *and*. Likewise, our collective understanding of feminism must stretch itself in much the same way to appreciate the fact that Black women are victimized by patriarchy in very different ways than white women are.

The unfavorable reaction of many white feminists to some of the choices that Michelle Obama made shows us that the women's movement still has some growing to do. She was criticized for dubbing herself "Mom in Chief," for not taking on a meatier policy portfolio, and for her magazine covers—all earning her accusations that she was a regressive version of a First Lady without any appreciation for the racial stereotypes she was challenging. Michelle's "mistake" had been simple: She'd been too authentic—she told the truth. Michelle was refusing to pretend that the ways misogyny had hurt her were identical to how it had hurt the First Ladies who came before her. Those women may have felt empowered by demanding to take on a bigger policy portfolio. But she—and many Black women who were watching—felt empowered by her doing what had been denied so many Black women and their families. She decided that her most important role would be as the mother to young girls. She did what I hadn't done. What Lisa hadn't done. She didn't pretend she was fighting the exact same fights as the white women. Subtly, quietly, *carefully*, she made her feminism Black.

Now as an adult, I can ask for more from white feminists than I ever asked from Jessie when she had judged Lisa. Maybe lying about her interests to attract a boy didn't make Lisa more of a feminist, but failing to understand Lisa's position compared to hers definitely made Jessie less of one. I needed the episode not to end before we got to hear from Lisa this time. *Please.*

Following the release of *Melania*, Melania Trump's memoir, I had a conversation with a friend about whether her first tenure as First Lady was actually more feminist than it would ever be given credit for because her husband's politics (and, as I would argue, *hers*) are so regressive. My friend, who is white, pointed out that Melania was criticized for refusing to move to the White House and give up her own life to be the nation's hostess. She hadn't chosen to run for office. She hadn't sought out power and truthfully hadn't exercised any. She hadn't asked for a policy portfolio and, according to the book, was only spurred to launch her anti-bullying campaign, the curiously named Be Best initiative, after seeing online speculation about her son's mental health. Moreover, my friend pointed out, Melania talked in the book about her pro-choice politics and how she never made that a secret from her husband.

LISA VERSUS JESSIE

"I don't *like* Melania," my friend argued, "but I do think as feminists we have to acknowledge that it's not fair to shame a woman for not wanting to give up her life to be a professional spouse."

"But we don't criticize her for not moving to the White House," I argued back. "Sure, we criticize the people around her who we *know* would have called for congressional hearings if Michelle Obama had suggested the same thing, but most feminist critiques of Melania Trump don't center on how quickly she moved to D.C."

"But she's the first First Lady to do that, and she never gets credit for it. She's basically a pro-choice woman who chose not to let her life and career get eclipsed by her husband. We can't say that's *not* feminist."

"I not only think we can, I think we *have* to," I insisted. "Wanting abortion rights for *herself* while her husband got rid of them for the rest of the country isn't feminism. And I have no problem with her individual choice not to move to the White House, but I'm not going to call it feminism unless it's a position she holds for anyone beyond herself. She started Be Best to protect her son against online attacks. I get that. But she and her husband also started birtherism, which made it harder for Michelle to do the same thing for *her* children."

I took a breath. We were at a party, and already the length and passion of the conversation were on the verge of making people uncomfortable. We quietly conceded we understood where the other was coming from and moved on.

What I didn't say, what I couldn't say because it would have sounded nonsensical to my friend, was *"I'm not doing this again!* I'm tired. I'm tired of being asked for my gender analysis to be used in service of women whose analyses don't include me. I'm tired of feminism being reduced to the point that it can be applied to anything a woman with power does, no matter the impact it has on any other woman. I'm tired of feminism that only sees Jessie and erases Lisa."

THE REAL ONES

Misogynoir is the portmanteau of *misogyny* and *noir*, coined by Moya Bailey, who used the word to refer to racialized misogyny directed at Black women. Misogynoir and misogyny can't be combated the same way because they do similar but qualitatively different damage. And the mistake the women's movement has made for too long is thinking of misogyny as the lowest common denominator—something that impacts all women equally, with other overlapping oppressions layered on top of that shared indignity.

But in truth, that misses the point. Misogynoir is not a version of misogyny that applies specifically to Black women: the result of sexism plus racism. It is the *way* Black women experience misogyny. Black women never confront sexism that is *not* racist sexism. Misogynoir is not an all-Black remake of *The Wizard of Oz*; it's *The Wiz*—a complete reimagining of the concept as something familiar but all new and undeniably Black.

And that's true for all intersectional identities. We can't dissect our identities and determine which oppression we experience is about our gender versus something else. That's not how identity works. We're always everything we are. And if our feminism can't make room for that, our feminism has to get much bigger. It has to be big enough for Lisa *and* Jessie.

Self-reflective authenticity can help us expand our feminism because it can allow us to accept multiple experiences from women that conflict with one another but that are all authentic.

For example, Lisa got called out for lying about who she was because she was presenting herself to Smart Boy as someone other than who she presented every day. But imagine Lisa's goal was self-reflective authenticity. When her friends pointed out that Smart Boy wasn't getting to know the "real her," she could remind them that she is the ultimate authority on the real her. And then she could engage in authentic self-reflection.

Perhaps Lisa, a rich Black girl who grew up with two surgeons

LISA VERSUS JESSIE

as parents in the predominantly white town of Bayside, realized that she was going to be an outlier. And in an attempt to give herself the best chance of fitting in, she knowingly adopted a flighty and superficial personality that would allow her to get along and be accepted by most people. Authentic self-reflection could help her recognize that, while she was pretending to be studious to get Smart Boy's attention, the version of herself that her friends were more comfortable with was just as much of a performance. Ultimately, self-reflective authenticity would allow Lisa to choose, after examination, what felt the most like the "real her." Maybe she ultimately would have chosen the same outcome and decided that the performance we all knew was who she was. Maybe she would decide that the girl Smart Boy was falling for was closer to who she understood her authentic self to be. But she would have felt like the driver in her authenticity journey rather than a passenger who had her authenticity policed by someone who didn't understand the nuances of what her identity meant to her. Obviously, it was a sitcom, and, in truth, we have no idea who Lisa was. But that's kind of my point: *We have no idea who Lisa was.*

In much the same way, I have developed greater comfort with my relationship with feminism as a function of self-reflective authenticity. I no longer feel the same pressure to pretend my struggles have to match the struggles of other women in order to be authentic, and in fact can recognize that they are sometimes diametrically opposed. I now work to be more honest about where they come from. The result has been that these spaces, which used to feel so narrow to me, have started to feel bigger. Like they're finally big enough for Lisa *and* Jessie. And Hillary *and* Michelle. And me.

6

CANDACE AND ME

One of my least favorite things about Candace Owens is how easily I think I could have become her.

Obviously, I don't mean her in particular. As far as a personal outlook goes, she and I have nothing in common. She is a far-right provocateur who is most known for being a Black conservative who is willing to offer anti-Black rhetoric in service of some frankly indefensible positions and I . . . am not that. But there's an uncomfortable familiarity that I recognize in her ability to slickly translate conservative ideology and make anti-Black racism sound like it comes from a place of care for the good of the Black community. There is a nostalgia I feel for the social credit I see her enjoy from white conservatives. As much as I hate to admit it, I remember the embarrassing satisfaction that came from winning the approval of a White Person and being seen as "one of the 'good ones.'"

Owens both infuriates and exonerates me. I'm always a little grateful that I don't feel tempted by the desire to revert to the respectability politics that I was taught growing up. I'm relieved when I don't seek out white approval, nor the role of the one Black person that White People will listen to on race. I want to distance myself from Owens in a way that betrays my secret fear that we're

CANDACE AND ME

not that far apart. I worry that if I spend a little bit too much time letting the Cool Black Girl run the show, I'll find myself chasing that seductive high I used to get every time I was seen as a special Black girl that White People aren't afraid of.

Many people of color have a complicated journey to our own self-identity, and that journey often includes a period where our own self-acceptance was tied to acceptance from white people. However, we are not often afforded the space to talk about that, because if our racial politics evolve past this, it becomes shameful to admit. Obviously none of us were magically born fully formed with our current lens for racial politics. We all crawled before we walked. And before we crawled, we fell. A lot.

This is another dynamic I don't think is unique to communities of color and extends to other people with underrepresented identities. Many of the sharpest cultural critics with the most finely attuned radar to privilege and power went through a growing period where they had to unlearn their allegiance to existing power structures. And as obvious a point as this is—that everyone who teaches us now went through a period where they had to learn—we are weirdly secretive about this reality. The power structures that we fight against are systemic, which means it's impossible to live in our society and get by unscathed by institutionalized biases. We all internalized the isms that we now fight against. In order to reject those systems of privilege and oppression, we have to acknowledge that at one point we accepted them.

The social justice movement would gain a huge benefit from us being more honest about this. Discovering that even the people whose instincts you trust the most on these issues had to go through an unlearning process may help people to feel less defensive about their own need to do that same unlearning. Transparency will help us get to a point where people feel more comfortable admitting their persisting biases and are more willing to challenge them.

THE REAL ONES

But that isn't what tends to happen. The social justice movement is actually surprisingly resistant to accepting the humanity of our thinkers. We ask for a level of perfection and deny a level of grace that is self-defeating to our ultimate goal. No one wants to admit to the ways they had to expand their thinking during their own growing periods. Instead, once we embark upon our evolution, we obscure the path behind us and pretend there was never a time when we too obsequiously sought the approval of the mainstream at the expense of our own selves and communities. And some of us hide this backstory by harshly judging those who internalized conventional thinking and never left.

Despite our saying we want people to be authentically themselves, it seems we really don't—and if you want evidence, I would look no further than the way society responds to the existence of Black conservatives.

And that brings me back to Owens. Following her surprising termination at conservative news site The Daily Wire, which came after she repeatedly embraced antisemitic rhetoric and tropes, she made an even more surprising appearance on *The Breakfast Club*.

The show is popular with its predominantly Black audience for commentary on politics, culture, music, and issues of the day. Owens has made much of her career being a conservative provocateur by doing things like dismissing concerns about police violence, sharply criticizing the Black Lives Matter movement, and urging Black voters to leave the Democratic Party with Blexit. However, she was not seriously challenged on her politics on the show. Instead, she was asked to play a Black pop culture game to prove her blackness. She didn't have to answer for why she said Martin Luther King Jr. would have voted for Trump. Or why she called BLM a hate group. Instead she was asked to rap the theme song to *The Fresh Prince of Bel-Air*. Her politics are preposterous, but this response to them befuddles me as well. A lot of the popular critiques against her center on whether her politics are a referendum on her Blackness.

CANDACE AND ME

There's a hard-to-describe but visceral discomfort I feel whenever I see this type of criticism of Black conservatives. It's not protectiveness, at least not really. In fact, I agree there is something particularly infuriating about the use of Black conservatives to validate the most racially incendiary positions of the conservative movement. It's transparently cynical but also ineffective.

"You can't call it racist if it's a *Black person* saying it!" is just the kind of anticlimactic trump card you'd expect from people who don't understand racism or our objections to it. Racism is a structural evil, not something that people of color can evaporate by virtue of their identity. Racist ideas aren't speaker dependent. They don't magically get more credibility if you can find the right messenger. Anti-Black sentiments can be—and often are—espoused by anyone, *including Black people*. Throwing down a token Black Republican who will say the quiet part out loud so the white people don't have to isn't winning the poker game; it's going all-in with a pair of twos.

But that's not the only accusation that Black conservatives face from progressives. What would be otherwise valid critiques of Black conservatives often carry an implicit—and sometimes explicit—attack on the racial authenticity of the person. This strikes me as deeply unfair. The argument essentially boils down to the insistence that there is nothing in the Black experience that would prompt someone to genuinely develop conservative politics, and their presence on the ideological spectrum is clearly the result of some other factor or falsity.

Sometimes the people leading these attacks are from outside the Black community. I'm not only condemning white outrage at the existence of people like Candace Owens or Tim Scott, but I confess I'm uncomfortable with the racial dynamics of some of those critiques. It is concerning to see white progressives feel such ownership over the loyalty and allegiance of Black voters that some would accuse Black conservatives of not being "Black enough."

THE REAL ONES

To be clear, I do not believe any Black conservative should be shielded from the natural consequences of their dangerous rhetoric. We should critique people on the substance of their arguments regardless of race. And Black conservatives should not be spared because they're Black.

But embedded in this critique of Black conservatism is an assumption that marginalized communities never buy into the marginalization of others. This is not only ahistoric but it imagines that oppression confers some sort of spidey sense upon those who have experienced it so they can sniff out and oppose it when it comes for someone else.

Marginalized groups do marginalize other groups, and this isn't rare or accidental. This is how power and privilege protect themselves in this country. The few people in a marginalized group who have achieved success often become the strictest gatekeepers of the systems of power that formerly kept them out. This is what respectability politics tries to sell us: that if we can simply prove to whiteness that we are worthy on their terms, they have to let us in. This doesn't work. And never will. But people have always tried to win equality in this way.

People in power can use a scarcity model and treat justice as a limited resource, then convince communities that their access to their own human rights is dependent upon someone else not getting access to theirs. It's the reason that Trump blames immigration for the loss of jobs in Black communities. It's the reason anti-trans activists co-opt feminist language to try to keep trans girls out of sports. It's the very reason whiteness was created. Power protects itself by selling the false promise that some of us who have been kept out can get in, but only if another group is kept at an even greater distance. So we fight for a slightly closer place in a never-ending line instead of joining forces and crashing the gates.

Stripped to its core, attacking the authenticity of Black conser-

CANDACE AND ME

vatives is an insistence that, after having faced racism, Black people are only allowed to have one type of authentic reaction to oppression. These attacks imply that it is possible to be Black the "wrong way." Attacking Black conservatives then becomes one more way to rob an already marginalized group of entitlement to interpret their own experience. It's basically *What's the Matter with Kansas?* for Black folks: In Thomas Frank's 2004 book, he attempted to explain the rise of populist politics in places like his home state of Kansas where most people would actually benefit from the same liberal proposals that were written off by an "anti-elitism" sentiment. The book armed many well-meaning progressives with a pedantic scold-turned-wistful-concern troll: They're voting against their own self-interest.

The confusion around Black conservatives is uninteresting and fails spectacularly for the same reasons. It is a condescending attempt to argue that someone else knows better what's in another person's self-interest. It's called *self*-interest for a reason. Much like authenticity, you're supposed to get to determine it for yourself. In order to make better and more coherent critiques of Black conservatives, we need to let go of the critique that conservative ideology makes someone less authentically Black.

I am constantly grateful camera phones and the social internet were not *a thing* when I was young. There are nights I bolt upright in bed, just as the tendrils of sleep are gently pulling me down, wide awake in a cold sweat remembering some of the most cringeworthy choices of my twenties. I can't imagine what it would be like to know those memories are readily available, free of the critical context that *everyone was dressing like that*, for anyone else to view.

But for all the unfortunate fashion choices (unironically worn cowboy hats) and wild nights out (I went to UC Santa Barbara) that could make me thankful that I dodged those particular technological bullets, I'm most grateful that my underinformed and overconfident hot takes from my younger years will never see the light of

THE REAL ONES

day. For someone who now pores over every tweet and post before hitting send, hoping to strike the right tone and include enough context, my thoughts in my younger years would never have reflected that care. They lacked grace and humility. They were laughingly simplistic. And they were overly focused on the racial feelings of white people.

I have prided myself on my progressive politics since back when we were calling them "liberal." But as a Cool Black Girl from way back, while my politics always fell on the hard left of the political spectrum, I often consciously centered my racial politics on a white gaze that ensured I never made it seem like white people—or honestly even White People—were the enemy. I was essentially a pick-me girl for white liberals, which is perhaps why I find myself feeling empathy toward women like Owens who strike me as pick-me girls for conservatives.

When she went on *The Breakfast Club*, Owens was asked if it bothered her to be called an Uncle Tom. She said no and noted that in the book, Uncle Tom was actually "the hero." It occurred to me that because many schools no longer teach the book, not only are younger generations significantly less familiar with the literary character but also with the use of *Uncle Tom* as a pejorative epithet. In fact, I once referenced the term to a group of undergraduates I was speaking to and someone asked me what it meant. I answered the question, tightened my shawl around my shoulders, grabbed my cane, and hobbled out. But Owens has a point: Few people are probably familiar enough to remember the details of Harriet Beecher Stowe's novel *Uncle Tom's Cabin*, the source of the insult.

In the book, Tom was an enslaved person who is portrayed as a noble and incredibly tragic figure. He is a devout Christian and throughout the book is subjected to and witnesses many of the horrors of slavery. He is savagely beaten by sadistic overseers, befriends and provides comfort to enslaved women who face brutal

CANDACE AND ME

sexual assaults, and is ultimately killed when he refuses to betray his friends and tell the overseer where they have escaped. In his final moments before he dies, he forgives the people who killed him. During the course of the book, Tom's goodness, his devout Christianity, and his enduring nobility and spirit change many of the white people around him. They are moved by his ability to take on the brutalities and abuses they mete out, and it inspires several of these characters to come to oppose slavery and change their ideas about Black people. The character had a similar impact on readers. This portrayal is credited with having humanized Black enslaved people to many white audiences who had never before identified with a Black character. Stowe, herself an abolitionist, is credited with helping to foment an emerging antislavery movement with the book. Over the years this complexity has become obscured, and *Uncle Tom* has simply become synonymous with a person so afflicted by self-loathing turned cultural Stockholm syndrome that they are willing to buy completely into the system that oppresses them.

Interestingly, Uncle Tom as a character bore little resemblance to the traitorous caricature invoked by the insult. The fact that he was ultimately killed when he refused to betray his friends undermines the idea of him as a sellout. Uncle Tom was a martyr, but he was no sycophant. Even so, the fact that in order to be an effectively sympathetic character he had to endure these abuses and never fight back, never become resentful, and ultimately forgive his murderers feels like an odd thing to be celebrated for. Creating a character who sacrificed himself so well that his captors saw him as human doesn't feel heroic to me. But it does feel familiar. Uncle Tom was the ultimate pick-me.

Whenever Black slang enters a wider—and whiter—lexicon, it typically loses much of its political context and power. Much like *woke* and *canceled*, which used to be incredibly useful terms before they got turned into caricatures of themselves and now carry

THE REAL ONES

essentially the opposite of their original connotation, *pick-me girls* used to be a much more interesting label that carried with it an important critique of power, a critique that has since been lost.

Pick-me as a moniker started on the Black social internet when that referred more to message boards than social media. I can't say for sure when it originated, but I first remember seeing it in the mid aughts. This was the time of countless think pieces about the falling marriage rates in the Black community. (I admit I was the author of at least some of those, and thank whatever internet gods there may be that my pieces from the *L.A. Watts Times* are no longer available online.) According to those think pieces, there were many possibilities for what was to blame for Black couples getting married in lower numbers than their white counterparts, including the criminal justice system and its overincarceration of Black men, Black women outpacing Black men in degrees and in earnings, interracial dating, and systemic racism. According to message forums on BlackPlanet and similar sites, the list of candidates for who was to blame was shorter: Black men or Black women, depending on who was typing.

These message boards were home to many nuance-free and vitriolic fights about the state of the Black community. They followed a frustratingly familiar cadence of observation: one-dimensional accusation that it is the fault of one gender, the ensuing fight escalates, moderators shut the topic down, and the same issue gets brought up a few days later. Because of how quickly the fights devolved into a battle of the sexes, anytime someone crossed enemy lines to defend the other gender, that person was immediately labeled a traitor by their side and a truth teller by the other. And that's where pick-me came from.

The fight would go something like this: Some dude with the user name HotepHomie, or something equally apt, would blame "Black females" and "white feminism" for why Black families were falling apart. He would end his screed with something like

CANDACE AND ME

"Black women don't want to submit anymore, and Black men can no longer be men." A number of women would come back armed with their own stories of being expected to do too much and asking why they should have to submit in their marriages if they out-earn their husband and carry the bulk of the domestic labor load. The fight would go back and forth for a while until a new woman would enter the chat.

She would offer a critique that links racism, capitalism, and misogynoir and explain how the undervaluing of domestic labor and the associated mental load that was disproportionately being performed by women of color is why we still undervalue this work and urge a focus on dismantling these systems rather than arguing within the community.

Nah, I'm just kidding. She'd very helpfully say something like this: "I don't understand you females. I am *happy* to submit to my king when I'm in a relationship. I cook and clean because that comes to me *naturally* as a woman, and especially as a Black woman, because we were the *first mothers*. If I work outside the home to help him hold it down, that's still not my real job. I am proud to let my husband lead our home as the head and I nurture it as the heart."

The men would fall all over themselves to commend her, to let her know how brave she was, and how she gets it. "Protect her at all costs, fellas," they would beg.

Then one of the women would digitally roll her eyes with a simple phrase, "They still not gon' pick you, sis."

A "pick-me" is not just a woman who wants male attention. She is a woman who—in response to misogyny or misogynoir—embraces the same rhetoric to try to get the approval, attention, and/or protection from the men espousing it. Because it was happening in real time, it was easier to clock. The pick-me was responding directly to the men who were giving her attention, so the connection was clear. This distinction matters more than it seems

THE REAL ONES

like it does because *pick-me* was never just a critique of the woman trying to get picked. It was as much about the men doing the picking and the power that allowed the picking.

As the phrase got more popular, it has become so separated from the original context that it seems to just be a way of making fun of women who want male attention. Often in parody videos portraying her, the whole gag is that the pick-me girl is being *openly rejected* by the man whose attention she is seeking, and she still tries to engage in the pick-me behavior. It may be cathartic to see a woman who basically embodies *I'm not like other girls* humbled for hating women. But this portrayal has robbed *pick-me* of much of its original bite. It's been transformed from a layered critique into just a way of insulting women who try too hard for male approval. Disconnecting the pick-me behavior from the immediate validation from the men loses a critical piece of the equation of the commentary.

The central conceit of pick-mes now is that they are engaging in this behavior despite the fact that it bestows none of the attention, approval, or protection that they seek. The pick-me girl is no longer a critique of misogyny and the self-loathing it encourages. The pick-me girl is just a . . . mean girl.

Imagining that there are just some women who are so hostile to other women that they, with no prompting, started defining themselves as "not like other girls" as a way to shade other women and to prop themselves up is such a lazy read of a complex situation. The reason women bought into that framing is that power structures begged us to, tricked us into it, and forced us to. So keeping the critique of the behavior while sanitizing the power structures that birthed it is dishonest. It makes the pick-me behavior more of a personality flaw instead of a perfectly rational, if misguided and self-sabotaging, response to misogyny.

I have a point: If you think Twitter is a cesspool, you never spent time on BlackPlanet in 2006. Those mid-aughts message boards

CANDACE AND ME

would make a YouTube comments page look like the Algonquin Round Table.

Fine, I have a second point: There is nothing inauthentic about a Black conservative. When power structures are anti-Black, it is a perfectly rational and authentic response to oppression to buy into the anti-Black rhetoric and try to gain approval and safety at the expense of other Black people. I vehemently believe it's a wrongheaded response. And that it's an ultimately futile one. But it's not an indictment of someone's authenticity as a Black person. In fact, seeking white approval in exchange for safety is a pretty common feature of that experience. And focusing on the shortcomings of individual Black conservatives as though their politics are evidence of a weak will is as pointless as imagining pick-mes as women with a preternatural hatred of other women. The political philosophy of an individual Black conservative is not interesting. The system that produces their anti-Blackness is. And to understand that, I don't need to listen to Candace Owens, I need to listen to everyone else who could have been her. Like me.

I think there are a lot of us who have had similar experiences at some point in our lives. I know I did. Fortunately for me, there are no recordings of my evolution. No self-righteous videos. No essays written in the ink of the internet and screenshotted for posterity where I recount how I accepted white approval at the expense of other Black people. So out of solidarity and a strong sense of "there but for the grace of god go I," I'll create a record now.

When I was in college, my social circle was overwhelmingly white. I went to UC Santa Barbara, where that's not uncommon, but there were ways I could have sought out Black friends. I just didn't. I wasn't active in the Black Student Union and I didn't take Black Studies courses until late in my college career. One night I was at a party with my friend. We were dancing to Nelly's song "Country Grammar" because it was 2000 and also because mind your business.

THE REAL ONES

We got to the part where he uses the N-word like nineteen times in a single verse and my very white friend rapped right along with it. A Black student at the party happened to see this, and I saw her point at my friends and say something to the Black students she was with. She caught my eye and gave me a sympathetic smile and an eye roll, clocking the microaggression and offering me—kindly—sisterhood. All I had to do was smile back, shrug, and have a moment with her. It wasn't even that deep.

But my friend happened to see this look and wondered if they were talking about her. Now this is a friend I love dearly to this day. And since that party back when we were two nineteen-year-olds, she and I have had a number of honest and painful conversations that have massively shifted her worldview over the years. But, at this point in her life, she had an extremely immature and problematic view of race.

At that point, we had had conversations where she had revealed that she thought I was too dismissive of the ways that racism impacted her as a white woman. She passionately explained to me how unfair it was that if she walked up to a table of all Black people she would be made to feel uncomfortable. This fictitious table of Black people that she was desperate to sit with would reject her, she insisted, because she was "a little white girl."

I didn't even bother with why we needed to engage in a thought experiment about this at all, seeing as I had never once seen her attempt to put herself in a situation where she would be the only white person. Instead, I explained that the situation she was describing was one I was in constantly—that I was always the only Black person in our friend group. She responded that the difference is that I didn't get treated any differently because of it. No one would ever explicitly bring up my race, she insisted. I was shocked that she believed that race never came up for me—explicitly or implicitly—but at the same time, I never went out of my way to tell her the ways that it did. It would make her defensive and uncom-

CANDACE AND ME

fortable, and I preferred maintaining the semblance of comfort, even if it created distance between us, which I also felt guilty for creating.

So that night at the party when she noted that these Black students were looking at her, I *knew* she was imagining herself the victim of some huge racial slight. And so I decided to defend her honor by glaring at the Black student just trying to love me up in an awkward moment. I made a point of putting my arm around my friend. The Black girl looked at me blankly. That poor woman. She must have been so confused and so disappointed. My friend and I bonded over the moment in a "see how race doesn't matter because we have each other's backs?" kind of way. Of course race *did* matter. The entire exchange—from the fact that she had just sung the N-word at a party to the defensiveness she felt that these people of color were staring at her to the fact that I overreacted to show her I was on her side—had been about race. But what I showed her was that *my* race didn't matter. I had sided with her over other Black people in a moment where my solidarity would have meant something.

And when I think about moments like that, I try to understand why I did this, but I'm being overly charitable when I try to make it more complicated than it was. I did this because in that moment, the approval of the white people around me felt more urgent and valuable than expressing solidarity with the Black people who were trying to express comradery with me.

It's hard to tell that story, especially knowing there are others like this one. But it's also freeing telling this story, especially *knowing that there are others like this one*. It's freeing admitting that there was a time when I was most comfortable in majority white spaces and most craved white approval because of the objectivity I believed that approval conferred. I appreciate being able to admit this because when I do, it becomes easier for me to trust that I am firmly on the other side of my evolution on this. And I feel the

THE REAL ONES

distance between Candace and me grow larger. Not in the artificial way that comes when I performatively *try* to distance myself from Black conservatives, but in a more authentic way that allows me to rightsize my relationship with them. I don't have to be extra critical of them, because I'm not trying to prove anything. There's no projection. I don't see a fun house mirror version of myself reflected in any of them.

This raises another question for me. If I can admit that there was a time that I was part of this problem, how can I respond to the moment when some of these conservatives who are publicly doing harm go through their own evolutions? If I was allowed my process, I sometimes wonder how I would respond if, for example, Owens looked at her current platform and realized this has all been a part of *her* evolution, and she no longer believed any of her rhetoric.

Public forgiveness is complicated, and we currently don't have a great process for allowing people's politics to grow and mature without indefinitely holding their prior positions up and insisting that they still have to answer for them. Many of us made our biggest mistakes in private before there were internet platforms where the damage we did could impact people beyond our immediate circles. So I recognize that part of the difficulty with public forgiveness is that the harm someone with a large following does continues harming even after they have disavowed it. But by the same token, it seems that a larger platform could likewise do a lot of good if someone expressed genuine regret and accountability, and took steps to affirmatively dismantle the dangerous arguments they engaged in.

I feel that today's social and racial justice movements have not given real consideration to how people who have done this kind of harm can be held accountable and seek forgiveness. There is no path to repair things. This is something that deeply troubles me. At the same time, the discussion on forgiveness often gets taken

CANDACE AND ME

over by people bemoaning "cancel culture" who simply want the freedom to do harm, give a cursory apology, and move on with no consequences. But I don't have a concept of justice—and that includes social and racial justice—that doesn't have forgiveness and rehabilitation at its core, so I'm deeply bothered by our inability to seriously grapple with this question.

I spend more time than I probably should wondering if I could forgive Owens if she decided to abandon her politics and apologize for the harm she has done. The amount of time I've spent on this hypothetical scenario is vastly out of proportion for a number of reasons. First, I don't know Owens. Second, she has never indicated to me or any of her nine million viewers that she has any remorse over her political positions or any harm that could be attributed to them. Even as she has more recently seemed to soft launch a rebrand, moving away from politics and more into celebrity gossip and cultural commentary, she hasn't alluded to any kind of evolution on her political views. And finally, I don't think whether I would forgive her or not would really matter if she ever did decide to publicly apologize.

But I care about the answer to this question. First, because Owens is not just a Black woman, she's a young Black woman. And while I have no desire to protect her from a reasonable response to her damaging and untrue political rhetoric, I know a lot of the responses she gets are not reasonable. In fact, they are downright dangerous.

Everyone gets people disagreeing with them on the internet, but when people disagree with Black women, they attack. When people don't like articles I have written, they call me racial slurs. They call me ugly. They call me fat. One time I got doxed because Trump supporters didn't like something my boss's brother said on Twitter. (That was it. That was *genuinely* the reason. Sometimes the fact that some people cannot tell the Castro brothers apart impacts my life too much.) They got my phone number and shared it

THE REAL ONES

quickly. They filled my voicemail with hateful, racist comments and my text messages with pictures of apes.

There isn't a Black woman on the internet who doesn't know the fear that online attention brings. In fact, I don't know women of any race who work in politics who haven't been subjected to vitriolic attacks online whenever they espouse an idea that some people could disagree with. One time a colleague announced online that he was getting hate for something he'd said. I immediately reacted with sympathy, texting him and asking if he was okay. The colleague—a white man—was puzzled by my reaction and explained that he was fine. In fact, he considered it a badge of honor. We laughed sadly over the misunderstanding and our vastly different experiences.

So despite not actually knowing Owens, I do know with absolute certainty that Black women on the internet get subjected to a level of virulent harassment and violence. And I think I would feel an obligation to publicly support her if she were to evolve her thinking, if only to help offset some of the negative responses I know she would get.

But the other reason I care about the answer to this question is that I'm not really thinking about forgiving Owens. I'm thinking about how forgiveness would work for any Black conservative provocateur who had a crisis of conscience and realized that they no longer believed their dangerous rhetoric and were ready to evolve their thinking.

I like to think that in the same way I was given time and compassion as my racial politics matured, I could grant that same compassion to someone else on a similar journey. And while it's no one's place to absolve others of harm on behalf of entire communities, my approach is this: If people with underrepresented identities make careers out of being "the good one" for a mainstream audience, and then ultimately decide they are doing harm, I *want* to forgive them. I want to forgive them because I think the forces

CANDACE AND ME

that prompted them to seek white approval are the problem, and their behavior was only a symptom. They were trying to survive. And if I pretend I can't understand and empathize with the impulse to do that *and* the shame of realizing how wrong you were, I'm doing something harmful. I'm furthering the dangerous erasure of the fact that a part of most of our evolutions involved a period of time when we knew less than we know right now. And we did the same thing in different ways and, in the name of pursuing our authentic selves, came out the other end changed.

7

BLACK GIRL NEXT DOOR

Like many Black girls, my young adulthood was spent experimenting with my hair. I've had my hair fall out from relaxers. I've lived and died between press and curls. I've worn wigs and been terrified they would fall off. I've worn weaves. I've had every variety of twists and braids they make. And after a lifetime of experimentation, I've come to a conclusion: There is no equivalent to a messy bun for Black women.

Let me be clear: There are some Black women who can put their hair into a messy bun, and while I've never been one of them, I know this possibility exists. But I'm not using "messy bun" to refer to a hairstyle as much as a cultural signifier. What I mean is that the thing that a messy bun *conveys* doesn't exist for Black women.

I am a fully grown woman. But if I so much as catch a whiff of VO5 apple shampoo, it's like a time machine. I'm suddenly fourteen again, and I am burning with envy. That shampoo had a *choke hold* on everyone at my high school. I remember I smelled it every morning when I got to school and greeted my friends, their hair damp from showers and smelling like apples. I wished so hard for hair that allowed me to run out of the door while it was still wet. I wished so hard for the deep claw marks their combs made through that wet hair. I wished so hard for the skill to gather all that hair into a messy pile on top of my head. And I wished so hard for that damn appley, chemically smell.

I remember times that I let details of how I cared for my hair slip out to my white friends, and the ungenerous reactions I received trained me to keep such matters to myself.

That I used grease in my hair prompted fake gags.

That I didn't use hair spray was met with disbelief.

That I didn't wash my hair every day was intentionally misunderstood as I *never* washed my hair.

Kids are cruel, and all of that, but my hair was always a huge source of insecurity and such a signifier of difference. Sometimes I watch Black hairstylists and creators on YouTube and TikTok, and I wonder if this means that young Black girls aren't having the same trauma around their hair that we older millennial (or, if you prefer—which I do—xennial) and Generation X Black girls did.

Please tell me that young Black girls don't have the same trauma around their hair that we did.

Before *Sesame Street* had Auntie Kayla come visit Gabrielle and tenderly detangle, wash, and style her hair, wash day used to be a secret. It was a cultural reference that many outside the Black community were wholly unaware of. And I kept it that way. Every other Sunday I was just quietly unavailable, and when I emerged on Monday, edges were laid, scalp was shiny. But it was more than just wash day. My hair became a magic trick, and magicians never reveal their secrets. I had been so scarred by the reaction I'd gotten anytime I'd pulled back the curtain that I simply did not let my white friends catch me slipping in the hair department. A headscarf or bonnet never made an appearance at a sleepover. I kept the existence of hair curlers a closely guarded secret under my bed. No one knew how much work went into my hair, and when I saw how little they were able to put into their own and still be safe to go outside, it made me hide my process even more.

THE REAL ONES

There could not have been a more stark difference between the casual way that my white classmates came to school essentially still doing their hair and how I would never be seen in public until mine was perfect. And that made the wet, VO5-scented hair of my white girlfriends so *fascinating* to me. Not only could they leave the house with their hair undone, that lack of being done was a *style*. And I watched with envy as they held their heads upside down, flipped their hair, did some kind of magic, and ended with a messy bun. We grew up, and went into professional jobs, and they could *still* wear their hair that way and have it accepted in the corporate world. Meanwhile, in my corporate law firm, my hair the way it naturally grew out of my head may well have been considered a violation of the dress code. *That* knowledge had a choke hold on me.

For Black people who grew up around other Black people, I'm sure this sounds at least a bit unhinged. But I don't think I'm alone among Black people who grew up in predominantly white areas. And I don't think *we're* alone in envying our white peers' casual ease. I've talked to queer friends about how envious they were of the casual way their friends would disclose their crushes. Meanwhile, they'd only confess a crush to a trusted confidant, and only then if they were 300 percent certain the object of their crush was also gay. When you *have* to put in so much effort to feel safe, it's understandable to envy the effortlessness others take for granted.

One of the most frustrating things about essentialist authenticity as a concept is its obsession with naturalness. If authenticity is who you are when you aren't concerned about what you're supposed to be, it is, simply put, who you are without trying. In this rendering, effort is anathema to realness. If you're trying to be something, it's not who you are at your core. But nature is actually pretty overrated. Or at the very least, it's misunderstood.

Imagine going to the grocery store with the goal to eat only natural food. You steer clear of the obvious problem areas—the frozen prepared meals section, the candy aisle, the processed and additive-laden cereal aisles. Then you head to what seems like safe ground, the produce section, and begin filling your cart. Apples, lettuce, carrots, cucumbers—easy choices that can be eaten and enjoyed in their natural form. But what happens when you get to the sweet potatoes or beets? In their raw state, these are actually inedible. But it seems wrong to say that cooking them makes them *less* natural. What is the value of keeping it in its natural state if it can't be consumed that way?

The problem with authenticity and its fixation on naturalness is that it assumes we are all apples when many of us are sweet potatoes. It assumes that none of us need any preparation. Who is to say that the way I present myself is less me than the way I'm found in nature? What about those of us who get closer to who we really are with some change or transformation?

This problem again reveals the value of focusing on self-reflective authenticity rather than an essentialist model. Self-reflective authenticity can let us bypass this issue by refusing to privilege originalism. In fact, it is sometimes the things we put the most effort into cultivating that reflect what we most value and, likewise, who we truly are.

When I talk about a messy bun, it isn't a hairstyle. It's a signifier of the ability to be accepted and desired without effort. It was clean beauty before clean beauty was an aesthetic. It was girl next door, another trope I was obsessed with because of its ubiquitousness and how beyond my reach it seemed, a natural beauty who stood in contrast to a more glamorous romantic rival. The girl next door's appeal derived from ease and effortlessness. And that beauty ideal doesn't exist for Black women.

A few years ago, Hasan Minhaj got some backlash for making a similar critique about beauty standards for men of color in Hollywood. In a *Vanity Fair* video, comparing attractiveness standards for white actors and brown actors, he took a lie detector test in which he was asked to rate Dax Shepard on a scale from 1 to 10.

THE REAL ONES

He rated Dax a 6.75, but when asked for an explanation, Hasan decided to do the lie detector proud and get honest, and that's what prompted the ensuing controversy. He described Dax as falling within a category of approachably attractive white men in Hollywood who look like someone who went to your high school. His point was that while these guys are undeniably attractive (it's still Hollywood, after all), they have what would be considered attainable good looks. He went on to note that for men of color, that category doesn't exist, citing examples like Daniel Dae Kim and Idris Elba. Men of color can't be average—even by Hollywood standards. They have to be attractive in a way that is so undeniable that it is completely unattainable.

There's a comparison here that I'm afraid to make because, in order to talk about it, I have to discuss two larger-than-life talents who have passionate and protective fan bases. Among them are fans who would react in fury over any perceived slight. So I will try to make this point with the disclaimer that I genuinely love the music and deeply respect the talent of both Beyoncé and Taylor Swift.

Despite them being two of the biggest and most profitable superstars alive, they have very different public images. Despite them having two of the most fiercely loyal fan bases, the relationships that their fans build with them are very different. And I think it's interesting to see the reasons for these differences.

Taylor Swift's image is based on an idea of relatability. In her lyrics, despite being an incredibly conventionally attractive woman, she casts herself as the plain or awkward or monstrous other. Despite being a woman in her thirties, she still regularly releases music invoking high school imagery and references. She's T. Swift. Tay Tay. Blondie. Despite being immensely powerful from an economic, social, and political standpoint, her persona communicates that she doesn't know she's Taylor Swift and is, in fact, just like you. This persona is effective. Her fans feel like they're friends. They engage with her music, her events, and what they know of her life as though they're rooting for their best friend. They love her boyfriends and turn on them when they hurt her. When they think she's made a bad choice in dating, they try to talk her out of it. They mean-girl the ex-friends who have wronged her. They are quick to point out when she has been victimized—particularly if it feels like misogyny is playing a role—and use feminist arguments to defend her against critiques. They root for her happiness with the fervor of your most supportive text chain hyping you up before a big presentation at work.

Beyoncé's public image is the opposite of "just like you." Her entire brand is based on being completely unattainable, the absolute paragon. She is otherworldly. Her songs catalog a deeply unrelatable superiority on every metric imaginable and rely on the fact that her lyrics are boastful but inarguable. Fact-check her and you'll find no lie: her wealth, her sexiness, her status, her peerlessness. Her fans love her because they'll never be her. She's Queen Bey. Hell, according to her husband, she's King Bey. Her persona screams that she is leagues above you, but don't feel bad, you're in great company, because she's leagues above everyone. This persona is effective. Her fans aren't friends. They're a hive. A collective who love her with no delusions about *their* role in *her* life, but they're a crowd still willing to make outsized space in their lives for her. They are aunties to her children and defend them as their own. In truth, they don't love her husband but harbor no false impressions that their feelings impact her choices, romantic or otherwise, so they keep it pushing. They defend her from criticism, injecting particular protectiveness when racism and misogynoir seem to underlie a critique.

Images are just that. They're images. Tropes. Neither of these personas is who these women really are, but they're the personas they've chosen. The diva and the girl next door.

Because they are both so successful, it's easy to forget that

THE REAL ONES

Taylor is succeeding at something (not musically, but in her persona) that is much easier than what Beyoncé is achieving. It is easier to be the girl next door than the diva. For the diva, perfection is expected. That's the baseline. For the girl next door, flaws are not just allowed, they're part of the appeal. Being human strengthens Taylor's image and harms Beyoncé's. Taylor gets to be an *Anti-Hero*. Beyoncé has to be *Flawless*.

Central to Taylor's ability to embody the girl next door is her whiteness. It's not another piece of the equation. It's core to the image, and therefore unavailable to a Black woman like Beyoncé. Obviously, this doesn't matter for Beyoncé because she is, literally, Beyoncé. But for other women who come after them who need to try to adapt these images to replicate their successes, this difference is stark. That's the point Hasan made: For white people, there exists a category of relatable appeal. For people of color, the appeal has to be indisputable to be recognized at all. There is no Black girl next door.

That means Black beauty often requires visible effort to even be recognized. And in a culture that claims to reward effortless beauty, that creates a problem. Because effort, when it shows, is seen as disqualifying. There's something quietly cruel about the idea that it's not enough to be beautiful; that, in fact, beauty should be obvious when unenhanced. It really is a brilliant trick of marketing to make it seem magnanimous to prefer women to be simply stunning all on their own. But I'll save that critique for another time. Right now what is frustrating me about the tyranny of effortlessness is how damaging it is that we equate effort with inauthenticity.

Effort has been taking a beating for a while, and I honestly don't know when this started. The myth of effortless beauty was always around. The late '90s and early 2000s were a constant barrage of famous women convincing us that they ate junk food all the time and still kept their rail-thin bodies. Plastic surgeries happened, but no one was supposed to admit that they had had them. Despite the fact that everyone *knew* effort was being put in, we all engaged in a bit of a shared delusion around it. But aesthetically, it was clear effort was being put in: Makeup was heavy, clothes were attention-grabbing. We may have been pretending celebrities were simply genetically blessed to look a certain way, but there was still an understanding that people were putting in work.

At some point, the beauty industry decided to co-opt feminism. It's as if the phrase "if you can't beat 'em, join 'em" became a business model. In this new beauty *and wellness* industry, the goal wasn't just beauty, it was health: mental, physical, and spiritual. And the heavy, caked-on makeup that they *used* to sell us? Who would want that? Not only was it not trendy and bad for your skin, it made you the wrong kind of woman. That's the kind of makeup vain women wore. Women who wanted male attention. Women who put in . . . effort. The beauty and wellness industry wasn't about that. Makeup should be natural. Simple. Effortless. Authentic. To be clear, there should still be makeup—just *different makeup.*

The vilification of effort didn't start or end with makeup. But it did provide a clear example of the shift. It continued to show up in a number of ways. I remember that in 2011 a lot of people decided Anne Hathaway was trying too hard to be good at her job, and she got a toxic amount of hate online. In 2009, J.J. Abrams rebooted the *Star Trek* franchise with a movie that retconned the origin story of Captain Kirk. The new version fit the hero model we are accustomed to today, in contrast to the heroes an audience would have identified with in the 1960s during the original series. In the original series, James Tiberius Kirk was a much more classic male lead. He had always dreamed of being a captain in Starfleet and had the track record to prove it. He had been an extraordinary hard worker in the academy and graduated at the top of his class. He took a role as a lieutenant on another ship before receiving his command as captain of the starship *Enterprise*, becoming the youngest captain ever. He took the role seriously, sometimes too seriously, and much of the action of the original series involved him having to learn how to lead and accept that he can't always make the perfect decision.

In Abrams's reboot, Kirk had to get talked into attending Starfleet Academy and basically agreed only to avoid getting in trouble. He was a talented student but a lazy one, coasting through his classes, cheating on tests, and generally not taking it seriously. He slouches into leadership instead of wanting it; and while he ultimately rises to the occasion, it's reluctantly once the role is thrust upon him. The trope is not unfamiliar—it's the reluctant hero. But that's *not* James Tiberius Kirk. The difference is now he represented a version of the character audiences would find it easier to relate to, and apparently that means someone who doesn't want anything too badly.

This shows up in politics all the time, and as I will discuss later, the way we talk about and judge effort in politics sets up completely unmanageable and unmeetable expectations. As voters, we like to imagine that our favorite candidates never planned to run for office, that it essentially happened by accident. People respond well to the idea that before a candidate was a candidate, it had never occurred to them to run for office. But something just called them to service, and the rest was history.

I understand the appeal of this story. We want leaders who don't set out to lead; someone who can get elected without the ego that makes them *want* to get elected. We want the humility and relatability of someone who never thought they could do this, mixed with the competence and natural leadership skills of someone who hasn't been preparing but is somehow ready to lead.

In real life, things don't work that way. First, for very practical reasons. The decision to run for office takes planning and foresight and endless conversations. Candidates have to talk to family and loved ones about what a potential run would mean for them. They need to save money because they can't work while they run. They need to plan around life issues, like kids changing schools and spouses changing careers. The decision to run for office—if it's made by someone thoughtful enough to be good in office—has never been made overnight.

But beyond the practical, running for office takes ambition. It takes the person who believes that in the darkest moments there is a way out, and that they can help us find the way. It takes someone who is used to being up against really tough odds *and trying really hard*. Obviously, there are people who don't fit this bill. Donald Trump has never struck me as someone burdened by an abundance of effort. I got the impression that he tried as hard to become president as he'd ever tried for anything. I think he put in what he believed to be a real effort.

The irony is that there are people who would be amazing public servants but are waiting for the stars to align the way people say they're supposed to in order to run. The fairy tale we tell about how things come together—*effortlessly*—is likely scaring away some of the people who would be most effective in office. This is why it's critically important that we are honest about the effort that goes into decisions like this. In much the same way that, despite knowing there are speechwriters, we like to believe that our leaders are simply telling us what's in their hearts, we seem to want to cling to the idea that candidates wake up one day and decide to run for office. Demystifying the process of running for office lets more people in on the nuts and bolts of deciding to run. This is especially valuable as we try to increase the number of people who have been underrepresented in politics.

I have spoken to so many would-be candidates who express a desire to run but tell me they are waiting for the right moment. When I ask what that would be, they recount stories they have been told about an open seat, a retiring incumbent reaching out to encourage a run, a donor willing to bankroll the entire thing based

THE REAL ONES

on an initial meeting. When I press, I find out these are stories they heard or read about how someone got their start. They are *shocked* to find out that retiring incumbents have lines of wannabe successors who begin planning years in advance for the hope of an endorsement. Or that big donors take multiple meetings, early poll numbers, and path-to-victory PowerPoint presentations to decide to support a campaign.

In addition to scaring some people from even stepping forward, the way we view effort in politics also creates an unfair bias that hurts people with underrepresented identities. People who had to work harder to get where they are can't hide their effort, and this is true of people with underreported identities. They don't accidentally end up in positions of power, but when voters are made aware of how long and hard they have been working for this moment, many are turned off by what they see as unchecked ambition. It creates an impossible quagmire for us.

Hillary Clinton famously got critiqued for how badly she seemed to want to be president, especially when compared to Donald Trump's seeming indifference to the job while campaigning. It's an odd thing indeed to hold a desire for a job against the person running for it. And after watching for a term and a half how someone who could take or leave the job leads, I would hope effort would be first on our list of qualifications for elected leaders moving forward. Why wouldn't we want the person who treats the job like this is the one they've been waiting for their whole life?

The problem with our cultural takedown of effort is that effortlessness is a privilege. It's the ability to not try and just end up at the top alongside people who have scraped and clawed to get there. It's the idea that a woman wanting recognition for her work makes her less deserving of acknowledgment. It's a candidate looking like he didn't plan to run for office because he didn't have to start three years in advance building up a donor base. It's getting to wear a still-wet messy bun to work next to colleagues who have been told their natural hair is unprofessional. Effortlessness is reserved for people who can do the bare minimum and still be accepted.

One of the most brilliant commentaries I've seen on this came from a TV episode with one of the silliest premises. Bear with me. There's an episode of the show *Community* that you should watch. Truthfully, you should watch all of them. We are standing at the brink of finally getting the *Community* movie we had been promised (#SixSeasonsAndAMovie), and it's worth the bingeing time, trust me.

In this particular episode, "App Development and Condiments," a new app called MeowMeowBeenz (listen, I know how it sounds but *watch it*, it's seriously brilliant) takes over the community college campus. It's essentially Yelp but for people. Everyone can rate one another and when your rating is higher, your ratings of others are weighted more heavily, so you have the ability to make other people more popular. Because this is *Community*, after having the app for a day, the campus fully morphs into a dystopian world where your app rating controls your entire experience on campus.

The central conflict in this episode is between Jeff Winger and Shirley Bennett. Shirley is a classic try hard. Everything about her screams effort. She goes out of her way to be nice to people, she gives away baked goods, she is overly friendly and outgoing. However, beneath that lurks a performative nature to her niceness—a manipulative, passive-aggressive behavior. And even though all she wants in return is friendship, it still feels transactional: She *expects* that friendship in return for her kindness.

Jeff, on the other hand, seems effortlessly charming and popular, especially since he is constantly trying to avoid participating in campus events despite repeatedly getting swept up into shenanigans anyway. He doesn't have to try, and he gets the friendship Shirley works for—even when he claims not to want it.

Shirley is a Black woman and Jeff is a white man. In this episode they are set up as foils to each other: Jeff trying to prove that Shirley's friendliness is phony and a way of gaining control, and Shirley trying to show Jeff is just as phony because, despite his insistence to the contrary, he desperately wants the popularity and control he claims to resent.

As their fight comes to a head, without once mentioning race or gender, this episode reveals the giant problem with effortlessness. *Jeff and Shirley are the exact same character.* They both want to be liked and they both want power. But because of who Jeff is, he is given it automatically, and because of who Shirley is, she has to scheme for it. But then she has to bear the burden of effort, while he enjoys the veneer of dispassionate effortlessness. They both want the same thing, but she is punished, while he is admired.

I used to work in a shared office space with a number of other companies. We all had separate offices, but because of a lot of collective space and, being young professionals, we spent a lot of time mingling. Another Black woman, Elle, and I became friends. Elle, a trans woman, and I bonded over our similar style and where we could find cute, plus-sized dresses. None of these companies were especially formal, so unless you were going to an out-of-office meeting, no one really dressed up. But Elle and I tended to wear dresses and skirts, which meant we tended to look dressier and more formal than many of our colleagues. And that was why I was so confused one day when Elle came into my office, closed my door, and started crying. She told me she had just gotten a warning from HR for dressing unprofessionally. My jaw dropped.

"What is considered unprofessional?" I demanded.

She shook her head. "They basically said I was dressed inappropriately for a workplace. My dresses are too low-cut and my makeup is too heavy."

I fumed. I asked what I could do, and she said she just needed to vent. She left my office soon after and her role not long after that. I was livid. Not the least of which because the same HR staffer who had issued that warning had come into my office a couple of days earlier in a T-shirt and sweats and boasted that it was a pajama top. I don't know what kind of dress code looks at those two employees and says Elle was the unprofessionally dressed one, but I do know unconscious bias when I see it.

The privilege it took to come into work in pajamas and then criticize someone else for their work attire is something else. But what's more is that Elle may not have felt as comfortable coming to work in anything other than a dress and makeup. Yes, she was a high femme girly to her core, but she was also conscious of the reality of being a Black trans woman and wanting to present in a very gender-conforming way in order to communicate professionalism. She didn't come to work in a full face of makeup and a dress just to be cute. She did it to fully embody her authentic self. Effortlessness was not a privilege she was ever going to be afforded. The double bind she found herself in is what happens when we encourage effortlessness without being honest that it isn't treated the same for everyone.

Social media has changed this conversation in a way that is actually really helpful. Our obsession with creating curated concepts of ourselves online gave way to the understandable backlash against the pressure this created. In a way, it democratized the pressure to curate a palatable version of yourself. It forced everyone—not just those of us with underrepresented identities—to be overly concerned with how we are being perceived at any moment. It made the tyranny of effortlessness more mainstream and thus understandable for more people.

Interestingly, this has sparked a number of discussions on the impact social media has on the development of young people. They are being shaped by a constant need to come across as effortlessly perfect. This dynamic impacts their mental health in serious and inescapable ways. In 2022, Caralena Peterson explored this phenomenon. As she argues in an essay for *Teen Vogue*, young women are facing the pressure of curating an identity online that appears simultaneously perfect and effortless. Further, the constant knowledge that they are being observed online can cause anxiety and increased stress.

The focus on young women makes sense. As Peterson explains, this is the point at which they are developing their identities. But people with underrepresented identities, whether growing up in the age of social media or not, were interacting with a similar dynamic. So while it is refreshing to see this damaging cycle get attention now that it is a more widespread phenomenon, I don't want us to lose sight of the number of people with underrepresented identities who grew up well before the age of social media who likely experienced very similar outcomes. The knowledge that we were constantly being observed, coupled with the need to reflect an effortlessly perfect image, created a pressure cooker during our formative years.

The same negative mental health outcomes, which we have seen associated with young people and social media use, are likely things many of us have struggled with in silence. Peterson points to the effortless perfection myth as a driver behind mental health issues like impostor syndrome and stereotype threat that young women are more likely to face than their male counterparts. Obviously, these are both issues that all people with underrepresented identities are likely to experience. In fact, the first time I heard it, I was shocked to learn "stereotype threat" had a definition: The fear of confirming a negative stereotype about Black girls was something I never thought would have a name.

People with underrepresented identities "who live with a mental illness are also more likely to be misdiagnosed or underdiagnosed." There are many reasons for this disparity, including cultural stigma where often people in underrepresented communities are told that mental health issues are simply facts of life that people can deal with through "mental toughness." If simply by trying to develop our identities we were facing pressures that could impact our mental health, it's no wonder the cultural skepticism around mental health persists within underrepresented communities.

By the same token, some of Peterson's recommendations for how to deal with this pressure can likely help people with underrepresented identities reach a healthier relationship with the pressure we face on and off social media. According to Peterson, shifting out of this cycle requires appreciating the difference between "pursuing an image versus developing an identity: An image is something one must constantly strive for" whereas "an identity . . . is something we are, simply by being and living in the moment—no proof or validation necessary because it doesn't have to measure up to standards defined by anybody other than ourselves."

Image versus identity is a useful way of understanding the pressures marginalized people face. Being constantly expected to appear effortless, while simultaneously receiving the message that our natural state was unacceptable, meant we could never relax. Many of us developed into a persona, instead of a person. And now the project before us is to try to retrofit ourselves into an identity that has always been marked by a need to curate for the consumption of others.

The similarity that life online has to the experience of many underrepresented people presents a real opportunity to better articulate the pressures and anxieties we have often been experiencing silently and unable to name. Effortlessness as authenticity has been a toxic myth for too long. Letting it go is going to take some work. We may have to let ourselves try really hard.

8

GOLDILOCKS

One of the clearest examples of how an environment can become more riddled with inequality and exclusion without a fuller exploration of authenticity is in creative spaces. The practice of critiquing art and creativity has created a process that is unconducive to exploring self-reflective authenticity because critique often allows us to police others' authenticity. If your authenticity can only be arrived at through personal reflection, my assessment of it should be seen as wholly irrelevant.

This is easier said than done. We are used to measuring how authentic something seems to us and judging things accordingly. As I explained earlier, it's possible that when we do that we are unknowingly reacting to some other aspect of a person. We should instead be more accurate in what we really mean when we ask for authenticity. But beyond this, in order to stop overcrediting our own assessments of others' authenticity, we must expand what we think can credibly be read as an authentic story. Especially for people with underrepresented identities.

Part of what happens when we assess whether someone seems authentic or not is that we are measuring them against our own ideas of what their authentic experience could possibly be. When

GOLDILOCKS

it matches our expectations, we read them as authentic; when it doesn't, we don't. For some people, our imagination for what those experiences may be is virtually limitless. White men with no other underrepresented identities can claim any experience and be seen as authentic because they have been given the freedom to embody so many different stories. That's not true for those of us with underrepresented identities and, accordingly, we have a much higher threshold to challenge people's expectations before we get read as authentic. The trick to expanding the range of experiences people will see as authentic is in telling more of our stories.

As humans, we are hardwired toward storytelling. It's one of the first ways we learned to order the world, and that tendency toward narrative shows up in how we understand one another. If I can make sense of your story, I feel like I can make sense of you.

This is one of the reasons diversity in popular culture is so important. In addition to creating more opportunities for creators and performers of color, creating better media, and showing young underrepresented people more portrayals of themselves in media, diversity in popular culture can change how we see one another and the world around us. This is especially important because we remain a very racially and culturally segregated society. On the social internet, we are often hearing only from people we agree with politically, creating an insular bubble where we rarely hear alternative viewpoints. According to research, 75 percent of white people report not having any non-white friends. All of this creates a greater need for representation. Popular culture is one of the few ways white people will hear stories from people of color. Culture dictates how we understand one another.

Many white people of my generation credited *The Cosby Show* with being their introduction to Black culture and President Biden name-checked *Will and Grace* as playing a role in his evolution on LGBT rights. While those shows weren't perfect and neither are the politics they sparked, it is undeniable that they shaped the

THE REAL ONES

worldviews of people who watched them. Giving people access to more stories that go beyond stereotypes helps people understand, and even empathize with, stories that are different from their own. We create character tropes that make these people seem familiar to us and, therefore, more believable as authentic when embodied by real people. The inverse is also true. When we have fewer stories that feature diverse groups of people, we have a much more limited vision of those stories. And when the few stories we see depict the *same* stories, our capacity for what can be considered authentic experiences for other people is flattened into only what we have seen.

This is a vicious circle when we are presented with a limited set of "authentic" stories: We think those are the only stories that exist. So we don't read contradictory accounts as credible and, as a result, they are not perceived as authentic. So even when those stories do make their way into mainstream consciousness, they are perceived as less authentic than the ones we are used to. Instead of challenging the dominant narrative, confirmation bias sets in and we simply see the new stories—and the people who present them—as less authentic.

The ubiquity of white characters means they are granted the assumption of authenticity because we have seen so many examples of their stories over years of television, movies, and literature. White characters have the ability to inhabit any world and tell any story. And the way that shows up in real life is that we have their tropes that seem familiar in *every setting*. White people can thus be credibly understood as authentic in a myriad of ways.

This transforms the authenticity discussion in popular culture to something that disproportionately limits rather than empowers creators of color. Whether something can be considered an authentic portrayal is not measured by whether it reflects a genuine and personal experience. Instead, the story is judged by whether it is recognized by others as matching an accepted authentic experience. That places an onus on these creators to comply with what broader—and whiter—audiences consider to be authentic. The acceptable stories are typically much more narrow and stereotypical. At the same time, creators of color take on the additional burden of cultural representation for their community, and have to make sure everyone sees themselves reflected.

This creates two often opposing forces that creators of color must contend with: a white audience that will feel most comfortable with stereotypes and an in-community audience that recognizes this may be their only chance to see themselves reflected in media and wants to see stories that tell *their* individual experience. So a creator of color who tries to tell their authentic story—which will naturally involve *some* tropes that are familiar both inside and outside their community but some that are not—is often met with criticism that is impossible to resolve, and as a result, struggles to find an audience anywhere.

In 2014, Cristela Alonzo became the first Latino to create, write, and star in her own show, the eponymously titled *Cristela*. It told the story of a young, Mexican American recent law school graduate living in Dallas with her family. The show navigated her getting her first job—an unpaid internship at a prestigious law firm—dealing with her white and privileged coworkers (including one potential love interest), and navigating her relationship with her mother, sister, and the rest of her family.

The show lasted only one season.

When Cristela spoke about her reactions to the challenges she faced on the show, she revealed the double bind many creators of color encounter. In the wake of the cancellation, she was asked about the fact that her show got considerably less money in terms of marketing than other shows on the network. Tellingly, she also noted that a lot of the marketing they did was in Spanish, which made no sense: "Why are we focusing so much on the Spanish-language promotion for an English-speaking show?" By focusing on marketing specifically to Spanish-speaking audiences, the network sent a message that the show was more narrowly targeted than it actually was, which hurt its ability for broader appeal. Further, that marketing campaign exposed the show to the added burden of cultural representation.

Latino experiences in this country are obviously incredibly diverse. *Cristela* was telling a story that was authentic to Cristela: a Mexican American woman in Texas, and her story of navigating family, work, life, and love. The episodes of that first season were heavily influenced by Cristela's own life and experiences. They were, by any measure, authentic. But because the show was marketed as a Latino show, the diversity of the Latino audience it was supposed to appeal to presented a challenge. Because her stories didn't feel authentic or familiar to *everyone*, Cristela faced criticism that "not all Latino families are like that." She pointed out how unfair that was, noting that white creators are not asked to represent an entire community. But the double standard persisted and the result is that the show never found an audience and was canceled too soon.

Or consider the 2015 sitcom, *Fresh Off the Boat*. That show, set in the 1990s, follows the Huangs, a Taiwanese American family who moves from Chinatown in Washington, DC, to a predominantly white community in Orlando, Florida. Parents Louis and Jessica are immigrants raising their three sons in an environment very different from the one they were raised in. The show ran for six seasons with much of the humor centered on the culture clash between the family and their white community, the fear the parents felt that their kids would be so Americanized they would forget their culture, and, well, Constance Wu.

When the show premiered, it was the first time a network show featured an all Asian American cast since 1994 when Margaret Cho starred in the short-lived *All-American Girl*, and many Asian Americans were understandably nervous about how they would

GOLDILOCKS

see this family portrayed. Comedian Jenny Yang coined a term for the anxiety: "rep sweats." But many reported feeling relieved after the premiere, and they saw themselves and their stories represented.

Interestingly, one person who was very vocal about *not* feeling represented was Eddie Huang, restaurateur and the author of the memoir the show was inspired by. The show was created as a televised version of his story, but he was very critical of the direction it ultimately took, claiming that the creators had whitewashed his story to make it more palatable to white audiences rather than telling his authentic story. Despite this, the show was generally well received and did well enough with ratings to get six seasons. It also prompted many conversations among Asian American viewers, including whether it was too concerned with catering to white people, whether it played into too many stereotypes, and whether Constance Wu adopting a Taiwanese accent was offensive.

This show resonated with many viewers and still felt offensive to many others. The show was perceived by many as authentic and yet the person whose story inspired it blasted its authenticity. Clearly these are very complex issues. And it seems to show the limitations of authenticity as the metric for this storytelling. If it's true that this story was inauthentic *and* that many people felt represented by it, it serves as further proof that the solution lies in telling *more* diverse stories.

However, diversity in storytelling doesn't guarantee positive representation, and diverse communities won't agree on what constitutes positive storytelling. A troubling dynamic can arise when creators of color present images that many within the community don't just find unrepresentative but as negative representation.

Tyler Perry has faced an intense amount of backlash among many Black viewers for what is seen as an overreliance on some troubling tropes in his movies and television shows. Despite this fact, Perry's work attracts a large audience of overwhelmingly Black viewers, revealing how often in-community reaction can vary widely and how often critique does not mean something will not still be marketable.

He has been criticized for his tendency to write Black women characters who embody bitter, angry Black woman tropes. That their anger is often a response to abuse, mistreatment, and trauma they experience in their romantic relationships is another source of criticism that has prompted many viewers to accuse Perry of exploiting the pain of Black women. There are other themes that run through his work that have prompted criticisms, specifically that he often presents a central conflict that follows the same pattern: a professional Black woman in a relationship with an abusive or manipulative dark-skinned Black man. Her other romantic option is a good-hearted but poor/down on his luck light-skinned Black man. The Black woman suffers abuse until she chooses the light-skinned man and learns to overcome her classist fear of being with a man who makes less than she does. Viewers have balked at these stories and argued that they show Black people in limited roles and trade on negative and outdated stereotypes, and that the comedy seems designed for white audiences to laugh at the expense of Black people.

In response, Perry has consistently invoked authenticity. He has said that he tells the stories that are familiar to him and the people he knew growing up. Recently, he made waves by arguing that a large portion of his fan base are Black people who are struggling financially, and they see themselves and their families represented in his work. He compared these to his critics—who he called "highbrow negroes"—who he argued don't reflect most of the Black community.

Similarly, Mindy Kaling has come under fire specifically from South Asian women viewers for her creation of Indian women characters. Kaling is known for being one of the more prolific creators of Indian American characters on TV, several of whom she herself has played. Her work, which has included *The Mindy Project*,

GOLDILOCKS

Never Have I Ever, and *Velma* have given us some iconic Indian American young women and stories. However, she has faced criticism that these characters present poor representations of Indian American girls and women who constantly ridicule their own heritage and racial identity, seem overly focused on the acceptance of white characters—especially white male romantic interests—and perpetuate some of the most troubling stereotypes that desi women face.

At the core of the critiques of both these creators and others like them is the fact that because they are putting out content that fewer people are putting out, they are subjected to a higher expectation of representation. And when we know that diverse content has narrow lanes to work within before being considered not marketable, the stakes get raised. It's a Goldilocks problem: Creators of color are being asked to create broadly appealing stories of people of color without relying on stereotypes, while making everyone in a community feel seen and still seeming authentic. There is no "just right" with this equation.

The real problem isn't any particular creator. It's the scarcity model that tells us there can only be a few creators of color telling their stories so they better tell them in a way that represents as many people as possible. If we had more opportunities to tell more stories that represented more people, there would be no reason to go back and forth about what the *real* experiences of these communities are. There wouldn't need to be a singular real experience because there would be more for everyone to choose from.

I understand the frustration of seeing the most well-known creators in our communities tell stories that feel limited or stereotypical or sometimes even regressive. But we have to remember that the creators of today had their formative experiences in a world where they didn't see *anyone* in pop culture who looked like them. There's a tension here. We elevate creators of color who reproduce the dominant images that are already held about us, rather than

THE REAL ONES

ones who challenge them. If the goal is authenticity, we can't begrudge them their real experiences, even if we wish they hadn't happened that way.

Tyler Perry has responded to his critics by saying he is telling stories that are familiar to him. And the fact that he is as popular as he is means that those stories resonate with other viewers, even if they don't resonate with me. To be honest, it deeply troubles me to see portrayals of Black womanhood inextricably linked to trauma, but his job as a creator doesn't have to be to create a narrative that ultimately provides healing.

Likewise, I understand how South Asian women and men can cringe when one of Kaling's characters overreacts to the approval of white men at the expense of her own character's dignity. But, as she has explained, some of those experiences are autobiographical for her. And I'm not willing to deny another woman of color her exploration of the messier and less evolved parts of her journey, because we all had them. They are a part of us, and for her, they are a part of her art. Put simply, Mindy Kaling didn't have Mindy Kaling when she was coming up. And if her authentic stories feel outdated to a lot of people, that's in part because of the battles she has fought that make them feel outdated.

Some of the ability we have to critique these creators is because we have access to more stories that feel authentic for us now—in part *because of them*. The way representation tends to work in media is that one piece does initial work, and then others can build off that. *Girlfriends* told the story of a group of young professional Black friends living in Los Angeles. Because of the groundwork it laid, *Insecure* could tell its story of young professional Black friends living in Los Angeles. And because of that, *Grand Crew*, the tragically gone-too-soon show could tell *its* version of a group of young professional Black friends in Los Angeles. Each show was able to do more, go farther, assume more from its audience because of the existence of previous shows. And each show had the ability to tell different stories and reflected a panoply of experiences so that I, a Black woman who lived in Los Angeles in my twenties, feel like there is a body of media that captures my experience, even if one particular show did not capture the whole of it.

Instead of placing one more barrier on these creators, we can simply demand more opportunities for creatives to tell these stories. This way, the demand to do more isn't placed only on creators of color but felt more broadly across the industry. But the commitment has to be sustainable. And it has to be real.

In the wake of the civil unrest and racial justice protests of 2020, we saw a demand across industries for more diversity in the shows and movies that get made. Top Hollywood executives made a number of commitments to increase racial justice and diversity efforts, both in hiring and in the projects that got green-lit. However, in response to conservative backlash against diversity, equity, and inclusion (DEI) efforts, many of those efforts have been shuttered and commitments left unfulfilled. Now that Trump has taken aim at all DEI efforts, we have seen many of these same corporations quickly walk back those commitments.

As for those changes that were enacted, too many of them felt superficial. Casting people of color in shows, but not changing the storytelling to accommodate them, doesn't offer new stories. It simply features more diversity in stories that don't feel familiar to people of color. There are limits to race-blind casting. It may result in fewer all white casts, but if the writing doesn't adjust to tell stories that make sense for people of color, it is simply casting actors of color to play white characters.

These changes also do little without also looking at questions of narration and point of view—and this is where racial erasure occurs most insidiously. The most obvious example of white storytellers displacing those of color is the ubiquitous "white savior" narrative, where a white outsider (almost always a man) joins or observes a community of characters of color. He quickly becomes

THE REAL ONES

a central figure, often taking on a leading or savior position in a fight for the survival of the group. *Dances with Wolves* and *Avatar* both famously employ this trope. Movies like *The Help* and *The Blind Side* also fall into this category, presenting white saviors—in these instances women—who learn about racism by seeing it happen to Black people in their lives. Ultimately, it is the white women who become the engines of social change and the heroes in a story about the triumphs of another community.

But a similar and less obvious example happens in science fiction and fantasy genres when stories of marginalization are handed to white men and women when their real-life corollaries are experiences borne uniquely by people of color. Comic books have famously done this; and with the popularity of the superhero movies, we have seen reboots of countless examples of stories that clearly are based on experiences that do not belong to the actors being cast. *Superman* tells an immigrant story of alienation and patriotism. The *X-Men*'s central conflict has been compared to philosophical differences within the Civil Rights Movement. Franchises like *Harry Potter* base their in-world power structures and systems of oppression off real-world racism and anti-Semitism but imagine the heroes to be non-Jewish white people.

These stories are not attacked for a lack of authenticity, because at their core lies the common assumption that whiteness is a neutral zone, a universally applicable state, whether or not it makes sense narratively to feature a white character or a white actor. If race truly were not central in these portrayals, then the racial identities of the characters would fit organically into the stories being told. Instead, whiteness becomes both required and assumed.

Likewise, when a character is race bent—meaning an iconic character who was formerly portrayed as white is rewritten in a reboot or subsequent retelling as a person of color—the response of critics is often an attack of authenticity. According to this argument, the character wasn't originally written as a person of color and therefore changing their race doesn't make sense. This debate reveals the central problem with how authenticity makes writing characters of color hard. Because we are so used to seeing white characters, there is no corresponding authenticity requirement for those stories because literally anything can be understood by an audience as an authentic experience.

This is one of the reasons we should have greater comfort race-bending characters when the original character was white rather than when the original was a person of color. Characters of color are written *as* characters of color. Their race is a part of their identity. Almost poetically, the same neutrality fallacy that accounts for the ubiquity of white characters makes it easy to change their race. It's the other side of the myth of the universality of whiteness: A universal story can, by definition, be told by anyone.

Instead of ignoring authenticity in storytelling, we should simply care about it equally. Pretending authenticity is only something that matters for creators of color undermines the quality and richness of storytelling in our society. It makes our stories less true, and it makes them worse. This can only be combated by an acknowledgment that race matters in storytelling. This first requires an admission that white is, in fact, a race. We must do away once and for all with the idea of white neutrality in storytelling; rather, we need to accept that white characters tell stories from a white perspective, in the same way it is always conceded that characters of color do. Instead of being portrayed as white by default, white characters should be written to be conscious of their whiteness, just as characters of color grapple with their own racial identities. Having white characters interact with their racial identity would make authenticity a more useful metric for our stories.

Consider *Doctor Who* and the controversy sparked the first time it was announced that the Doctor would be a white woman and then again when it was announced the Doctor would be a Black

THE REAL ONES

man. Up until that point, the Doctor had only ever been portrayed by white men, despite the fact that the mythology of the Doctor is that he is a time- and space-traveling being with the ability to reincarnate and appear as a different person throughout his lifetime.

Critics complained that it wouldn't make sense for the Doctor to be a woman or a Black person, which was a hollow complaint for a science fiction show about an alien who flies in a ship modeled after an English police box (don't worry, it's bigger on the inside). However, it could make sense narratively for a time-traveling being to choose to only ever appear as a white man, because when traveling through time and space, it is the identity that would afford him the most immediate safety and acceptance. That could be a conscious choice and one that is explored canonically to justify a decision to cast diverse actors as the Doctor.

However, that would require the Doctor to at some point be confronted with this choice of seeking privilege that many of his companions, who are often women, do not enjoy. It would require him to grapple with the reality of racism and misogyny in our world and to wonder if his choice to protect himself from this reality is a moral one. That would be an interesting exploration. This would require him to interact with more people who are different from him, and to care about them genuinely in ways that will allow them their own arcs and rich characterizations. The result of writing authentic white characters will actually support authentic characters of color as well. It would be emotionally resonant and thought-provoking. It would make the Doctor a more nuanced and three-dimensional character. This is the crucial point. Not only will requiring authenticity in white stories ultimately produce more diversity in film and television but, more importantly, it will also lead to richer and more complex characters and storytelling. It will make all of our stories more authentic. And it will make them better.

One of the challenges inherent in telling authentic stories that focus on race and racism is that it actually takes a lot of work to

GOLDILOCKS

present these stories both authentically and understandably to a diverse audience.

In 2023, *The New Yorker* published a bombshell piece accusing comedian Hasan Minhaj of lying during parts of his stand-up routines. Ordinarily, this wouldn't be a problem for a comedian. It's generally understood that comedians lie—and are allowed to lie—for comic effect. I don't know if Chris Rock's neighbor is really a dentist, but the joke still worked. The reason this was so damaging for Minhaj was that he has carved out a space in stand-up that is a mix of political commentary and comedy to a huge amount of success. His first stand-up special, *Homecoming King*, is one of the most poignant and powerful performances I have ever seen. And one of the first descriptors he tends to get when people describe his show is that it is powerfully authentic.

He derives a lot of his humor from cultural jokes and references that are less familiar outside the desi community, but he brings his audience along regardless of how much prior exposure it has to the community. His comedy is touching, informative, and laugh-out-loud funny. And according to an article in *The New Yorker*, it's a lie.

In the piece, writer Clare Malone fact-checks Minhaj's routines and concludes that some of his stories are untrue. Importantly, her implication is that the fabrications aren't there to make the jokes funnier. They're there to make the political commentary land with more weight. For instance, the article implies that a powerful story he tells about being stood up by a friend on prom night because her mother was uncomfortable with him being Indian was untrue, citing certain disputed facts from the woman involved in the story. Minhaj responded brilliantly by taking each accusation in turn and responding with proof—proof that he gave the reporter and was often left out of the article—that while he exaggerated in some places for comedic effect or to make a point land, the stories he tells, he argued, are essentially true.

Minhaj labeled his exaggerations—not about the facts but

about the details—an effort to get at the "emotional truth." He told the story about his prom date as though it happened the night of prom instead of a few days before. He described an Anthrax scare as opening a letter and having white powder fall on his daughter instead of falling right next to her. His goal, he explained, was to place the audience in the frame of mind that he was in while these things happened. It worked. It's why his comedy has been so powerful.

Here's what I find interesting about the *New Yorker* story: nothing. Mostly because after reading the article and listening to Minhaj's rebuttal, I'm convinced the reporter had to know her story would, at least, leave us with the impression that Minhaj lied about racism and death threats against his family to make himself look noble. And I don't think misleading articles are all that interesting. But what is interesting to me is the reason she decided to tell this story and not include some contradictory information. Because the *reasons* we mislead are very interesting to me.

The New Yorker stood by its story in the face of Minhaj's response because—as the reporter noted—he did admit to lying about certain details of his show, and that's technically all the article said. If you're ever curious about why stop and frisk was such a dangerous and racist policy, this story actually offers a great illustration of how it worked. Minhaj's stand-up likely got fact-checked in part because he talks about race and issues of social injustice, which, as the article noted, seems to "change the stakes." While it's common for comedians to lie or exaggerate in narrative details in their shows, he was held to a different standard because the implication was that he was lying to make the racial commentary powerful. But when he argued that he wasn't doing that, and that his exaggerations fall within the familiar and understood vocabulary of stand-up, instead of getting an apology, he is told, *Well, technically you did still lie.*

This is a danger of our overreliance on authenticity when it is

GOLDILOCKS

disproportionately asked for from people of color in a way that it isn't for other creators. It sets an unrealistic standard for our stories that isn't demanded of other stories. No comedian can tell entertaining stories if they are going to be strictly fact-checked, but not everyone is being asked to. Singling Minhaj out *because* his comedy is rooted in his experiences as an Indian man, raised by immigrant parents, living in white communities after September 11th, and experiencing racism means holding him to a standard that no white creator would have to, or arguably could, meet.

After *The New Yorker* piece but before Minhaj's response, "emotional truth" was becoming a meme. Like "alternative facts"—a comedic attempt to cover a lie that becomes a parody of itself. But I actually understand precisely what Minhaj was trying to say, and if we want storytelling—especially in stand-up comedy—that captures the experiences of people of color, emotional truth sometimes feels like a better metric than authenticity.

This dynamic is especially troubling when the suspicion about whether the stories are true comes from someone outside the creator's community. Talking about racism to white audiences is tricky. White supremacy and white guilt often work together to cast doubt on the veracity of claims of racism. I went on a date once with a white man who, after *several* drinks (and I suspect a few more that I hadn't been present for) told me he was glad I was Black because he couldn't have pulled a white woman of my caliber. "It's like you're on sale," he slurred at me as though it was a compliment. My genuine reaction in that moment was relief that he had been drunk enough to say it so plainly. This wasn't the first time I had felt a dynamic similar to this, but I never before had proof that that's what it was: a man who thought he was dating down simply by virtue of my race, so he felt like my other attributes put us on the same level. But I had never had the courage to talk openly about this particular microaggression among my friends because I knew I would have to defend my read of the situation to white women who would argue tooth and nail that no white man could think that way. I had never been so casually insulted by someone who still expected to date me after it, and my genuine reaction was happiness. Because he had said the quiet part out loud, I had proof.

This is the challenge of talking about racism to white audiences. It needs to be clear enough that there is no other plausible—or even possible—explanation. But it can't be too clear—too cookie-cutter perfect to prompt a white person's suspicion that it wasn't *exactly* how it went down. We need to experience Goldilocks racism, and that very often conflicts with wholly authentic storytelling.

Sometimes it's something small: I tell a white girlfriend that a waiter was rude to me because I'm Black and she cheerily suggests, "I bet she was just having a bad day!" And sometimes it's something big: A white reporter hears Hasan Minhaj's stand-up special and, for whatever reason, questions its veracity. So, she starts investigating. And to be clear, when that happens, the consequences are big, too. Minhaj has confirmed that he was set to take over as the new host of *The Daily Show* until the article came out and prompted his offer to be rescinded. He lost a dream job and we lost out on one of the few voices that could have helped us navigate our current political moment with humor, intelligence, and truth—both factual and emotional.

The solution is more stories, but my fear is moments like this will lead to fewer. That the threat of unevenly applied and out-of-context fact-checking for certain storytellers will lead to fewer creators taking risks and combining comedy, storytelling, and commentary on their unique experiences. And fewer voices make the landscape less complete and less *true*. Because if we lose those efforts to get at an emotional truth, it takes us further away from a factual one.

9

FOR THE FUTURE

On November 6, 2018, against a smoky black backdrop at his election night rally, as he conceded a surprisingly competitive Senate campaign, Beto O'Rourke declared he was "so fucking proud" of his team on live television and the crowd went wild.

He had already captured enormous attention following a viral video of him talking passionately and seemingly extemporaneously on the Civil Rights Movement. That was quickly followed up with a number of media moments that proved he wasn't a regular candidate. He was a cool candidate. He air drummed. He skateboarded. He was quick to jump on a clearly unscripted Facebook Live and pull back the curtain for his followers. Dropping the f-bomb on national television was the capstone.

He's so authentic, the internet gushed. Meanwhile, I seethed.

My anger wasn't with Beto, not really. I didn't know him at all. His relationship with Julián Castro, my boss and the only reason I was as invested as I was in Beto's trajectory, had always been good. In fact, earlier that fall the two of them and Julián's twin brother, Congressman Joaquin Castro, had gone on a campaign bus trip together for Beto's race. Beto had then taken to introducing Julián as "the next president of the United States." That alone was enough to make me appreciate him, as I would later go on to manage Julián's presidential campaign.

But Beto kept attracting more and more attention. Meanwhile, Julián's early interviews and his book tour, which previewed his upcoming run, didn't garner the excitement I felt they deserved. My resentment came from something much deeper than anything about Beto. My resentment was apparently with authenticity. But more than that, how easy it was for white men to showcase it, and how difficult it was for anyone else.

If authenticity is an amorphous concept in general, in politics it is quite simply ineffable. Political authenticity can make or break a campaign and a candidate, but it's not really clear to anyone precisely what it is. It somehow simultaneously seems to mean everything and nothing. Interestingly, it doesn't seem as connected to genuineness as it perhaps should. An authentically boring candidate doesn't get credit for being themselves just because it's an honest personality trait.

Or consider Joe Biden and Donald Trump. Both are constantly credited for their ability to appeal to white, working-class voters, despite the fact that they have little in common with the lived experiences of people in those communities. Biden may be from Scranton, but he became a senator at twenty-nine years old, then vice president, and then president. Each time he has run for president, he has run as an insider, and yet is still described as being able to authentically appeal to white, working-class voters.

Before he got into politics, Trump's name was synonymous with over-the-top opulence and showy wealth, a far cry from the working class and rural white voters that would form his most devoted fan base. And yet his unapologetically tribal appeals to these voters through an us-versus-them lens are called authentic without a trace of irony or explanation as to why the New York City hotel and real estate magnate could authentically claim an "us" with the voters he is talking to.

FOR THE FUTURE

In addition to being hard to define, political authenticity is confusing because it requires a healthy degree of self-contradiction. Gilad Edelman of *The Atlantic* discussed this contradiction during the 2020 Democratic primary: "When we talk about authenticity in politics, it turns out we're usually describing something specific: Candidates from Obama to Trump to the Democratic presidential hopeful Pete Buttigieg seem authentic to the extent that they seem to be saying what they're really thinking, rather than what they're 'supposed' to say. The key word here is *seem*."

Edelman goes on to note that according to research, "listeners perceive[d] speakers to be less authentic when they were told that the speakers were repeating themselves." As he notes:

> *Self-repetition, the researchers argue, "confronts observers with the performative nature of the interaction" and challenges our assumption that social interactions, even those that are typically performed and repeated, are assumed to be unique. In other words, we're wired to assume that all speech is extemporaneous. When that assumption is revealed to be false, we penalize the speaker. This is true, the authors found, even in contexts where it makes no sense to expect speakers not to repeat themselves. . . . Authenticity is not about being honest; it's about seeming unscripted.*

People want authenticity in a politician because we want to believe that the person we are seeing is who they really are. When the doors are closed and the cameras are off, people want the version seen in public to be the same person they will be in private. It's an understandable desire, but the wheels come off the wagon in the execution. Because the only way to prove authenticity is to see them when the doors are closed and the cameras aren't on. So political authenticity becomes measured by who can best publicly present private interactions without letting the knowledge of an audience transform it into performance. Or at least, who can best convince us they can. The measure of authenticity is how much we believe a performance. And that belief is as much about us as it is about the politician. Thus, authenticity is about subverting expectations. If we have a certain image of a generic politician, seeing them smash that image makes us feel like they're being real.

The bias at the core of this definition of political authenticity is almost palpable. First, the mere act of being—or even seeming—unscripted is itself a privilege. Candidates of color are consistently penalized more harshly for missteps, which makes being unscripted a much bigger risk. Consider the media narratives that emerged about Kamala Harris and Donald Trump during the 2024 presidential race. Soon after becoming the Democratic nominee, Harris was frequently criticized for not giving as many long-form, sit-down interviews as Trump was giving. Obviously, the massively abbreviated campaign gave a skewed impression: By the time Harris became the nominee, it was the time in the calendar when most candidates began focusing on events with more voter contact rather than the interviews with legacy political media outlets that tend to mark the early months of a campaign. However, even as Harris consciously began sitting down for more interviews, this impression dogged her—the implication being that she didn't feel comfortable being unscripted: that she was inauthentic.

This was in contrast to Trump, who had the reputation for having a robust media schedule. In truth, that reputation was unearned. While he ramped up media and interview appearances immediately following Harris's entry into the race, those appearances flagged as the race went on and Harris's increased. But the impression persisted for each of them and played into an existing narrative that Harris's preparedness undermined her authenticity, while Trump's meandering and unhinged remarks proved his.

There was another infuriating dynamic, which was that Harris was subjected to a sharp scrutiny in the media that was simply

FOR THE FUTURE

never applied to Trump. Trump released a skeletal policy platform that contained virtually no details as to what he would do as president nor how he would pay for the proposals he did offer. He contradicted himself in what his policies would be, taking credit for ending *Roe* and then promising to be a champion of reproductive rights just days later. He exhibited a frightening lack of policy understanding and consistently made demonstrably untrue statements. In response, he would sometimes be fact-checked (but alarmingly sometimes would not be). And while some pieces may have been written about a particularly unhinged screed or bafflingly uninformed comment, the news cycle tended to move on quickly.

Meanwhile, Harris navigated a completely different press environment. Her policy proposals had to stand up to the rigor of real and pointed questioning. She had to explain how she would pay for them and how she would pass them. She was asked to explain why she hadn't already accomplished her goals since she was the sitting vice president, a question that would have been equally telling from Trump who wasn't being asked why he hadn't accomplished any of his priorities while he had been president. If she misspoke, she was asked to explain: Was it a misstep? Or did it reveal a gap in policy knowledge? Or was it a flip-flop on a previously held position? When Trump misspoke, as he did regularly, his statements were reimagined as more coherent than they were, and it was that version that was understood to be his real position.

Harris and Trump were not making the same calculation when they considered whether to participate in an interview, because the stakes were entirely different from them. Trump could give interviews, be completely unprepared, and not pay a political penalty. In fact, his willingness to be unscripted contributed to his reputation as authentic, but he was only able to be unscripted because the press would be so forgiving of him. Harris, on the other

THE REAL ONES

hand, would be subjected to a higher standard, so she needed to be incredibly prepared for interviews. In response, she got critiqued for overpreparation, for sounding too canned, for being inauthentic. But if she had gone off script, that same media would—as we saw them do—critique her for any misstep.

It was more than a double bind. It was a triple bind: If she sat for the interviews and was prepared, she was inauthentic. If she refused to sit for the interviews, she was inauthentic. If she sat for the interviews but did so without preparation and let herself speak extemporaneously, she would be critiqued for any misstep and it would follow her campaign and she would get no credit for authenticity. This is how political authenticity is weaponized against candidates of color and women of any race. And it wasn't Harris's first experience with this because we saw these same dynamics at play in the 2020 Democratic presidential primary when she initially ran.

In 2020, the Democratic presidential primary boasted a historically diverse field of candidates; and during that race, the difference in how we metabolize the concept of authenticity for political candidates was on full display. I was lucky enough to work for two of these candidates during the campaign. I managed Julián's campaign, and when we withdrew from that race, I joined Elizabeth Warren's team as a senior adviser. I say this with complete bias but also complete confidence: In the 2020 primary, I had the opportunity to work for two of the most genuine people I have known. And, despite that, both of these experiences were marked by far too many conversations about how to make sure they each came across as authentic.

During the 2020 primary, *Vox* writer Tara Golshan wrote a piece on authenticity in politics, attempting to showcase the gender divide in the perceptions of authenticity in the race. In her piece, she settled on four broad buckets of "what authenticity looks like, according to political science":

FOR THE FUTURE

1) **The ability to interact in an informal way.** . . . This speaks to a candidate's performance style. . . . Do they sound like they're speaking off the cuff, rather than rehearsed?

2) **Having a credible personal narrative.** . . . Biden talks politics with stories about his family, riding back and forth on the train between Wilmington, Delaware, and Washington, DC, or his memories of the late Sen. John McCain. He's selling a personal narrative for people to have an emotional response to. [Senator] Sanders recalls fighting for the same issues in the 1970s as he is today, creating what appears to be a credible political record.

3) **Aligning with voters' perceptions.** "Authenticity" becomes more complicated when it gets into people's biases and preconceptions about what a politician should look and act like. Can a politician fit the mold of how an average voter thinks a president should look and act?

4) **Electability.** In many ways, the previous three attributes determine this last factor. Is the candidate presidential? Can they win?

This definition of political authenticity perfectly illustrates how difficult it is for any nontraditional candidates to be read as authentic, because of the number of biases built into its very definition.

If you close your eyes and think of the word *presidential*, what image comes to mind? With precisely one exception, our historical collective answer to that question has been a white man. Put him

THE REAL ONES

in a suit, give him an Ivy League degree and a successful background, and that basically defines our expectations of presidential candidates. This is critical because it means without having to try as hard, there are some candidates who will already be assumed to be presidential—intelligent, respectable, serious. Thus showing a more casual side is all upside for them because the hard work of proving their worthiness has already been done for them by us. We *assume* they're worthy. Beto's skateboarding and unrehearsed remarks didn't undermine him because we already assumed he could fit within our expectations, so it was enjoyable to watch him subvert them. That's not true for candidates of color, and it's not true for women of any race. They have to be more careful about showing casualness, because it can undermine their argument for being presidential. But the unwillingness to do so undermines their authenticity.

In order for voters to determine whether a candidate has a credible personal narrative and aligns with their perceptions, we first need an expansive imagination for what candidates can look like. For white men, that is easier to pull off because we have already seen—in politics and in culture—so many narratives that they can authentically embody. We have seen so many examples of this candidate, there are a number of visions to choose from. We have a cultural and political appetite that can tolerate a white male candidate as a plainspoken truth teller, an erudite wordsmith, a professorial policy wonk, a tough and principled war hero. But when it comes to people of color and women of any race, our collective palette is much choosier. These candidates are unceremoniously shoved into the few narrow models of candidates we have seen before, and failure to fit within those visions means voters are less likely to find their narratives resonant.

So voters are asking these candidates of color to interact informally and still seem qualified as leaders; they are asking them to align with voters' perceptions but maintain a credible personal

FOR THE FUTURE

narrative. This is a trap. And when candidates find themselves stuck in that trap, they are deemed either underqualified and not ready or too rehearsed and fake. Their personal story is either too hard to relate to or unbelievable as a personal narrative. And voters conclude they are unelectable. And that is blamed on a lack of authenticity that they never had a hope of meaningfully showcasing.

And thus, despite its beginning, our historically diverse field of candidates ultimately got whittled down to Joe Biden as the nominee. And his decision to step aside in 2024 and allow Harris to become the Democratic nominee was game-changing. But I cannot help but fear that had she competed in another primary like the one we had in 2020, it would have been impossible for her—or any candidate of color or women of any race—to surmount the authenticity gap that tends to plague them. In fact, watching her struggle in the general election and ultimately lose to Trump while her authenticity was once again questioned, while he was able to lie with impunity, is further proof that we have a problem with how we understand political authenticity. We need a more nuanced approach to the way we approach authenticity, or it will be incredibly difficult for underrepresented candidates to break out of a Democratic primary.

I met Julián Castro when he was secretary of the Department of Housing and Urban Development (HUD). I was a senior policy adviser for him, so my job was to lead the department's efforts around some of his key policy priorities. We worked together on a number of projects that revealed how much we had in common in our theories of how to approach governing, particularly around racial justice. And none so resonant for me as racial justice in the wake of an influx of police violence.

In 2015, we were in the midst of a spate of shootings of unarmed young Black men and women at the hands of police. It was a frustrating time to be a part of the administration. As the Black

THE REAL ONES

Lives Matter movement was drawing attention to just how often these extrajudicial killings were occurring, our first Black president was in an impossible position. Any statement from him on the issue was treated as an all-out attack on the police and the utterance of "Black Lives Matter" from him would have been ungenerously interpreted as an insistence that *only* Black lives matter, instead of a plaintive plea that Black lives matter, *too*.

But the double standard that defined Obama's presidency defined this moment as well. And as a result, the entire administration had to be very careful about how we responded publicly. But internally, it was a different matter, and Julián expressed a desire to do anything he could to respond to this moment without creating a problem for the administration. When I found out he was looking for ways to quietly engage, we created a small, sad tradition out of the tragedies. He and I—sitting alone in a large conference room—would call the field offices that were in communities dealing with unrest stemming from these shootings. On those calls, he would acknowledge the difficulty of the staff doing their jobs while they and their community were grieving. He would remind them that their jobs at HUD were about building safe communities, they were about racial justice, and so they were about this moment.

As meaningful as I found these calls, I want to be clear that they were a far cry from soaring moments that make a political drama. Think less *The West Wing* and more *Veep*. In truth, these calls were usually *super awkward*.

This was 2015, and the BLM protests were very politically fraught. That meant that a conversation about this moment was just as likely to center concern-trolling whispers about the effectiveness of the protests, the destruction that protesters were causing *in their own communities*, and how Black on Black crime was the real problem. The composition of the calls was up to leadership in each of the offices, so while sometimes we were talking to a big

FOR THE FUTURE

and diverse office of people, we were also speaking to a small group of senior leadership. So we were often met on these calls by awkward silence.

Once, when Julián opened the call for discussion, a member of senior staff used the opportunity to ask him about his future political plans. Julián and I stared at each other, baffled, as he diplomatically handled the non sequitur. Once, following one of these calls, Julián turned to me and wryly remarked, "I think we were the only two people of color on that entire call." But while it rarely sparked a robust conversation about racial justice and the legacy of HUD on the calls, I heard from several people that following those calls, people felt freer—among their trusted colleagues—to talk more vulnerably about these issues since the secretary had given them permission.

The fact that we even had those calls was never supposed to be talked about publicly. Part of the conceit of what we were doing was finding ways that we could, with no fanfare, participate in this moment. If this got out, it would undermine what we were doing and likely cause a problem for President Obama, who had to be overly cautious around this issue. There was, I calculated, no political upside for Julián. Which is why it was during those calls—those awkward, off-the-record calls that no one even knew we were even doing—that I realized how much I trusted him, how authentic I found him. And how much I wanted to work with him on whatever he did next.

In August 2017, Julián had pulled together a small circle of advisers to discuss his next steps after the Obama administration, including the possibility of him running for governor of Texas in 2018. I had been in favor of it—I saw it as an opportunity to raise his profile and the possibility of having the race elevated to a national stage if we were able to strategically provoke the notoriously thin-skinned Trump.

THE REAL ONES

But running statewide in Texas is incredibly challenging, and every cost-benefit analysis weighed against running. First, it's expensive, and we didn't have the deep network of donors needed to mount a meaningful challenge against Governor Greg Abbott and his $40 million war chest. Besides, Julián had young kids and he bristled at the idea of being away from them—and saddling his wife with the lion's share of the childcare—for a grueling gubernatorial race with the ever-increasing likelihood that he would then turn around and have to immediately do it again for a presidential run. And finally, there was genuine skepticism about whether an unsuccessful statewide bid would make it easier or harder to run a bigger race.

Like most people of color of our generation, Julián was raised being told he had a higher threshold to meet than his white peers, and that lesson has stayed with him throughout his political career. His successes would be more fragile; his losses would be more tarnishing. And the idea that he could lose one race and be encouraged to run a bigger one was anathema to how he understood his political future. Failing forward doesn't really exist for candidates of color. The sacrifice would be too great. The risk would be too high. So he didn't run in 2018.

So while I watched my fantasy for Julián play out for Beto on national television where breathless commentators couldn't stop labeling him the most exciting 2020 prospect a full six months before he would enter the race, I couldn't help it: I was *jealous*. But it was more than that. It was the first time it crystallized for me that authenticity is at its core a privilege. Being "who you are" is an indulgence afforded only to those whose identity does not invite the question, "Who do you think you are?" For many people of color, particularly those raised by baby boomers, authenticity is a cardinal sin.

Like many things in the race, it created a double bind for us. This amorphous concept of authenticity is inextricably linked to

FOR THE FUTURE

the kind of performative casualness, the kind of off-the-cuff cool that you can embody only after a lifetime spent never questioning—or having it questioned to you—whether you belong. Thus, the yardstick for authenticity had whiteness as its true zero. Which means that even while many voters decried the knee-jerk credibility afforded to white men, we designed a system that perpetuates it. And Beto became an avatar for me of the way that privilege shapes the concept of authenticity.

So while Beto was extolled for a meandering youth that made him seem like he reluctantly accepted leadership instead of having planned for it, Julián's book was criticized for not having any bombshells—for his having a past too perfect, too designed to get him where he was. People of color don't end up in power by accident—it *is* carefully calculated, but that says more about how power is conferred than it does about how it would be wielded. Beto was excused his youthful indiscretions—including a drunk driving arrest—whereas Julián, who doesn't drink in part because he witnessed his mother struggle with alcohol when he was growing up—was criticized for being too "squeaky clean," making him "less relatable." I couldn't help but chafe at that characterization, wondering how quickly those same pundits would label him unelectable at the slightest slipup, authenticity be damned.

One particularly painful comparison was that Beto was willing to take a risk in 2018 and run for a race that he might lose, while Julián had turned down doing the same, putting an even finer point on the comparison and their courageous-versus-cautious reputations. But that analysis failed to capture the rather obvious difference that lies at the core of this entire discussion: *It wasn't the same risk they were assessing.* A loss simply wouldn't impact Beto's reputation the way that it would Julián's, and we know that because Beto was not the only surprise competitive candidate who ran for statewide office in 2018. Andrew Gillum and Stacey Abrams both also ran in red states and came incredibly close to beating their Republican opponents. And yet there were no comparable high-profile "Draft Andrew" or "Draft Stacey" movements for 2020.

In fact, despite the over-the-top hero worship that Stacey Abrams has received any time someone wants to say that Black women saved democracy in 2020, that gratitude only extended so far. As soon as Abrams publicly acknowledged that she would be honored to serve as vice president if Biden selected her, many in the establishment expressed skepticism of her candidacy and described her approach as "brazen" and "aggressive." Chatter behind the scenes pointed out that she had no real experience and had lost her most high-profile race. Which was also true for Beto, who did not get the same behind-the-scenes skepticism at the idea that he would run for president. Losses feel more permanent for candidates of color because they don't subvert expectations—they confirm them.

On Christmas Eve 2018, I sat in my mother's car, parked in the driveway, on the phone with Julián and Joaquin. We were about two weeks into launching our exploratory committee and a little over two weeks away from our official launch event, and I was scared. Announcing the exploratory committee had done little to encourage Julián to draw back the curtain, and I had started getting calls from people in our orbit expressing concern that he wouldn't break through if he stayed so—well, (this is where they would draw back their breath and whisper like they were betraying some secret) *boring*.

After a few missed opportunities in some early interviews and a column in *The New York Times* by Charles Blow that hit way too close to home in its description of Julián's tendency to self-censor and mentally edit before speaking, I fired off a missive at 2 a.m. with the subject line "a few thoughts on authenticity," and we set a call for later that day.

Once we were all on the phone, Julián asked where I was.

FOR THE FUTURE

"I'm home—I'm in California," I explained what I thought was an obvious point that I had gone home for the holiday.

"No, you sound weird," he pressed.

"Oh! Yeah, I needed quiet so I'm taking the call from the car."

"The car?" His delivery was dry. "You?"

"Oh my god." I groaned, realizing where this was going and hoping my eye roll was audible over the phone.

"You can't drive!" he reminded me laughingly, landing on one of his favorite reasons to tease me—that I didn't have a driver's license.

We joked and laughed for a bit before getting down to business, and I was struck by an irony—his actual personality is one that many teams would need to manufacture in order to create apparent authenticity. We didn't have to work at it. He had it. But he hid it.

I had gotten to know this version of him: quick-witted and sarcastic and uproariously funny, a pop culture and sports junkie who would debate Jordan versus LeBron with me, and a guy with the most uncanny memory for 1980s television I have ever seen. This version was nowhere to be found in his public persona. There, he was only a policy wonk who, more than having hobbies or other interests, just wanted to be president.

I explained my concerns that a narrative was developing that wasn't going to help us. We needed him to be less scripted and more casual. He was immediately resistant. He was afraid of looking unprofessional if he dressed down, unserious if his tweets were more conversational. He wanted to be seen as intelligent and thoughtful, and that left no room for error when he discussed policy, particularly where he hadn't already taken a well-considered position.

"I already don't look like what they expect," Julián reminded me. "I can't give them any more reason to discount me." I could practically *hear* his mother's voice in his, and it's not like I didn't understand his concerns. There was no reason to believe, and every

THE REAL ONES

reason to doubt, that the honesty people clamored for would actually serve him if he displayed it. In order to be successful, people of color listened to our parents, and we learned how to make White People feel comfortable. We learned how to code-switch. We learned how to protect ourselves by never *really* saying what we think, all in order to get ahead. That's the cruel irony of the authenticity question for candidates of color: Many of them got to where they are only by being careful, by never appearing unrehearsed or unprepared. In short, by being deliberately inauthentic. And now, once they got to where they were going, people asked them to shed the armor that had protected them through all their battles leading here.

We announced Julián's candidacy on January 12, 2019. The day went about as well as I could have hoped. We turned out a crowd of three thousand people on the Westside of San Antonio where Julián and Joaquin had grown up. He arrived at the site with his daughter and brother, the three of them having taken the bus—the same route they had ridden as kids countless times when their mother had to take them with her to work during the summer. He shook hands on the bus and told them this time, he was riding the bus downtown to announce he was running for president.

He announced his candidacy in English and then in Spanish. He told his story, which is also the story of his mother and of his grandmother, a Mexican immigrant who came to the United States as an orphaned, unaccompanied minor to live with distant relatives, who made a life for herself, and helped her grandsons believe they could be anything they wanted. He decided to run to make sure that sense of hope extends to many more generations. He named issues that he would focus on that no one else was making a centerpiece of their campaigns—immigration, homelessness, police violence, and bail reform. I snuck away from backstage to listen to the speech from the crowd. Surrounded by an audience of

FOR THE FUTURE

people who had no idea who I was, I cried. A high school mariachi band played. And he left the next morning on his first campaign stop: Puerto Rico (against the advice of conventional wisdom and the pleas of many people who said our top priority *had* to be Iowa).

Our first policy proposal was immigration reform, and we had a plan that would change the way the field talked about immigration. Julián would propose decriminalizing border crossings, a bold proposal that would reshape the conversation Democrats were having around immigration. We got plenty of input that we shouldn't start off talking about immigration, because people feared commentators would imply that we'd be pandering and, as the lone Latino candidate, it would look self-serving. We ultimately decided to lead with our immigration plan for the simple reason that in Trump we faced a president who was historically hostile toward immigrants, particularly those from the southern border. It felt like political malpractice to start with anything else. I was proud of that decision and realized our skeptics had been wrong. People, it turned out, wouldn't imply that we were simply pandering—they would say it outright.

Enter Bill Maher. Julián went on his show following our immigration announcement and immediately got the question we expected: Why start with immigration? Maher compared the decision to if Barack Obama had started with reparations or affirmative action. Interestingly, Maher didn't draw comparisons to the number of white candidates—including Pete Buttigieg, who he'd interviewed the week before—who were campaigning on their ability to appeal to working-class white voters. Instead, Maher had seemed compelled by Buttigieg's potential appeal to the industrial Midwest.

Now, there's an obvious question that arises here that I, frankly, think we should ask ourselves more often: Who cares what Bill

THE REAL ONES

Maher thinks? In fact, it's a question I pose to myself rhetorically whenever his name comes up. But the problem is, he's not alone. There is a crucial divide between those reactions—that a Latino candidate talking about immigration is pandering, while a white candidate appealing to Midwest working-class white voters is authentic. This gap is the problem at the core of political authenticity. Authenticity doesn't have an objective definition, only a subjective one, and that means biases distort a candidate of color's ability to be seen as authentic.

Interestingly, Julián didn't give Maher the real answer to his question. He saved that for *Latino Rebels Radio*, where when he was interviewed, he said one of my favorite things I've ever heard him say: "I'm not going to run away from standing up for immigrants just because they look like me."

I don't have a workable definition for political authenticity. But if I had to offer an example of what it entails, I would cite that sentence. And the decision to flout political conventional wisdom and make his first campaign trip Puerto Rico. I'd point to mariachi bands at an announcement speech. I'd mention phone calls after racial justice protests, where the point wasn't a solution but permission for more conversation.

And yet, we continued to be hounded because of his apparent lack of authenticity. And all the commentary was entirely context-free. While many questioned the wisdom of a Latino candidate talking about immigration and questioned whether it would pigeonhole him as the brown candidate, in the next breath the same analysts would predict we couldn't get anywhere unless we carried the Latino vote.

We got a constant barrage of bad faith speculation about how damaging it was that he didn't speak fluent Spanish—and critiques of his comfort level when he did. But none of that commentary pointed out the history that is true for *many* second-generation

FOR THE FUTURE

immigrants: In order to ensure acceptance and to shed stigma, they often don't learn any language but English.

And it takes some Hogwarts valedictorian–level rhetorical wizardry to cite an over-focus on the Latino community *and* an underperformance with Latino voters, a lack of fluency in Spanish *and* willingness to speak Spanish anyway, and conclude a lack of authenticity. But get them some wands and sort them into Slytherin, because the political media figured out a way to do it. It was infuriating to watch, but there's only so much critique of the media a campaign can do without looking like we're just arguing with the ref. So I saved my simmering rage for the truly egregious examples of bias and racism.

I knew how to handle them. I could be Cool.

The race is over now, so I can say what I wanted to say every time we got this criticism: Demanding someone's authenticity, fully knowing that same authenticity would be weaponized against them, and pretending not to understand that reality is journalistic malpractice.

This problem wasn't unique to our campaign. This was a common theme throughout the cycle. Cory Booker campaigned with a relentlessly hopeful message. But his refreshing positivity and message of radical empathy and love, particularly when he turned that message toward how he wanted to address the racial divide in this country, was called phony in a moment where people expected a Black man to campaign with a fiery message. Interestingly, Pete Buttigieg had a similarly hopeful and unifying message about healing a divided country, and often used his own experiences of discrimination to help him make the point that there is still more that unites than divides. But that message was heard as inspiring, not fake, coming from him.

Kamala Harris was criticized relentlessly for misstating or readjusting policy positions, causing people to question her commitment to any particular ethos. Meanwhile Biden was allowed to about-face on positions within the same news cycle and is famous for a steady string of gaffes, which somehow just make him *more* trustworthy instead of less. Until it didn't.

More recently, we have seen just how dangerous the consequences of this kind of selective relationship with authenticity can be. Following the midterm elections in 2022, Biden turned eighty, and there were widespread and legitimate concerns among voters about his age and capacity to serve another term. While the White House pushed back vigorously against the idea that the president was too old to run for reelection, the issue came up often. The media covered the story. Voters were polled and overwhelmingly expressed serious skepticism about his candidacy because of his age. And yet, there was no serious effort to primary Biden or publicly urge him to stand down until the disastrous debate performance against Trump in the summer of 2024 that created a groundswell and public pressure campaign. His decision not to run for reelection came so late that there was only time for a hyper-compressed campaign from Harris. And people were left asking a very fair question: Why didn't anyone say anything sooner?

As early as the 2020 primaries, there were whispers suggesting voters had serious, and underexplored, concerns about Biden's age. And those concerns were met with intense pressure for opponents to avoid raising the issue. It was seen as a mean-spirited and bad faith attack against a good man. So we had a tightrope to walk during the primary: Biden's frequent misspeaking opened him up to fair criticism that he wouldn't make a strong candidate, especially against someone like Trump who would be quick to exploit such foibles. But if a criticism from a Democratic opponent seemed to imply Biden hadn't simply misspoken, but more problematically had *forgotten* something—an issue attributed to age and not simply carelessness—the critique would backfire.

FOR THE FUTURE

So when Julián challenged Biden on the debate stage in September 2019 on an inconsistency in describing his health care policy, there was a slim margin for error. Biden described his own health care policy as giving people who lost a job the ability to buy into a Medicare-like plan. Julián countered that would leave too many people uninsured and that his own plan wouldn't make people buy in, they would be automatically enrolled. Biden shot back that *his* plan would automatically enroll people as well. Julián pounced on the clear contradiction of what he had just said earlier in the debate.

"Are you forgetting what you just said two minutes ago?" Julián asked incredulously. The auditorium erupted into a chorus of "ooohs," and in the spin room, my stomach sank. I saw what Julián saw—a clear opportunity to point out a genuine policy disagreement between himself and the leading candidate. But I heard what he hadn't been able to hear from stage—that it was being taken as a personal attack about Biden's age.

The response was swift and lacked any nuance. He was accused of taking "a cheap shot." He was called "too aggressive." To be clear, Julián hadn't referenced Biden's age. But it was such a preoccupation in the minds of the media and voters that they projected the implication onto his words. Despite the fact that, as I said at the time, "anyone who reverses their position like that onstage in real time would have been open to that type of criticism," the attack became about age and was assumed to be in bad faith. The backlash wasn't rooted in policy—it was rooted in tone. In perception. In norms about who gets to challenge power and how. But that backlash sent a chilling message to anyone who may have publicly challenged Biden earlier on what would become an increasing political liability for him.

In early 2023, Julián made waves again for suggesting on Astead W. Herndon's podcast *The Run-Up* that the Democratic party *should* have a primary, and then again in 2024, when he became one of the first significant Democratic leaders to say he should step aside and endorse Kamala Harris to be the Democratic nominee.

Once the voices pressuring Biden to step down as the nominee reached a fever pitch, it can be hard to remember there was ever a time before. But there was. And it took courage, moral clarity, and *authenticity* to get there first.

There is a real tension that no one seemed willing—or politically able—to name. The very people with the proximity and profile to raise concerns about Biden's electability were also the ones who would pay the highest price for doing so. And so, almost without exception, they didn't. But the cost of that silence is being felt now: growing public frustration with the Democratic Party's lack of boldness, a sense that no one was willing to speak uncomfortable truths to power.

In other words, an authenticity crisis.

Honestly, I see this as an opportunity. While voters may enjoy long-form podcasts and unscripted asides, they're telling us that this moment clearly demands more than charm or relatability. It demands courage. What people are hungry for now isn't just personality—it's principled leadership. And if the Democratic Party hopes to recover from this authenticity crisis, its leaders will need to stop looking for moments to showcase realness and start embodying it in action.

10

FOR THE CULTURE

Once Julián decided he was going to run for president, there were a million decisions we needed to make very quickly. And as I often do in moments like this, I focused on one of the least important decisions: what we would name the campaign.

"Julián for America" seemed too obvious after Obama, Hillary, and—let's be honest—*The West Wing*'s Jed Bartlet. "Julián for President" was too on the nose.

I took an early liking to "Julián for the People," which thankfully we didn't use because Kamala Harris used the same slogan and it had the clever reference to her time as a prosecutor to make it particularly fitting. I loved "Julián for the Future" the first time Julián suggested it, but we wanted some more options and were working with consultants who would do mock-ups with our favorite suggestions.

"What about 'Julián for the Culture'?" I suggested one day on the phone, and the call fell silent while I waited for feedback from our consultant team.

One consultant said, "It's so—I know you guys are going to talk a lot about race, *which is great*, but it kind of seems too . . ." She trailed off because there is no end to that sentence that wouldn't

THE REAL ONES

have been painful for both of us. As I listened, I did what I am accustomed to doing whenever I hear a white woman try desperately not to sound racist. The Cool Black Girl to the rescue.

"No, I know, it has the potential to sound really alienating. I'm just brainstorming!" I allowed.

"Right, totally, and look, he's going to probably be the only Latino candidate. He's going to have you and a really diverse team. You guys will be Julián for the culture no matter what!"

I laughed out loud and sighed inwardly. I hadn't known at the time how weirdly poignant that remark was.

We would launch "Julián for the Future." And somehow I would need to run "Julián for the Culture."

On our campaign, it wasn't only Julián's authenticity that was being put under a microscope. My authenticity was also under scrutiny.

Given the size and diversity of the 2020 primary field, diversity of staff was a major issue for the first time during the campaign. There were a number of reasons for that. With such a crowded primary, *everything* was a way to stand out—or get called out—and so there was more pressure than there had been before to diversify staff, especially at the senior levels. Moreover, in Trump we had a president who was making directly racist appeals to his base, and there was a lot of early commentary on who could get support from voters of color.

But it was more than that. The rise of the alt-right and the way Trump had fanned the flames of white supremacy had made issues that used to be limited to critical race theory classes a matter of public debate. Words like *intersectionality* and *white privilege* had entered mainstream political lexicon. Candidates released plans to combat the legacy of white supremacy and hate violence; and several followed Julián's lead and supported reparations. They became conversant in the language of movement politics.

FOR THE CULTURE

I always assumed that by the time these concepts had permeated popular discourse, we would have a deeper understanding of race, racism, privilege, and oppression. Concepts like this without nuanced understanding are meaningless. I hoped our national conversation around these issues would have gotten sophisticated enough to make social progress. However, that wasn't really what happened. The new vocabulary wasn't backed up by a real or lasting shift around these issues, and not many candidates seemed ready or willing to translate this discussion happening within the Democratic primary to voters outside the party. It felt like we bought a racial justice word of the day calendar and adopted the language of a racial understanding that we collectively still lacked. So racial diversity of campaign staff then became one more marker of candidates who lived out their values, but it wasn't accompanied by a real analysis of what that would mean for the campaigns.

Alongside this media coverage about diverse staffs, there was no coverage about whether that meant new or different issues would be prioritized. There was no attention paid to whether campaigns that "looked like America" would have different relationships with supporters who were less used to feeling seen by presidential campaigns. There was no reporting about support from unlikely voters who would be important but wouldn't be captured in early polling. There were no articles about whether the consultant firms were likewise diversifying, or about the inevitable clashes between the consultant class and the newly diverse cohort of campaign leadership.

Instead, diverse campaign staffers just faced conflicting pressure: to run campaigns that felt authentic to the communities we represented but that didn't deviate from the status quo. Even though we already knew that the status quo had never really felt authentic to those same communities.

As you can imagine, the result was just a raging success. You should have seen it.

THE REAL ONES

There are a number of reasons there will never be another Barack Obama. He was the first Black president. A once-in-a-generation political talent. And he also had the benefit of a Black and multiracial coalition of progressives that largely agreed they would not be the reason that he wasn't successful. This cohort gave him allowances that no other candidate of color is likely to ever enjoy.

In 2007, Obama had considerable support among Black voters, even before his Iowa victory. But there was a shift after he won in Iowa. While Black voters may not have been waiting to coalesce around him, the Iowa win did seem to confirm him as the presumptive front-runner. That precarious bounce of credibility could have easily been upset; and there seemed to be a tacit agreement among Black voters that if he lost that primary, it wouldn't be because the Black community had weakened him. There seemed to be a tacit agreement among Black voters to allow him to run as the post-racial Black president without asking a lot of questions—at least publicly—about what that meant for us. Criticism of Obama was sharply discouraged by many Black leaders at the time. It was understood that he needed to spend a lot of time convincing white voters, and that left little room for him shoring up support within the community.

His Philadelphia speech on race gets compared to Kennedy's speech on religion, and that comparison is apt: Kennedy wasn't speaking to Catholics, and Obama wasn't speaking to the Black community. Instead, appeals to the Black community happened through references to shared culture—his taste in music, his love of basketball, his style, his swag. We took those as coded messages that while his policies did not reflect the priorities of many in the Black community, once in office, he would be freer to recalibrate. Support among the Black community continued to soar and led to a decisive primary win in South Carolina, and ultimately to winning the primary. In the general election, it was even easier for

FOR THE CULTURE

Black voters to grant him leeway; and ultimately, Black voter turnout for Obama broke records when he won.

Authenticity was measured differently in that race. Obama was assumed to be—at least on some level—inauthentic. Much of the willingness of Black voters and progressive voters to support Obama came from an assumption that he wasn't being completely honest about his positions, especially around issues like racial justice, marriage equality, and other issues of identity politics. Many seemed to understand that a Black man could not ascend to the presidency and at the same time speak openly on race and identity policies that felt authentic to many in the Black community. Voter pragmatism shielded Obama from this requirement. The assumptions that he was further left than he came across and that he had a sharper racial justice lens than he was allowed to reveal were based on little more than an assumption about Black people. It was authenticity with a wink, a nod, and an understanding that we had to let him pretend if he was ever going to win. Four years later, Black voters were more disenchanted, even as support remained high, particularly as the racist backlash against him made supporters protective and unwilling to join any unfair critiques.

This is all to explain, despite the fact that we had elected a Black president, no one had walked the particular tightrope of running a campaign that expressly appealed to voters of color and their issues while remaining focused enough on the white electorate to seem viable. To build a campaign like that isn't just to build the plane while we're flying it but to pave the runway as well.

Harris's 2024 campaign doesn't change this calculus for a very specific reason: She was unopposed in the abbreviated primary. When Biden stepped down, all the serious would-be contenders almost immediately endorsed Harris. She was spared the tightrope that we all—Harris included—faced in 2020. Importantly, when she ultimately lost in 2024, President Biden shocked a lot of people

THE REAL ONES

by admitting that he wasn't surprised that Harris lost specifically because of the sexism and racism she faced.

We were trying to elect candidates of color in 2020, and whenever we pointed out the challenge that presented, we were confronted with a chorus of "Obama did it." But the model he used wouldn't work again. Not only were communities of color not willing to grant the benefit of the doubt again, the expectations were even higher for the next candidates of color. And as a Black woman running one of those campaigns, I felt that pressure acutely. The campaign brought into stark focus for me how much *authenticity* could feel like a weapon against which I would need to defend myself on multiple fronts. Depending on who I was talking to, people had different expectations on the role my authenticity should play in my position as campaign manager. And I just tried to keep up.

Whenever I'm asked how I started working in politics, my first instinct is still to respond that I don't work in politics. My background wasn't in electoral politics, and it still feels a little unearned to me that I don't have the history with campaign work that many of my colleagues have. Most senior operatives can trace their political careers back several cycles—starting as volunteers or interns, then organizers, rising through the ranks. They have paths that feel designed for them to end up where they are—they feel *earned*. They compare battle scars and remember obscure races—some races they loved even though they lost and others they hated even though they won. And I always feel embarrassed by my admission that the first campaign I worked on was the one I managed.

Typically, my explanation comes out sounding like false modesty. It's acing a test without studying, and lamenting that you didn't get to stay up late and make flash cards with your friends. And I'm sure impostor syndrome contributed to my tendency to feel professional shame where most people would feel pride. But I actually think it's more straightforward than that. I genuinely still

FOR THE CULTURE

think of myself more as a movement person or a policy person than I do an electoral politics person.

So when I was named campaign manager, it's unsurprising that movement leaders expected a campaign that reflected my career as a social justice leader. I was immediately beset with requests for Julián's time: for him to attend events and give keynotes sponsored by every progressive group, for his endorsement for every progressive candidate, and for sweeping progressive policy positions.

There is a concept in public policy called the Overton window. Basically, it refers to the range of issues that are considered politically palatable to a mainstream audience. Over time, that window widens or contracts based on issues like changing norms, popular culture, shifting discourse, political shifts.

We had already decided that we would run a campaign that centered social and racial justice in a way that we had never before seen at the national level. But we were also still conscious of the fact that to remain politically viable, we needed to be strategic about when and how we pushed the envelope. We wanted to run a courageous and viable campaign. We were not running a message campaign focused on staking out radical positions with the goal of pushing the Overton window as far as it could go.

One of the challenges of progressive politics is that, by its nature, once anyone states a position, the movement has to ask for the next thing. It's in the name: *progress*. Today's victory is tomorrow's bare minimum. And I would never ask anything less from activists than this kind of zealous advocacy. But while we generally think of our feelings about various issues as our "position," there are often different approaches and strategies rolled up into one "position."

On any given issue, there are actually three positions most people hold: A philosophical position (what we believe), a political position (what we can vote for, given our choices), and an activist position (what we want our voting choices to be). For instance,

THE REAL ONES

take an issue like the police state. I hold a philosophical position of being a prison and police abolitionist. Based on what I have read, I believe that a society is at its best when it is a non-carceral state and aimed at justice rather than retribution. I can understand that the racist origins of our policing and prison systems in this country, and their current furthering of structural racism, make them inherently unjust.

This is an academic position I hold as my goal for the kind of society I think we should aim at creating through politics, activism, culture, and policy. It is not a description of the one I believe we live in now. As a practical matter, I do not support simply dismantling these institutions and expecting a workable system. Instead, I will support policies that create the circumstances that make us less reliant on these institutions. For instance, policies that redirect funds into strategies like targeting the root causes of crime rather than simply focusing on enforcement, limiting the situations in which we rely on police, and supporting alternatives to incarceration. And I will agitate for causes that make these positions more politically popular, so I have more values-aligned candidates to choose from.

Notably, not everyone who pushes those policies forward shares my philosophical position. That's fine. In fact, it's good because it means there are more people I can agree with on policy strategy even if we don't share the same ultimate philosophical goal. In turn, I will support candidates who run on these policies. And my activism will focus on pushing for more candidates to embrace these and even more progressive policies to expand the Overton window even more.

Because I work in politics, I have to be conscious of how all these issues intersect and, importantly, how they don't. I hold a number of philosophical positions that I would never advise a candidate I worked for to publicly express, because they aren't yet politically viable. In order to make them more politically viable, we

FOR THE CULTURE

need activists always pushing the Overton window toward greater justice. And we need politicians who we are confident we can work with. But we make a mistake when we assume that a philosophical position, an activist strategy and a policy strategy, and our political choices all must perfectly align. And thinking that they do is one of the challenges that the left is going to need to overcome in the near future in order to build lasting progressive power.

But I also know many in the progressive movement do not share my thinking on this. So early on in the campaign, my job was to have conversations with leaders of organizations and would-be validators, and listen intently without promising any specific positions until we made further decisions. It was also my job to assure these people that the campaign we were going to run was one they would want to support, a job made more difficult because not everyone was familiar with Julián's actual politics, only his reputation as mayor of San Antonio, where his ability to appeal to business leaders and make progress via bipartisan compromise made some progressives nervous.

His profile had earned him a number of comparisons to Obama, and clearly people's antennae were up. Progressives who were ultimately disappointed by Obama's record on some priorities were convinced the movement had been asleep at the wheel and so they were not going to make the same mistake again. They planned on fully vetting every candidate, and no one was getting a free pass.

In these conversations, my politics could be a liability because if we deviated from my stated positions on issues, this would make our campaign seem inauthentic. That frustrated me for a few reasons, but most notably, I wasn't the candidate, and the assumption that I personally agreed with every position we would take during a campaign was, I'm certain, not something generations of white male campaign managers had to confront in order to credibly represent their candidate.

There was an assumption that my decisions weren't political

but personal, and the controlling factor in my decisions would be my deeply held and unimpeachable values. And while I'm certain those assumptions were made about me with the best of intentions, they still stymied my ability to do my job. The Authentic Black Queen would be a horrible campaign manager with her unwillingness to compromise, and yet that is what I was being asked to be.

I let these conversations serve as a reminder that both my and Julián's racial identity wouldn't give us a pass on key issues and, in fact, would raise the bar.

As we build an increasingly diverse pool of leaders, it's worth thinking about how we can avoid making matters inadvertently harder on the left for candidates of color to be successful. White candidates can more easily talk openly and honestly about race without alienating white voters. When candidates of color do the same thing, they are often more quickly met with pushback that they are being too divisive or only trying to appeal to communities of color. Likewise, candidates of color are also expected by voters of color to be more conversant and comfortable talking about race.

The challenge for these candidates is to feel authentically comfortable and familiar to the voters of color without alienating the white voters. If they are too focused on race, white voters will punish them. If they ignore it, voters of color won't trust them. However, white candidates enjoy support from voters of color when they speak openly about race and racism. This creates a benefit for white candidates in progressive circles because there is no conflict between what voters are asking for of them. They do not have to constantly seek an impossible balance and face accusations of inauthenticity when they fail.

Obviously, voters should be able to vote for candidates who share their values, and I am not suggesting that candidates of color should be held to a lower standard. But injecting nuance into the demands we place on candidates does not undermine the ability to have expectations of them. It simply recognizes that not all candidates have the same freedom to express their authenticity; and that in order to accurately judge their values, we have to remember that.

Another frustration revealed in these conversations with movement leaders was the conflation between authentically held values and political positions. I want to be clear because I think it's important that voters can assess candidates based on whether they will fight for the values that voters care about. But a stated political position is an imperfect proxy for telling us a candidate's values. For example, no one truly thinks that Donald Trump is the social conservative he pretends to be in order to assuage the religious conservatives in the Republican base. Likewise, it was abundantly clear that President Biden had greater discomfort with abortion than his pro-choice stance made room for. Even so, both of them have received the benefit of their political position, and regardless of the fact that their values don't seem entirely aligned, this has not caused an authenticity problem for either of them.

As more candidates of color rise to political leadership, we will see more instances of the inverse of those situations: candidates whose values have clearly always aligned on an issue but who have refrained from taking a political position until recently in order to remain more broadly viable. Some people fail to understand that there are reasons to have held positions that do not align with their values early in their careers and to have those positions change as the electorate has changed. When voters refuse to understand this dynamic, they make things harder for candidates of color to succeed—because they will have either been deemed too radical at the beginning of their careers or inauthentic at the end of their careers.

To be clear, this is not a critique of anyone who refuses to vote for any candidate who they disagree with on an issue. My concern is more nuanced than that. There seems to be a greater suspicion of candidates who we believe agree with us, but who don't publicly do so until later in their careers, than there is of candidates who simply don't agree with us but vote with us out of political expediency. And the expectation that candidates of color will simply be more willing to lose than to compromise—that they are always driven by values rather than votes—will often result in them losing.

During one discussion with a movement leader, she asked me if Julián was going to call to abolish ICE, a popular refrain at the time among progressives but one that met with intense political backlash. When I refused to commit, I was met with a disbelieving look. "Come on," she chided me. "He hired a Black woman! He has to let you be you!"

It wasn't meant as an insult, so I didn't take it as one, but I did bristle at the implication. I wasn't trying to run a message campaign. My goal wasn't a critically acclaimed show that wins an Emmy the same year it's canceled. We were honestly trying to win. And I chafed at the suggestion that as a Black woman I should be willing to sacrifice my candidate's viability for a principle.

When it comes to recognizing Black women as the backbone of Democratic electoral politics, 2018 was the precursor to 2020's #LetBlackWomenLead moment. Following Stacey Abrams's surprisingly competitive race (surprising to those of us not in Georgia, anyway. I always say a political miracle is just organizing explained by a non-organizer), there was an outpouring of support to recognize the leadership of Black women instead of just relying on them to deliver victories on election day. I know that was one of the reasons I got the attention that I did for serving as a campaign manager.

I was only the third Black woman to have run a major presidential campaign. Donna Brazile was the first. She managed Al Gore's campaign in 2000. Then in 2008, Maggie Williams had the daunting task of managing the sunset of Hillary Clinton's first presiden-

FOR THE CULTURE

tial bid. And then there was me. I know that Julián hiring a Black woman would excite not just Black voters but progressives who saw hiring me as the ultimate proof that he too believed that Black women would indeed save us.

To be clear, that didn't bother me. As I will discuss later in this book, being hired because I'm a Black woman has never been something that troubles me. I *am* a Black woman. It's a core piece of my identity and dictates much of how I understand and move through the world. I would never want any opportunity that wanted me *in spite of* my being a Black woman. But what occurred to me in that moment, and many more like it, was that the expectation placed on me wasn't something I was comfortable with.

The willingness to see Black women as political superheroes ironically has allowed people to value our leadership less and to use us as political tools. The memeification of Black women has a long history; and in popular culture, images of Black women have fallen into specific and frustratingly familiar tropes. Mammy—the ever-smiling, nurturing, maternal Black woman who was quick to sacrifice her own comfort for the good of (white) others. Sapphire—the hypersexual, animalistic Black woman who is objectified as a sex symbol but not recognized as a romantic interest. And Jezebel—the angry Black woman whose finger-snapping, neck-rolling distortion of Black female strength is typically played for laughs.

These caricatures ironically undo themselves: Sapphire was overly sexualized and resulted in Black women being seen as less desirable romantic partners. Jezebel's overblown anger doesn't get read as real strength but as an impenetrable hardness that robbed Black women of the ability to be seen as vulnerable or needing protection. Mammy was nurturing and maternal to the point of self-sacrifice: Her caretaking undermined her ability to engage in self-care and self-love. The common theme of these tropes is that they shove Black women into cartoonishly narrow boxes and the result is to undermine the one perceived strength that formed their basis.

The idea of Black women as political saviors has created a new trope and essentially allows us to only metabolize a certain type of Black women's leadership, one focused on service and sacrifice for a greater good. And for me, that meant I was being faced with an expectation that authentic leadership as a Black woman would result in my unapologetically pushing forward positions that ultimately would make Julián unsuccessful. And my refusal to do so was read as a lack of authenticity.

One thing I've learned is that the best and worst parts of running a presidential campaign often happen at the same time. It's called call time, and its grab bag approach of talking to supporters each week left me vacillating between hearing from our most ardent supporters, who inspired me and reminded me of what we were fighting for, and from those who simply wanted a few minutes to tell me everything I was doing wrong.

The people who thought we were doing the right thing had reasons for being inspired by Julián's unlikely, long shot but compelling campaign. Those reasons were as diverse and varied as they were. The people who were less convinced largely and ironically coalesced around one common theme: We were too divisive.

Racial justice was a central theme of our campaign—by far the one that got the most media attention—and it was being read as too divisive to bring people together around a candidate. Truthfully, I didn't get it. Our entire theory of the case was to push as ambitiously unifying a message as has ever been seen at the presidential level. Our approach to the campaign—what we termed *People First*—involved centering racial and social justice and elevating core issues of inequality that are often left unaddressed by presidential platforms, despite the fact that they connect to every other issue. And while I knew that conventional wisdom and polit-

FOR THE CULTURE

ical cliché told me engaging directly on issues of race and racism was a third rail, it still felt like our goal was being deliberately misinterpreted. What could be divisive about an insistence that "everybody counts"?

But the critique I faced was more than simply that we talked too much about race. It was that *I* made him talk too much about race. Interestingly, we had a group of supporters and donors we were courting who were almost the mirror image of the voters we were courting. These were people who had followed Julián's career and also knew his reputation as a bipartisan mayor. They were convinced I was leading him astray by forcing him too far left, and I was doing it because—surprise!—of my commitment to authenticity. Somehow I was being accused of running a campaign too focused on being authentic to communities of color *and* not focused enough on that same authenticity.

Like I said, the whole thing was just an unmitigated success. How could it not have been?

The assumption was that I was so committed to my politics that I was pushing Julián to the left at the expense of our political viability. There were so many reasons to be annoyed by this characterization. First, on behalf of Julián, who didn't need me to push him anywhere. Our campaign's politics reflected his values, full stop. And while he and I largely agreed on a number of issues, we landed where he wanted us to be.

Moreover, we never really got to test how much any of this really cost us politically. During one particularly tense phone call with a donor, I was being lectured about how often Julián was talking about identity issues.

"He's only ever talking about immigration and race issues! He needs to talk about bread-and-butter, kitchen table issues," he hissed at me.

In order to bribe me into doing my call time, our finance team would always get me a Diet Mountain Dew as a treat on call time

THE REAL ONES

days. I love Diet Mountain Dew despite J. D. Vance's recent attempts to ruin it for me. I blame the caffeine for my response.

"Well, bread-and-butter issues depend on whose table you're eating at," I quipped. "I promise you a lot of families sit around their kitchen table talking about immigration."

The silence that followed snapped me back and I let out a laugh, trying to lighten the mood. "I hear you," I cut in as I heard the anger rise in his voice. "Listen, you know we just put out our housing plan?" I redirected the conversation as best I could, but he ultimately hung up without saying goodbye.

What I couldn't say to that (probably former) donor was that when you're elevating the issues people aren't used to hearing about, the polls don't reflect the real breadth of support. My theory had been that we actually had hidden support among people who loved what they'd heard from him but weren't going to support someone so low in the polls. But if we had been able to climb a few points, I suspected those few points would be catalytic. The challenge with early polls, press, and fundraising is that they actually aren't separate measures—they are one measure that reinforces itself. Early polls are entirely a function of money. Buying digital ads and increasing name ID makes the poll numbers go up, which in turn makes the press write stories, increasing name ID more and giving the candidate an appearance of viability. This makes it easier to fundraise, and so the cycle continues.

Further, the idea that I couldn't separate my personal politics from that of a campaign seems to be a major misread of what authenticity demands of a campaign manager, and I can't help but wonder if this assumption would have been made about me if I weren't a Black woman. There was a quality that was being assumed about me and whether I was being asked to assert my values more or less, my presence was understood as a moral presence, not as a political strategy.

While it's true that I'm a progressive, my strategy about the

FOR THE CULTURE

orientation of our campaign was a political one. The idea that Julián could succeed running as a moderate Democrat seemed naive to me. People who were drawn to a moderate in that race wanted someone with the best chance of beating Trump, and low name recognition kept us from being competitive in that lane. In a crowded field, Julián was most competitive as a progressive who represented generational change, diversity, and racial and gender justice. And fortunately that was who he was at his core. It would have been politically unwise to try to capture any other identity in that field. And we got lucky that authenticity and smart politics aligned.

But more than anything, what troubled me in all these conversations was that authenticity was being used as an accusation against me. The assumption that I could not hold my beliefs and still run a political campaign was at the core of these criticisms, and it made me wonder what value authenticity had for me if it could so easily be used as a cudgel. It's a similar concern that I have for the way authenticity is demanded and assessed in pop culture. People of color cannot be uniquely and solely charged with injecting authenticity into our politics, nor should we be treated like we are only able to work in politics as a function of our values.

In the moment, I didn't have time to unpack these frustrations. Instead, I focused on finding an ethos and making sure we stuck to it. It was the only way I knew to run an authentic campaign. Our political positions would be part values and part strategy, but our organization would reflect Julián's values. Of the first decisions we made, we decided to pay our interns $15 an hour despite our fundraising, meaning we wouldn't be able to hire interns for a while. Neither he nor I could have afforded to work for free when we were of intern age, and it made working in politics seem really distant. We committed to building the organization that would bring in people who had never before seen themselves reflected in politics.

THE REAL ONES

We hired those people, too. Our senior team was majority women and majority women of color. We talked about issues no one else was talking about, and he met with people no one else was meeting with. During a campaign stop to Las Vegas, he went under the glitz and glam of the casinos and toured the flood tunnels filled with homeless encampments. He defined the field on immigration and forced a conversation about decriminalizing border crossings that changed the way Democrats talk about the border. He brought up issues on debate stages that don't usually get that kind of attention. At his first debate, he rattled off a list of names of unarmed Black men who had been killed by police when talking about how he would target and address police violence. I thought back to our phone calls at HUD. We had done it. Whatever it meant, we were running an authentic campaign.

I'm sure there were still issues where some people thought we went too far and others where people thought we didn't go far enough. But we built a base of supporters who felt seen by our campaign. The first time we failed to qualify for the debate stage, Julián's name trended on Twitter with people talking about how they missed him because without him onstage, they didn't hear their issues reflected. When we ended the campaign, we did it in the most humane way we could, telling people as soon as the decision was finalized and forgoing some last-minute priorities so we could afford to pay out a small severance and keep people's health care going for the month.

Julián had no desire to sit out the rest of the race or strategically wait to endorse. He wanted to stay in the fight and that's one reason I'm so grateful to Elizabeth Warren. The campaign she had been running made us feel like we could do just that. I remember talking to Roger Lau, Warren's campaign manager, about Julián's desire to endorse her. Roger and Faiz Shakir, Sanders's campaign manager, shared the distinction of being the first Asian American presidential campaign managers. It was one of the many reasons I

FOR THE CULTURE

think I immediately felt seen by Roger, a sentiment that has never gone away. He just got it. When I told him how impressed we were by what they were doing this cycle, he immediately turned the compliment back around.

"We've been so impressed by the campaign you guys have been running," he told me sincerely. "Really, I hope you're proud of it."

I thought back to earlier that month during call time. I had called a supporter, but he only spoke Spanish, and since I only spoke English, we couldn't understand each other. I tried a couple of ways to express my gratitude for a $10 donation he had given us, but ultimately, I hung up without feeling like I'd been able to communicate my appreciation. An hour later, my phone rang. He'd had his daughter call me back to translate. I thanked her profusely for the call and told her I'd just been trying to tell him thank you and that his donation meant a lot. She told me ours was the first campaign he'd ever contributed to. She told me a bit about their family; they were Texans and her dad had loved Julián since he was the mayor of San Antonio.

"He's so happy whenever Julián is on TV!" she said laughing. "He just can't stop smiling."

"Well, let him know his donation is what keeps him on TV. And let him know we are going to keep fighting for your family and so many just like you."

"He says we're praying for him. And for you!" she told me.

I was so moved and didn't know how to respond to that kind of kindness so I just said, "Tell him Julián has a daughter, too. And you just keep making your dad proud."

That was the memory I went back to when I told Roger, yes, I was proud of our campaign.

Like I said. Just an indescribable success. You really should have seen it.

11

JUST, ONLY, TOO

"*YOU ARE ANOTHER DEI HIRE!!!!!*" the stranger yelled at me in closing from an Instagram direct message request. And I laughed.

Messages like this always confuse me for a few reasons. First, I don't always see them. I only recently discovered that people you don't know can send you requests to message you, but you have to check a special inbox in order to view those messages. It was like discovering a little DM purgatory, where I was given the power to decide if each message gets accepted, rejected, or stays there for eternity. Fortunately, I don't rule over any real afterlives because, as it turns out, I'm kind of an absentee deity. I check only about once a month or so.

Second, I don't know what prompts someone who—judging by their message—*does not like me*, to see me on TV or read something I've read, remember my name, look me up online, see that we don't follow each other (because why would we?), request to send me a message, and unleash a tirade of vitriol at me. I got bored halfway through typing that sentence. Surely people have better things to do.

But the biggest reason these messages confuse me is that they never seem to know how to close them. It seems like you'd want a

JUST, ONLY, TOO

message like this to go out on the worst insult, but they never do. I've had people wish me physical harm and then wrap things up with "learn how to write!" I mean, *okay*. But it kind of feels like the violent threat takes the wind out of the sails of a literary critique.

This one was particularly acerbic and, after he called me a litany of really awful slurs, he ended with the sole all-caps accusation: that I was a DEI hire. Now I know what he *thinks* he's saying. Diversity, equity, and inclusion has become a conservative bogeyman in recent years. Even though DEI simply refers to efforts that many employers have gone through to increase diversity of their teams and to ensure that the people they hire feel empowered and engaged in their jobs.

The 1990s conservative ghost story about the less qualified Black woman who was promoted ahead of every white person's father/uncle/neighbor has given way to the bizarre insistence that DEI is responsible for every hire of people of color and women of any race in fields that are still dominated by white men. There are many people who seem to genuinely believe that any consideration of identity given in a hiring decision is foul play and that seems to mean, to be safe, we need to give opportunities only to white men. And so seeing me on television triggered this man, who felt that I was obviously taking that opportunity from a more deserving white man. Calling me a DEI hire *was* playing his trump card. For people like him, DEI has become a slur.

It feels obvious, but it clearly needs to be stated: There is nothing wrong with DEI efforts. They are good, they are needed, and there is nothing about them that means that those who benefit from them don't deserve to be there. But the reason that the vilification of DEI has been so frustratingly damaging is that we don't have an effective way to talk collectively about the fact that merit and identity aren't opposing forces when it comes to hiring.

This dynamic was on full display during President Biden's tenure, in part because of his own commitments to diversity and his sometimes clumsy statements around it. When he secured the Democratic nomination in 2020, he immediately committed to selecting a woman running mate. He also promised that his next Supreme Court nomination would be a Black woman. Both were done with a spirit of genuine commitment to inclusion and representation, a healthy dose of political realism, and the finesse of someone whose racial politics are the product of a very different and less nuanced time.

Predictably, Republicans responded to these announcements by prematurely declaring that these women should essentially go down with an asterisk after their names since they weren't being made to compete against the entire field of possible picks. This was particularly pronounced when Biden made the pledge that would ultimately result in the selection of Ketanji Brown Jackson to replace Stephen Breyer on the Supreme Court. The *Wall Street Journal* editorial board called Biden's commitment to appointing a Black woman the elevation of "skin color over qualifications." Senator Ted Cruz called it "offensive." Senator Roger Wicker called it "a quota."

When Biden ended his 2024 presidential campaign and Harris became the Democratic nominee, this argument resurfaced, with several Republicans declaring that she was a DEI pick because Biden only chose her because she was a woman. The line of attack became so popular that House GOP leadership had to host a meeting to urge Republicans to stop making this accusation because they feared it could backfire and make them look racist.

This kind of cynicism was frankly unsurprising from conservatives. I have been more concerned by the progressive response that I think inadvertently conceded the point that acknowledging the role KBJ's or Harris's identity played in their selection was akin to acknowledging that they were, indeed, less qualified than a hypothetical white man.

Among many progressive commentators, there was a sentiment that by making a pledge to nominate a Black woman, Biden had actually undermined KBJ, because now people could say that was the only reason she was selected. According to this logic, he should have simply not made a commitment and selected KBJ anyway. Likewise, many had wondered why Biden made his preference for a woman known before selecting Harris.

And among progressives, I'm confused by our confusion. We're comfortable saying that authenticity matters. We're comfortable saying diversity matters. And we're comfortable saying we need political representation that reflects the communities being represented. And we're comfortable saying that people from underrepresented communities bring a perspective that is missing from much of our current political leadership. But somehow, the logical extension of all that—that identity should matter when choosing our political representatives—still makes too many people feel like we're saying something inappropriate.

It's especially troubling because it seems to be true only when the selection is someone with an underrepresented identity. From the moment Harris became the nominee, the veepstakes began, and it was almost universally understood that all her options would be white men. The memes this prompted were hilarious. Twitter users posted pictures of wine bottles with signs like "Interesting Whites," "light crisp dry whites," and "rich whites" with the captions indicating this was Harris looking for a VP. And while an early list included Gretchen Whitmer, once she made clear she did not want the role, the short list was solely white men and it remained that way.

However, that Harris considered only white men for her running mate and that she ultimately selected one of the "Interesting Whites" did not prompt any hand-wringing from worried progressives. It's important here to note something that seems so obvious it doesn't need to be said and yet it does: "White man" is an identity. Limiting the search the way they did was a consideration based on race and gender. No one thought the fact that the short list wasn't more diverse undermined Governor Tim Walz's ultimate selection. And no one—not even conservatives who seem to love the insult—have accused Walz of being a DEI hire.

But he was.

Now to be clear, *I* don't mean that as an insult. He was my first choice for her running mate, and I think he was an excellent one. But Walz was hired, in part, because of his identity. So was Harris. So was I. Saying that isn't actually insulting any of us, but I know Walz is the only one who wasn't called a DEI hire as an insult.

The difference is unfortunately simple. There is an assumption that white men are qualified. For anything; for everything. So limiting the search to white men didn't require anyone to endure any cognitive dissonance that maybe he wasn't being considered against the best. The assumption was that if the pool were limited to white men, the best was among them. But that simply isn't true when the pool is limited to women or, further, to Black women. We don't get the assumption of qualification. When our identities are considered, they are treated as if we are *just* that identity.

I didn't say just.

That was the thought that crystallized as my face burned as I sat on a panel next to the woman who had, with the absolute best of intentions, just deeply embarrassed me.

After the Castro campaign, I became a regular fixture on an unwieldy number of panels detailing how women—in politics, business, wherever—were taking on more leadership roles and what we should be doing with all this power. I was incredibly interested in this topic, though I had wanted to explore some of the nuances of this moment that I was afraid could get overlooked in a rush to congratulate ourselves on all this diversity. I wanted to talk about how it wasn't enough to hire diverse leaders if they weren't fully empowered and would still be undermined by other voices. I wanted to talk about the trend I was starting to hear about how candidates wanted women of color to come in as figurehead campaign managers while paying white male consultants twice the salary to really run the show. I wanted to talk about how if a campaign or a company wasn't prepared to really show up for diverse leadership teams, then they shouldn't prioritize their own desire for diversity over the well-being of the leaders they wanted to bring in.

Unfortunately for me, the panels tended a little less toward the questions I wanted to explore and more toward the "girl power" angle. I rolled my eyes but bit my tongue, especially when people reminded me the goal was to inspire young women in this political moment. Fine. Girl power it was. I could be Black Lady Spice.

On this particular panel, I was matched with some other "onlys," as in "the only woman serving as [fill in the blank]." I thought back to elementary school and my Only Games and was struck by the fact that, once again, everyone was staring at us. It felt less lonely now.

The panel was going well enough when I fielded a question from a young woman of color who had been a fan of Julián and asked me if I ever got tired of answering questions about the place that being a Black woman played in my ability to do the job.

"Never," I replied emphatically. "I *am* a Black woman doing this job." Before I could continue, I felt the energy shift.

That's when the older white woman sitting next to me interrupted. "Wait," she said kindly. "I'm not going to let you reduce yourself. You're not just a Black woman doing this job." She went on to compliment my résumé and note that, as women, we are often too quick to diminish our own accomplishments.

I smiled and reached out to squeeze her hand while people whooped loudly in response to what was clearly intended as an act of sisterhood, but inside I was humiliated. If celebrating that women were holding roles that hadn't always been available to us didn't diminish us, how did my proudly calling myself a Black woman do so?

I didn't say just.

I hadn't felt reduced. But I did now.

If my co-panelist hadn't been so eager to defend me from myself and let me finish, I could have explained that, to me, there had been no contradiction. If in politics, authenticity matters, and our authenticity and how we express it is inextricably linked to our identity, there are some professional opportunities that will be extended to us, in part, because of our identity. And treating that admission as an insult that needs to be explained away is part of what is so confounding about our discussion of authenticity in politics. I felt no more diminished by the acknowledgment that my identity played a role in how I performed my job—and even my selection for the job—than I felt diminished by a similar acknowledgment about any other fact in my background. I was the only Black woman managing a campaign in that cycle, and I never bristled at questions about that, because being the *only one* to do something doesn't mean you're *only that*. And now, because I can't be interrupted and because I don't have to worry about a moderator moving on, I will answer that young woman's question in its entirety. Because I think it's important, and I don't think we've gotten this particular question right just yet.

I have never received a professional opportunity just because I am a Black woman, but I know I have received some because I'm a Black woman, too. In fact, I hope I have received them all because I'm a Black woman, too, because I would never knowingly accept one that came to me *in spite of* being a Black woman.

When Julián asked me to be his campaign manager, I did something I have spent countless conversations with young women I've mentored begging them to never do: I tried to talk him out of it.

JUST, ONLY, TOO

There's a tendency women have to talk ourselves out of job opportunities, convincing people who would hire us that they haven't thought it through. We overfocus on the parts of the job where we don't have expertise at the expense of the parts where we do. We don't apply for jobs unless we have every qualification and, as a result, we lose out on *a lot* of opportunities. I know this. I talk about this. I warn other women against this. And yet, when confronted with accepting one of the most consequential opportunities of my life, I did exactly this.

The first time he broached my being the campaign manager, I had all but scoffed. "We'll get you a real campaign manager," I'd promised. We were still weeks away from our launch event, and I wanted someone who would convey that this was a serious campaign, and I feared my lack of experience managing a race wouldn't do that. Further, I had told him, I don't know all the elements we need for the campaign. "I'm a policy person," I'd insisted. We had already begun talking about a platform and sketching out in broad strokes what would become the element of the campaign we'd be best known for.

I began having conversations with people who had expressed interest in potentially leading the effort. It was during one such conversation, which came after a meeting with Julián where he hinted again that maybe I should just do it, that I considered for the first time maybe I could. I was speaking with someone—a white man—who was explaining how he would build out the operation.

"I know you guys want to focus on policy. I'm not a policy guy, but I know what it's going to take to build this." He had sounded so confident as he casually dismissed his lack of expertise in my exact area of expertise.

If he doesn't have to be a policy guy, maybe I don't have to be an early states guy, I thought. Maybe in the same way he could hire around his shortcomings, I could hire around mine.

THE REAL ONES

The next time I was on the phone with Julián and Joaquin, Julián was more explicit. "I want you to do it," he'd said. And I said yes.

If you asked Julián why he picked me, I think he would say it's because of my policy expertise, my experience managing teams, my temperament. I *know* he would say it was because of our relationship. (Someone once said to us, "You should have a campaign manager you're comfortable fighting with." We didn't skip a beat before exchanging a look. "We're good," he said wryly, and we both cracked up.)

I think he'd say it's because of my politics. He knew he wanted to run as a progressive, and that was somewhere I could help. And I think he'd say it was because I'm a Black woman. I don't know what position this would be on the list, but I hope this would be somewhere.

And I don't think its inclusion undermines a single other thing on that list. My identity is part of who I am, and if there is value to my authenticity in how I lead, then there is value to my race, my gender, my background, my experiences. And if admitting that feels like I'm reducing myself, then we are failing to capture how expansive that realization is.

My being a Black woman impacted every way that I led on that campaign. It impacted our decision to focus on the policies that we focused on and highlight issues that usually didn't get talked about during presidential races. It impacted the way we brought social justice and community leaders into our movement and treated them as experts. It impacted the way I felt accountable to everyone who powered our campaign, regardless of how much they were able to give. It impacted the way we hired our incredibly diverse team. It's why I insisted that we create a strict pay scale and paid people according to it and didn't ask people to negotiate their own salaries. It's why we committed to paying our interns a living wage as one of the very first decisions we made on the campaign. It's why we saved money at the end of the campaign to pay a small severance and continue health insurance for a little longer for our team. It's why I fought to make sure we prioritized the issues that we did. It's how I led because it's who I am. That's not a small thing, and I don't want to have to act like it is.

So, to the sweet young woman who asked me if I get tired of being seen as a Black woman in politics, because I didn't get to answer your question, I'll try to do it now.

No. I don't get tired of being seen as a Black woman in politics, and I hope I never will because I don't think I'm ever seen as *just* a Black woman in politics. And I hope that when you get your first job that prompts strangers to compliment you so kindly and ask you questions, they will ask if you get tired of getting asked about your identity, I hope you'll say no. I hope on the undoubtedly long list of reasons you got that job, because you're a woman of color is on that list. And I hope you hear that as the compliment it is. Because who you are is important.

There's a critical next step for anyone reading this and thinking about their own hiring decisions. Hiring people because of their identity is great, but to make sure you're not making them a *just*, you do have to make efforts to ensure that they are not just brought in but fully empowered. And that often requires some work. So now, I would like to talk to the person who will one day employ the young woman who asked the question on my panel. I want to talk to you about how you hire her and how you empower her.

If identity matters. If representation matters. If what we say on the left is really true, we have to get more comfortable with the way that shows up in hiring. To be clear, there is nothing illegal in most states about considering a person's identity along with other factors when making a hiring decision, but there are still ways to do it in a useful and respectful way that sets new hires up for success.

I once had a white woman ask me while I was working at a legal organization if I had a law degree. I was shocked she would even

THE REAL ONES

wonder until I spent some time advising people and companies on hiring and saw firsthand that some places are willing to throw out their most basic job requirements in order to hire a person of color. That is incredibly dangerous.

Just to be clear, I am a big proponent of eliminating any job requirement that is not absolutely essential. You will get a much more diverse candidate pool by only listing what you absolutely can't live without. One thing that always strikes me when I speak with potential job candidates is that women see job requirements as a checklist. Men see them as a word cloud. If you want people with underrepresented identities even entering your candidate pool, take a fine-tooth comb to your job description.

But once you edit and finalize that job description, stick to it. Being willing to lower your requirements in order to diversify your team will only set those candidates—or employees—up for an uncomfortable environment. People notice if all the people with underrepresented identities don't have the same quality of experience as everyone else. And it makes people respect them—and their work—less. It is a surefire way to perhaps hire, but never retain, this talent. Instead, consider whether you want to let go of some of those requirements for everyone. Recruit from more schools. Hire people with different fields of expertise. Trade a degree for a certain number of years of work experience. Diversifying your environment in more ways will help you recruit and also retain people with underrepresented identities.

Once you hire diverse talent, there are a number of ways you will need to support them.

Julián didn't stop picking me when he asked me to be his manager.

I remember one day later we had met with a number of people from his circle in San Antonio after I had been announced as campaign manager. After the meeting, I was swarmed by people who clearly felt very strongly that I should not be in this role. One man

JUST, ONLY, TOO

in particular backed me into a corner, demanding my résumé, explaining to me that some of them were just confused because I was so new to the inner circle. I'd like to believe I held my own, but I didn't. I shrank. I let him question my qualifications and answered the questions rather than challenge his place to question me. It was an awkward exchange, and I was in my head until Julián, after saying goodbye to everyone including this man, asked me to walk him out.

I was grateful for the rescue but curious as to what he needed. We chatted for a bit until we were out of the building, where I expected to hear the real reason he'd asked to talk. There wasn't one. He just shrugged and said he wanted to debrief in case I had anything to discuss. It was one of the most meaningful things he had done for me without it really being anything. There's power to being the last meeting the candidate has. It means you're the person they want to meet with after the meeting is over—to translate, to advise, to agree or disagree with anything that was said in the room. Silently, he had signaled to everyone the role I played for him, and it never would have occurred to me to ask him for that as a power play. But he gave it to me, and that move signaled to me and anyone else who doubted what my role was.

Julián isn't really a hugger. I am a giant hugger. Overall, we met in the middle. I learned to be judicious about the times I made him hug me, and he learned to get more comfortable with it. But this time, I didn't care. Before he left that day, I hugged him.

Similar dynamics played out other times on the campaign. I remember once we had an adviser—a white man—who felt very strongly that he should have a direct line to, if not Julián, our campaign chair, Joaquin. He felt like his advice wasn't being heard and that he should not have to work within the campaign structure to make suggestions. I tried to be an honest broker, and over the email setting up my next routine call with Julián and Joaquin, I explained this adviser's concern that his advice needed to go directly to the top. I remember being scared that I had inadvertently made his case so well that no one would see a problem with it, and within a week it would be impossible for me to do my job effectively. When we got on the phone, we discussed a number of things before getting to this issue. Before anyone had a chance to broach it, Joaquin ended it. "Everything goes through Maya," he said firmly. And that was it.

To be clear, anytime this adviser had advice that wouldn't need a campaign-wide response, I put him on a call with all three of us. My goal wasn't gatekeeping access, it was managing the operation so that anything suggested to the candidate was actually possible to execute. But the fact that Joaquin made it clear that I *could* gatekeep that access ensured that my efforts were read by the adviser as collaborative rather than obstructionist.

Julián never made me feel like he was taking a chance on me. Sure, I hadn't run campaigns before, but I had managed big teams and projects before, and he didn't treat me like I was an experiment he was running. That gave me the freedom to make mistakes, to be human. Every decision wasn't a test as to whether I should be there, and that allowed me to stop focusing on proving that I should be where I was and just be there.

There's a story I will never tire of telling. In one of our debate prep sessions, we had a higher number of consultants in the room than usual, which meant that a lot of people were throwing out suggestions and directions, and these ideas weren't all getting captured. Julián was getting overwhelmed, I could tell, and I felt like I needed to take control of the flow of information. At some point, I flipped the chart at the front of the room and started taking notes, making an effort to capture the points that were being fired off. The room soon adjusted to this, and people started flagging me, to get my attention so I would make sure to jot down the point they found most critical.

This went on for a bit, but soon Julián stopped prep and asked me what I was doing. "You're the campaign manager," he said. "You shouldn't be taking notes." He made a joke of it and we both laughed and teased, but he made it clear he was serious. "I want your thoughts on this," he insisted. "I need you participating."

He didn't let it go. He held up prep and didn't allow us to continue until I had relinquished the Sharpie, sat down, and shared my thoughts rather than transcribing what was happening.

I love to tell his story even though I look back at it and cringe that I thought I *should* be taking notes. I love to tell it because it's a familiar experience for a lot of women—especially women of color. We aren't often seen as visionaries in professional settings, which stops us from seeing ourselves in high-level strategic roles like campaign managers. We count our value by the practical tasks that we can complete: take care of the logistics, synthesize the discussion, take the notes. I know a lot of women who would have instinctively grabbed the Sharpie in that moment, and that's the same reflex that stops a lot of us from going for campaign manager jobs—because we don't see ourselves as the big picture thinkers.

It's a trap to tell ourselves that the trick is simply to change the way we see our leadership, because it's not a failing of ours that we see things this way; it's systemic misogyny and racism that professionally socialize us not to see our own judgment as a skill set. Instead, the trick is to remember that everyone has moments like this—even when we're doing the job—and hopefully that tells women who don't necessarily see themselves in these roles that they should. What Julián did was one of those really small, really big things. As I'm writing this, I realize I never explicitly thanked him for any of it. And maybe that's the point. He never asked for gratitude, because he didn't think he was doing me a favor.

This is what is required of the people who hire us, the people who crave our authentic leadership and experience. You have to recognize that that authenticity very often comes with a professional socialization to not see ourselves as the visionaries in the room. So it's not enough to just hire us. You have to empower us.

The support we need may look different than what you're used to, and that's okay. The goal shouldn't be to hire people with underrepresented identities and then treat them exactly the way you would treat cis, white, straight men. We have been professionally socialized differently, and that means we will show up in different ways. That's why you hired us, so just keep that in mind.

While it is important to never make hiring someone feel like a favor, it is equally important not to fall into the trap of treating diverse hiring as a cure-all. I have too often seen Black women brought in under the expectation of perfection, and that is likewise a recipe for disaster. It creates a dynamic where we never have the freedom to be flawed and, if we ever do make mistakes, we do not receive any protection.

I have seen this happen a lot in the social justice space. Despite the politics of the movement, many social justice organizations, particularly the bigger ones, have historically been white led and have not had a lot of diversity at the leadership level. There have been a number of movement shifts over the past several years, and many of those organizations—across issue areas—have started to bring in leaders of color for the first time. However, these decisions have often been made without the thoughtfulness that would be needed to ensure that these new leaders are not being treated like *justs*.

For example, organizations who have faced criticism for not having a leader of color can't expect that hiring one will fix things automatically. Further, not being able to attract leaders of color is often a symptom of other issues that will need to be addressed before the culture of the organization begins to change. A single new hire—regardless of the level—will not be able to transform organizational culture. Additionally, I have seen so many women of

JUST, ONLY, TOO

color set up for failure because an organization places them in a leadership position with absolutely no support and let them sink or swim. If they swim, great! The entire organization shares in the credit. But if they sink, that failure is theirs alone, and can follow them the rest of their career.

These issues are not unique to social justice or political spaces. Regardless of where you are building a team, if you have a desire to build diverse teams, there are things you should keep in mind when empowering leaders with underrepresented identities.

Recognize the moment that we are in politically, and take that into account if you hire leaders with underrepresented identities. In a moment when leaders are dealing with an increasingly mobilized workforce who are placing new demands on management, this will create new challenges for leaders, especially those with underrepresented identities who will face a double standard from employees who may feel more empowered making demands on them than they would have a cis, straight, white man in the same position. Moreover, despite the fact that they will be newer to their roles, the expectation will be that changes happen immediately. Help manage those expectations and protect your diverse hires from the unfair assumption that their mere presence can transform organizational culture, because they will be faced with that expectation.

Acknowledge when their identity is relevant to something. Don't pretend it never matters, and don't pretend it's the only thing that matters. But if you were trying to solve a calculus problem and someone on your team had majored in physics, you would bring them in on that case. Treat their identity and lived experience the same way you would treat any other area of expertise. Recognize they have something valuable to contribute, but it's not the only reason you hired them.

Don't treat every leadership difference you observe as a problem to be solved. People with underrepresented identities often

THE REAL ONES

lead differently, and that's one of the benefits of a diverse team. If they have a more collaborative leadership style, see if they get better outcomes from their teams that way.

Don't assume impostor syndrome is to blame for any opportunity that they don't immediately take. Build a workplace where everyone feels safe taking risks and be available to help if someone is questioning their own skills. But don't assume you know better than they do what is best for them.

But above all, make your peace with a simple fact: If you are invested in diverse leadership, at some point you will hire someone because of their identity. Don't be ashamed of that fact. It's not a problem unless you stop there. Hiring diverse teams is a piece of the equation, but honestly it's the smallest piece. Making sure people don't feel like tokens, even if they're an *only*, making sure they don't feel like a *just*—that's the rest of it.

12

COME AS YOU AREN"T

Shifting our discussions of authenticity from an essentialist framework to a self-reflective one will do a lot to make these discussions more inclusive and, therefore, more useful. Still, I have to admit I have another bone to pick with authenticity. She's doing too much. She doesn't have to be *everywhere*. And one of the places where she just doesn't belong is work. It's time to dispense with the idea that we should bring our whole authentic selves to our jobs.

At some point, authenticity became such a ubiquitous concept, and was understood to be such an unmitigated good, that it seemed able to describe absolutely anything and make things immediately better. We started being told that authenticity should be the standard for our professional lives, and we got the idea to bring our whole selves to work.

Initially, one could easily understand the appeal. Most of us spend a lot of our lives at work. If we are seeking authentic lives, it seems odd to simply exempt our professional selves from that goal. Plus, there are obvious benefits to being authentic at work. As Mike Robbins, the author who popularized the concept of bringing your whole self to work in 2018, explains:

THE REAL ONES

When we don't bring our whole selves to work, we suffer—lack of engagement, lack of productivity, and our well-being is diminished. We aren't able to do our best, most innovative work, and we spend and waste too much time trying to look good, fit in, and do or say the "right" thing. For teams and organizations, this lack of psychological safety makes it difficult for the group or company to thrive and perform at their highest level because people are holding back some of who they really are.

It makes sense that we would all benefit if workplaces were safe enough for us to bring our full, authentic selves to work. However, what makes a workplace safe is an incredibly subjective metric, and just as quickly as employers started saying "bring your whole selves to work"—and employees started listening—problems started to reveal themselves.

While the goal behind bringing our authentic selves to work is often described in terms of the employee, the employer gets a huge benefit, too, and not simply from a team of people unencumbered by the psychological toll of trying to hide their true selves. When people with underrepresented identities bring their whole selves to work, they benefit the work. Often these workplaces are lacking in cultural fluidity, and that makes it hard for them to relate to clients, beat out competition, and participate as a competitor in their field.

People with underrepresented identities are often relied upon to bring a fresh perspective and showcase the employer's values by presenting a diverse workforce. But these benefits often create challenges for those same employees when the workplace doesn't adjust to accommodate the reality of the authenticity those people are bringing. As a result, bringing an authentic self to work actually winds up hurting people with underrepresented identities in a number of ways.

Jodi-Ann Burey expertly breaks down this cruelty in her TEDx-

COME AS YOU AREN'T

Seattle talk. Burey draws a comparison between being invited to a party that takes place on Halloween. After the host's assurances that there is no need to dress in costume, she shows up dressed for a night out and is confronted by a roomful of people in costumes. The guests all vote for the best outfit, and she of course receives no votes. She compares that anxiety, upset, and confusion—of being the odd one out for doing what she was told to do—to the feeling she gets when she is told to bring her whole authentic self to work.

As she explains, as a Black, immigrant woman, there are too many pieces of her identity that, when she doesn't adjust them for the workplace, leave her exposed to criticism and, as a result, she is overlooked for advancement opportunities. She is thus punished for the authenticity she was encouraged to bring.

"We cannot compete in the costume contest with no costume and hope to win," she explains.

It's an excellent comparison, and one that plays out often in professional environments. While employers say they want our authentic selves, there isn't room for them in most workplaces. And the responsibility falls to us to figure out when we are supposed to actually be authentic and when we aren't.

The fact is that professionalism is still defined in most workplaces as whiteness, and just because a workplace wants to benefit from the authenticity of people of color does not mean it's willing to adjust for it. Workplaces use the authenticity of people of color as a cultural good. But that doesn't exempt those same people from being punished for that exact authenticity that their bosses claim to want.

In 2019, on the heels of the viral success of the Popeyes chicken sandwich, thanks to the organic marketing prowess of Black Twitter, in this case, led, if memory serves, by the hilarious Damon Young, a lot of companies were trying to find ways to tap into that success. At the time, a white colleague who worked at a big company called me. They were launching a new product and she

THE REAL ONES

wanted my advice on how to bring fresh voices on their team to help with marketing. Once we got on the phone, it was clear she wanted me to help her identify young, Black, social media–savvy people who could help come up with funny memes that would take off on Black Twitter.

At the time, Black Twitter seemed to many outside of it as this magical and specific place. People seemed to believe that when we logged into Twitter, it let us press an extra button and the app logged us into Black Twitter, where the memes were hilarious, the slang cutting-edge, and the people were ready to shape culture. In truth, as Tressie McMillan Cottom put it, "Black Twitter is not a place. It's a practice." In order to be effective, a user cannot simply glom on to a hashtag. It requires learning and participating in a set of communication practices, shared knowledge, and understanding. To be most effective, it requires a relational understanding of other users and a historical context. This lack of transactional interaction makes it essentially exploitation proof. It is incredibly difficult to hack Black Twitter because there is no passcode. You don't get in the door; you help build the space around you.

This fact didn't stop many companies from trying to crack the code, and hiring people who could help them navigate Black Twitter seemed like a great first step. Which is why, when this friend called me, I initially thought it was a good first step. I began listing people I had seen online who seemed like they had the fluency she was looking for but admitted that I knew nothing about these users, and she'd probably need to research to see if any of them would be the right fit for a role. That prompted a pregnant pause.

"I don't know if that would work. We'd still need people who . . . We're still pretty picky about how we hire here."

"Right, but if this is a skill set you need, do you think people would be comfortable with you hiring a little differently? For instance, I think most people you would be looking at for this are

COME AS YOU AREN'T

going to be pretty young. Can these be entry-level positions? Do they need degrees?"

I heard the telltale click of being taken off of speakerphone. "I—honestly, this place is . . . it's really hard to make a hire without a really strong résumé and . . . yeah, probably some experience. And a . . . culture fit. Not that they wouldn't fit culturally . . ." Her voice trailed off as it seemed that she was considering for the first time that hiring people who could navigate Black Twitter meant hiring young Black people. She was uncomfortable with the implication of what she was saying, or rather trying very hard not to say that she didn't know if her workplace could appreciate—or even tolerate—the Black youth culture it was asking for, outside of their marketing value.

Ultimately, I advised her to consider hiring people as consultants rather than bringing them in full-time. This obviously isn't the real answer. The real answer is that organizations like that need real culture change so that they hire and retain people of color. They need to have tough conversations about why their hiring practices and the resulting workplace feels so unwelcoming to staff of color. They need to listen to the answers they get, however hard they may be to hear, and commit to making real change. And until they are able to do that, they don't deserve the benefit of those same employees' cultural fluency for their own financial gain. But I didn't say all that. At least this way, maybe some of those creators could get a consultant gig. I could play it Cool.

But that was such a telling conversation for me. The people who will be culturally fluent in the language she was trying to employ would likely have had a nightmarish experience at that company. The way the same companies that fear Black culture want to devour it is truly something for a horror movie. People's authenticity isn't just for someone else's consumption. It defines how people move through the world. There is something especially cruel about

THE REAL ONES

asking for a trait in order to perform a professional service, and then deeming that same trait unprofessional.

And to put a finer point on it, it's not Black culture they fear. It's cultural Blackness. Black culture can be adopted—and has been adopted—by non-Black people. It's hard to define the difference; it's easier to draw the distinction. If Black culture is urban, cultural Blackness is ghetto. If Black culture is soft life, cultural Blackness is gold diggers. If Black culture is Gen Z slang, cultural Blackness is Ebonics. Put plainly, Black culture is box braids, acrylic nails, and lashes. Cultural Blackness is any of those things on Black women.

Another challenge arises for people with underrepresented identities being authentic at work: when they are called upon to speak on behalf of an entire community. Often, when employers encourage people to bring their authenticity to work, it's because of a belief that their authenticity will help the employer tap into some community—whether as potential clients, consumers, hires, or partners—they currently cannot reach. However, no community is a monolith; and simply because people with underrepresented identities are hired and encouraged to bring their authentic experiences to work doesn't mean they will have the cheat code for how to reach everyone else in their community. And when they fail to meet the employer's unexpressed expectation, they can sometimes be penalized for it.

I have had several roles where I have often been confronted with the expectation that I can single-handedly increase the diversity of hiring by my presence and network. This is an issue I have discussed extensively with other women of color. There is often an assumption that our hiring will automatically lead to more diversity in new hires, and that we will be able to cultivate and retain this diverse team where other leaders in the same organization have failed. Many of us have had our hiring decisions questioned by white leaders who, despite the lack of diversity on their own teams, expect that every new hire we make will be a person of color. This is an unrealistic expectation for a number of reasons. First, a single leader can't transform culture, and if a workplace has had difficulty recruiting people with underrepresented identities, one new hire will not immediately make those people comfortable in that work environment. Further, we face the same barriers to recruiting and retaining a diverse workforce that other leaders at the organization face. If there are a number of hiring preferences and requirements that limit the pool of applicants, we won't have any more success than anyone else in diversifying that pool. But that failure is attributed more personally to us. Finally, the expectation that, as people of color, we will be able to bring in other people of color ignores the fact that our network may contain people with other underrepresented identities that will also contribute to the diversity of the workforce but are being overlooked.

Finally, when underrepresented people are encouraged to bring their authentic selves to work, it is often assumed there will be a number of additional tasks—wholly unrelated to the reason they were hired—that they will be asked to perform. This dynamic was explored in a Refinery29 article aptly titled "Be Your Authentic Self at Work—But Only If You're White":

> *Emma Bracy, 31, a media professional, believes that many workplaces become toxic and inhospitable to people of color because there is a near-constant expectation of keeping white colleagues and employers feeling comfortable. "I'm generally expected to present as articulate, sometimes I'm expected to be the 'cool' one, the one who can dance and knows about hip hop and has an opinion on why blackface isn't cool. . . . Sometimes I'm expected to validate my non-Black colleague's political opinions [and] make them feel like they're being*

THE REAL ONES

'good' allies. But I'm almost always 'supposed' to be docile. To be safe."

The emotional labor of having to show up as a certain kind of Black person for the education and comfort of coworkers is not the labor Bracy was hired to do and isn't what she is being compensated for. This dynamic plays out often—people are "voluntold" to help with affinity groups and celebrations, to mentor new hires from their communities, to speak at company-wide trainings. While these tasks are all incredibly valuable, it's up to the employer to make sure that value is felt by the employee. Tasks like these should be compensated or weighted into a yearly evaluation that recognizes the additional labor and commitment it takes to do them. Otherwise, it's one more reason people with underrepresented identities may want to leave their whole selves back at home.

Thankfully when I was working at a law firm in my twenties, authenticity hadn't yet gone corporate. No one disingenuously implored us to bring our full selves to an office that clearly didn't have space for us. We were all quite comfortable being inauthentic and employed, which is fortunate because I honestly can't imagine a metric that can credibly call a corporate law firm an authentic environment.

My first interaction with authenticity in a professional setting came when I was on the management side. I was meeting with a white management coach who was working with all the supervisors of the organization on something called "authentic conflict resolution." It was all about encouraging team members to give direct feedback, be honest about impact, and handle conflict one-on-one instead of triangulating or escalating. It was a good idea that was going to be incredibly difficult to implement at the organization for a number of reasons, notably because of the impact these changes would have on some of the team members of color.

COME AS YOU AREN'T

At that point, I had heard from several staff members that when they were direct about issues, they were read as aggressive and the culture of the organization encouraged a more passive-aggressive confrontation style.

I raised the concern with the management coach that staff of color were worried that they were going to be perceived more harshly with this conflict-resolution style, and I told her I had given advice on how to raise issues more gently that still didn't involve escalating to supervisors or talking to other peers instead of the source of the conflict.

"No," she chastised me. "That's not right. They need to bring the issue up transparently with the person; otherwise, it's not authentic conflict resolution."

"But I honestly agree with them," I had insisted. "I'm concerned that there will be a steeper penalty for staff of color if they don't couch their critiques."

"But just by thinking about that, you're being less authentic. Authenticity isn't about how anyone else sees you," she told me shortly.

"I don't think you're giving enough credit to the fact that this *is* a difference for people of color in the workplace. Our bluntness is often seen differently, so we need to be thoughtful."

The phone was quiet before she took a deep breath. "It feels like you're saying I'm encouraging you to do something racist—or I'm being racially insensitive—and that isn't fair."

"No," I explained with all the inauthenticity I could muster. "I didn't mean that." I mumbled something cool and trailed off. After that, I started blaming my schedule for the fact that I couldn't meet with her anymore. I guess I never did master authentic conflict resolution, but I felt resolved enough.

Authenticity at work feels like one of those perks that seems like a good idea until you examine it more closely. Like when you find out a job offers free meals throughout the day. At first you're excited about your chicken panini, until you realize that this "perk" only exists because they expect you to eat every meal at your desk.

Perhaps a better comparison is the idea of unlimited paid time off (PTO). In theory, it means you can take off as much time as you want. But in practice, it becomes much more fraught to schedule time off. This is because *obviously* unlimited PTO isn't really unlimited. Imagine the reaction if a new employee took a three week vacation during the first week on a job. Or if during the busiest time of a quarter, an employee took time off and stuck their team members with a heavier-than-usual workload. Or after getting a less-than-stellar performance review, an employee took a vacation and posted beach photos on Instagram. Despite the fact that none of these violate the policy, they all will likely contribute to how these employees are perceived at work. And those perceptions will likely lead to their work being viewed with a more critical eye and their commitment to the job being questioned.

It's these unspoken rules that make it difficult to navigate a policy like this. The expectation is that the employee will be the one to recognize this fact, despite a policy to the contrary, then anticipate when would be a good time to take off, what would be considered reasonable, and then read the often unspoken expectations of their supervisor in how to facilitate taking that time off. It creates an incredible amount of psychological stress and places it all on the employee to read between the lines of what is *really* being communicated by an unlimited PTO policy. A much more humane system would be to acknowledge that PTO is limited, but employees are entitled to take all that they are given without having to worry if they are overstepping.

Authenticity operates much the same way. Obviously, there are limits to how authentic anyone can be at work, but a policy to bring your whole self to work places the onus for figuring out those limits on employees, who are not best equipped to do this. For people with underrepresented identities who know that being truly authentic means showing up without a Halloween costume to the costume contest, they are already anticipating the ways they will need to adjust their authenticity in order to fit into a workplace. The pretense that they are failing to take advantage of an authentic workplace is ignoring the real societal structures that disincentivize people embracing their authentic selves at work.

Instead, we should dispense with the pretense that people should bring their whole authentic selves to work, which simply creates psychological stress on employees to figure out how to be sufficiently but not overly authentic. They need to decode the unwritten rules so they will neither get penalized for failing to be real or for getting too real.

When we complicate authenticity and stop imagining it as an unmitigated good in every scenario, I think we'll find it is both being over- and underused. And there are a number of ways to address that. First, we have to be honest about when authenticity is a useful or relevant component in different areas of life.

Authenticity at work, for example, may be a nice-sounding idea, but the reality of the concept falls apart pretty quickly. Of course colleagues should be transparent and honest in dealings with each other, but it's actually dangerous to encourage a type of unapologetic authenticity that could result in blunt honesty without attention to tact or care in the workplace. Moreover, bias *does* make a difference in how things are perceived among colleagues. It's unfair and dishonest to call for authenticity for everyone, while at the same time people with underrepresented identities are burdened with having to figure out when their authenticity will be held against them.

Additionally, we have to dispel the myth that whether or not someone is perceived as authentic at work is solely a function of whether they are *being* authentic. When a manager ignores the biases that can result in someone seeming inauthentic, the manager is placing the responsibility solely on the individual and that's unfair and ineffective. If we first encourage people to be authentic at work, and then allow this to reflect badly on them if they are not being read as authentic, this furthers the risk that people with underrepresented identities will be punished because others do not recognize their authenticity.

Instead, employers should focus their energy on making workplaces psychologically safe for whatever level of authenticity people *choose* to bring to work. As counterintuitive as it may seem, this will require more specific policies and clearer, stated boundaries. The idea that no expectations allows for the highest degree of safety because it's leaving it up to the employee's discretion is actually incorrect. This is because there really is no such thing as no expectations; unlimited PTO doesn't mean *unlimited*. Whole authentic self doesn't mean *whole*. It means that the onus is on the employee to crack the code and understand the understood but unspoken expectations. And when the employee has an underrepresented identity, chances are the unspoken code has been inaccessible. Employers should simply eliminate the guesswork and not leave things up to interpretation.

If people choose to bring their authenticity to bear in the workplace, value it. Call it out. Adjust their workloads if they are taking on a mentoring project. Pay them more if they are the only bilingual person on a project that requires their language skills. Consider standards of professionalism and whether they are inadvertently punishing the authenticity that you want to encourage. Create an environment where authenticity is always welcome, but let people ultimately decide when to celebrate Bring-Your-Authentic-Self-to-Work Day.

Conclusion

WHO I THINK I AM

One of the central ideas I explore in this book came from the worst date I'd ever been on. (And that's saying something. I've been on some bad dates.) But this time, I went on a date with a white man who had a Confederate flag tattoo. And he felt the need to tell me. On our first and only date. Over coffee.

His confession came after I blithely commented on another tattoo he had; this one was visible. And he said he had one other. He said it with a sheepish and guilty pause that alerted me it was going to be offensive.

In my head, I imagined imagery that would be offensive to other communities. I would have had no qualms about getting up and walking out if he confessed to having some of the possibilities my mind immediately conjured based on his reaction. He knew it was offensive, but he was still telling me. Surely, he couldn't be about to disclose a tattoo that would be a direct insult to me. I recounted the date in the *Salon* essay:

> *"I have a tattoo of a Confederate flag," my date tells me. I look up from my coffee in disbelief.*

THE REAL ONES

In his defense, he says it sheepishly, like he's confessing something he knows he should be ashamed of.

In my defense, he says it at all like he's asking for an absolution I should never grant.

I stutter, and he rushes on, assuring me he was from Texas and got it out of Texan pride, not any other association. I don't ask why he didn't just get a Texas flag tattoo.

He promises me that he has only used the "n-word" once in his life, when he was young, and his mother slapped him so hard he never used it again. I don't ask if the fear of being slapped is still the only reason he doesn't use it.

He prefers dating black women; he says this like it's a compliment. I don't ask if they prefer dating him, or if when they see his tattoo under his shirt they recoil.

He looks at me and levies the accusation that I fear most in moments like this: "I feel like you're treating me like I'm racist."

When he said that, like so many times I'd done before, I immediately switched gears. I trained my face to remove all signs of the bafflement it showed. I smiled. I got self-deprecating. I made a joke. I talked about a show we both loved—*Community*. That's funny to me now. I wonder if he watched the MeowMeowBeenz episode.

That moment stayed with me not because it was unique but because it wasn't. At that point in my life, that was usually how I responded to someone accusing me of calling them racist after they had said something racist. But I had maybe never been so conscious of how quickly the Cool Black Girl could work. I immediately stopped thinking of my own deep discomfort and tried to respond to his. And I was so effective at it that he texted me the next morning with an invitation to hang out again. It wasn't until I explained to him how chilling it would be for me to see a Confederate flag etched onto the skin of someone I was dating that it occurred to him that I just might not be interested.

He was offended and fired back a missive that he couldn't believe I was judging him for something he did twenty years ago. His expectation of my interest and his feeling that I was somehow being unfair made me even angrier that I had been so quick to prioritize his comfort over mine, and it got me thinking about why.

My prioritizing his comfort was a learned behavior, and it was, in fact, one of my very first. And there has been something simultaneously distressing and validating in realizing I wasn't alone. Many of us learned how to prioritize the comfort of the people with that dominant gaze—those stares that were always watching us. To fix it, we first need to acknowledge it. This means people within the dominant groups have to acknowledge the ways they have derived a social benefit from the social inauthenticity that we were forced to embrace. This does not require an admission of active racism, sexism, homophobia, transphobia, ableism, or anything else. It's not about blaming or shaming anyone. Rather it is about making labor seen that has largely been made invisible. We need a recognition that engaging in social inauthenticity is work. Some enjoy a comfort in not having their preconceived ideas challenged. Some people are able to engage in gatekeeping around the ways that others can show up authentically. These comforts have come with a cost. And that cost was paid entirely by people with underrepresented identities.

Next we have to recognize that, despite that social benefit, this kind of social inauthenticity actually hurts everyone. We have all lost something from the ways that minorities have been forced into boxes and robbed of the freedom of exploring our self-reflective authenticity—our true authenticity. Our politics would be better and more worthy of us if our candidates were being measured by a standard that meaningfully told us who they would be as leaders.

THE REAL ONES

Our culture and our art would be richer with an understanding of authenticity that allowed deep and complex stories to be told by all creators and allowed them the freedom to expand their storytelling. Our friendships would be deeper and more honest. Dismantling the pressures around pursuing a flawed concept of authenticity would allow us to more successfully pursue equality and inclusion and belonging.

Our authenticity is valuable enough that it produces a material benefit to everyone around us. Our path forward cannot focus on demanding authenticity from anyone. Instead, our takeaway must be that minorities have the right to demand—and we as a society have the responsibility to respond—that our culture becomes safe and supportive before anyone offers up their authenticity. It is, after all, a collective benefit. Nurturing it should be shared and ongoing work. And that also means that when it doesn't feel safe enough, we will not bestow our authenticity upon anyone who doesn't deserve it.

That has been a powerful revelation for me. Authenticity is expensive. Sometimes prohibitively so. And if I choose not to spend it where I don't think I'll get my money's worth, that isn't a failure. It's a calculus. And far from not being ashamed, I can be proud of that. Authenticity may not be free. But I am.

It honestly never used to bother me how often I would lie about race. I actually thought it was a kindness. These awkward interactions came up for me constantly, and if I forced a conversation every time, it would get tiresome and counterproductive. I was fine taking on the awkwardness and discomfort to avoid having a Very Special Episode on a weekly basis. It wasn't until authenticity became a buzzword that seeped into every aspect of life—work, health and wellness spaces, pop culture, literature—that I started feeling weird about the fact that I avoided having authentic conversations about race and steered clear of giving honest reactions that aligned with my values. I was actively avoiding authenticity in favor of comfort in my relationships. But because I felt forced into this response, it seemed deeply unfair that the failure of authenticity was mine alone to bear. Sure, I was lying, but we were all benefiting. They were noble lies. Freedom fibs.

I have since given more thought to authenticity, and to why it has so deeply troubled me for so long, and how I can choose a new framework to make it work for my life. I have spent a lot of time disappointed in myself for being so comfortable with inauthenticity. At points in my life, I have let it create distance between myself and friends instead of having a hard conversation. I have let it stop me from better understanding myself because I let someone else be the arbiter of what authenticity can mean for me. I have failed to let people get close to me. I have shrunk from vulnerability. I have failed to pursue opportunities. I almost didn't write this book. I have let my comfort with inauthenticity cost me so much, and, even as I write this, I realize I'm still blaming myself for it. Punishing myself for not embracing authenticity sooner is like being mad I have to carry an umbrella on a nice day because the weather report was wrong. I had every reason to believe that my actions kept me safe, and finding out now that was untrue doesn't retroactively obviate the fact that I acted on the best information I had at the time.

Our cultural awakening around authenticity coincided with my professional move into social justice movement work. There, authenticity wasn't just prized, it was almost fetishized. And there was a weird, special priority that my authenticity as a Black woman carried. Because of the micropolitics of movement spaces being a direct response to broader power structures, for the first time, white people didn't seem to just tolerate my authenticity, they craved it. But my authenticity didn't seem authentic enough for them. They expected a sure-footed racial analysis from someone

THE REAL ONES

who embarrassingly still could go on a date with a man with a Confederate flag tattoo and make him think I was still interested. We were in the thick of callout culture, and they expected me to lead a charge, when my default was to forgive before an apology had even been uttered. I saw it in their faces. The disappointment. So I did what I did best. I lied about race. I created the Authentic Black Queen and was able to, once again, make white people feel comfortable.

There are times where I am at a loss as to how to handle a situation that calls for a set of skills I don't naturally possess. And in those times, I could make a compelling case to let the Cool Black Girl *or* the Authentic Black Queen handle it.

Passive-aggressive colleagues. Do I smooth out the tensions with blithe friendliness, pretending not to notice the sweetly combative tone? Or point out that this kind of behavior is white supremacy culture at its finest and the progressive politics she espouses don't mean anything if this is the way she treats actual Black women she works with, not just the ones she retweets on Twitter to #signalboost?

An offensive comment on a first date. Do I make a joke to get through drinks and politely decline a second outing? Or leave in the middle and tell him exactly why? Which raises another real concern about physical safety: Will my walking out anger him enough that he'll get violent with me? Authenticity can be dangerous on a date with a stranger.

In these moments, I imagine the Authentic Black Queen and the Cool Black Girl arguing for the right to run point on the interaction, each making the case for her respective side. I've done this often enough that I have given them personalities and an adversarial but begrudgingly loving relationship. They are the angel and demon on my shoulder, handing the halo and horns back and forth depending on the situation. I like to check in with them on the big moments, though I've found myself less comfortable through the years letting either of them take the wheel, and instead sanding each of their reactions down to something approaching what feels like my own voice.

Engaging in that thought experiment was how I first started to understand what I would eventually call self-reflective authenticity.

The pursuit for authenticity felt oppressive to me because of society's refusal to acknowledge that authenticity hasn't always been safe or encouraged for all of us. And that reality made the call for greater authenticity seem painfully out of touch and irrelevant. However, because authenticity is presented without nuance as always being good, I felt disconnected from that cultural obsession. I couldn't see my inauthenticity as a form of repression that I needed to shed, a lack of empowerment that was stopping me from embodying my true self and living my best life.

Freed from an essentialist understanding of authenticity, I have actually found myself fascinated with it as a concept. My aversion was always based on the fact that it just didn't seem relevant to me. Admitting that I wasn't interested in living an authentic life made me feel ashamed. So I avoided the issue. But since I stopped avoiding it, I haven't been able to stop thinking about it.

Because so much of what we read and understand assumes we are trying to uncover a "true self," I want to offer some guidance on how to explore self-reflective authenticity. By its nature, this is not something I believe should be overly prescribed. Instead, people should feel empowered to create their own journeys and inquiries and share what has worked—and hasn't worked—for them. In that spirit, I think it's helpful for me to share what has worked for me and where I have placed the guideposts as I think about self-reflective authenticity.

First, I think it's critical that we rightsize our individual versus collective relationship with authenticity. For too long, we have

THE REAL ONES

treated authenticity like it is an individual pursuit but one we can collectively comment on and assess.

In actuality, authenticity is a personal goal and a cultural good. We as a collective are better when people are able to live authentic lives, but we can't contribute to that process for anyone but ourselves. I like to think of the pursuit of authenticity as a team sport, but it's a team sport like baseball, not like basketball.

In basketball, imagine you're our shooting guard, and I'm our point guard. If I notice your shot is off, I'm going to take more shots than I normally would. I'm going to try to step in for you and make up for what you are unable to do on the court. In baseball, imagine you're our pitcher, and I play third base. If I notice your arm is off, I can't come pitch a few innings for you. But what I can do is assume everyone will get a hit off you, but I will make sure they won't get past third base. It's still a collective goal, but the way I contribute to the collective is to focus on my role, not yours.

I can work on my own self-reflective authenticity journey. The way I can contribute to yours is to create the conditions in order for you to feel fully comfortable pursuing your own authenticity. I can't judge your authenticity, and I can't define it. But I can create space for you to do those things yourself.

There are conditions we can create in our lives and personal relationships that make it easier for people to explore and embrace their own self-reflective authenticity. First, it is critically important that we allow ourselves, and others, the freedom to change. One of the most alienating things about essentialist authenticity is how permanent it seems. Once you declare something your "true self," it is treated as a betrayal or as a lie to change it. This makes exploration difficult because it seems far too easy to become stuck in an identity that doesn't actually fit. Self-reflective authenticity necessitates revisiting the choices we make about who we are and seeing if we would make them again.

Next, self-reflective authenticity requires inventory but doesn't compel an answer. In other words, if you are trying to understand why you want something that you are working toward, it is important that you interrogate the conditions that led you to want it: when you started wanting it, if you were conscious of ever not wanting it, if there are perceptions of you that you believe will be changed if you get it. There was a point in my life when taking an inventory like that would have really intimidated me. This is because conversations like this around authenticity were usually aimed at determining whether a desire was authentic or not.

This is easier to illustrate with a fictitious example. Let's imagine I have a desire to go back to school and get a PhD (it doesn't get more fictitious than this) and I want to understand why I have that desire. First, to be clear, the question isn't whether this is an authentic desire or not. That's not a useful framework for self-reflective authenticity. Rather, we will focus on understanding the desire, not assessing whether it reflects a "true self" or not. I will ask myself questions that get to the core of where this desire came from:

- When did I start wanting a PhD? When I was in college, I heard a professor called "doctor" and saw him treated with respect.

- Do I remember a time before I wanted this? This goal wasn't on my radar until I met this professor.

- Do I think there are people whose perceptions of me will change if I get this? Yes, in the same way I saw that professor get more respect, I imagine I will get more respect.

Hearing this laid out plainly, I can now understand where this desire comes from and situate it next to my other desires. To be clear, if I'm being faced with two options—go to grad school or

THE REAL ONES

take a dream job—the next step will likely need to be to decide whether, upon self-reflection, I want to keep this desire or let it go. But if there is no urgency attached, I can simply engage in this inquiry as a way of understanding this desire without making a further decision about whether I should pursue it or not.

This is important. Engaging in this inquiry does not require you to make an ultimate decision. The goal is to understand where the desire comes from and your relationship to it. That is valuable in and of itself.

When we are asked for our authenticity, it is a huge demand for vulnerability. So, if we aren't quick to give it, that should be understandable. And instead of endless think pieces on how we should learn to embrace that kind of radical vulnerability, the conversation should be focused instead on whether those demanding it of us have earned that. I want people to give real thought to why we may not in any given situation show up authentically. And, if ultimately, we as a society value authenticity, we need to focus on fixing the external factors that complicate our relationship with authenticity rather than treating it as a wholly internal struggle that must be individually overcome.

The Cool Black Girl made me Superman to my friend at happy hour. The Authentic Black Queen made me Wonder Woman to my movement colleague. But in truth, maybe I'm Mystique.

Mystique is an interesting choice for a superhero alter ego because technically she's as much villain as hero. She was an antihero before that was the model for every single character the way it is today. But as far as super alter egos, she's a solid option. She was no sidekick or love interest. She was one of the most feared mutants in X-Men mythology. She also resisted stereotypical female archetypes and was both notoriously ruthless and incredibly loyal, resulting in a complexity that allowed her to be one of the most complicated characters in the stories.

WHO I THINK I AM

She was complex: canonically queer, blue, powerful, loving, deadly. She was also kind of a liar.

Mystique was a shape-shifter who was able to perfectly impersonate anyone, allowing her to move about seamlessly without ever being noticed. She could figure out exactly who she had to be at any given time. She may have been onto something.

In the 2003 film *X2: X-Men United*, Mystique is played by Rebecca Romijn, and now that she is slated to reprise that role, it's a perfect time to revisit her characterization. Brilliant and blue, this is probably my favorite iteration of the character, in part because of one line. At one point, another character, Nightcrawler, who is also blue and easily identifiable as a mutant to anyone who sees him, asks her why, if she can be anyone, she chooses to look like herself so much of the time. He wistfully notes she could always be in disguise and just look like everyone else. Her response always kills me: "Because we shouldn't have to."

As an aside, I met Rebecca Romijn at an event once and after some wine it became *very* important to me that she know just how much this line meant to me. And how much I loved it. And the movie. And her. And her portrayal of Mystique. And . . . the color blue, I think? She was an unbelievably good sport.

Defending Mystique's version of authenticity is why I wrote this book.

I wanted to argue for an understanding of a pursuit of authenticity that still allows you to shape-shift even though you'd rather not. One that recognizes that, in a world not safe for mutants, being willing to be who you have to be to survive doesn't undermine the idea that you can still be unapologetic and self-loving. We can be complicated. We can also kind of be liars.

Authenticity is a currency that isn't accepted everywhere and choosing not to spend it because of how it may be received does not transform your entire bank account to counterfeit money. We can acknowledge in moments when we don't feel safe to be our authentic selves that it is not a crisis of confidence but a response to a situation that was often not designed to make us feel safe to do so. And we can rightly focus our efforts on alleviating the external pressures that make it hard to be all that we are.

Authenticity isn't an identity. It's not like you are either authentic or you're not. It's also not something you believe in. It's something you engage in. It is methodology, not ideology. And like any methodology, all that can be provided is the equation. We get to plug in our values.

Sometimes my authenticity calls for me to lie. Sometimes it calls for me to burn things down. It almost always calls for me to extend a little more grace (*please, let it almost always call for me to extend a little more grace*). Sometimes my authenticity isn't an outcome at all.

I think that's it. For me, authenticity isn't the answer to the question *who am I*, but rather it's an open question about why, for some of us, there is a socially necessary overlap between *who I am* and *who I have to be*. That feels a little like cheating, keeping the central question unanswered, but I guess that's fair. This is a book being written by a liar, after all. Or at least kind of a liar. But I know I'm happier when I feel less averse to the idea of authenticity, even if I don't think it's a useful tool in a given situation. Even if I want to change almost everything about how we collectively talk about it. Even if I don't want to use it, I don't want to avoid it anymore. Maybe that's my version of growth. Or maybe that's just me.

ACKNOWLEDGMENTS

To Mom and Dad: Look what you did. The solace I take that you aren't here to read this is that you don't have to be for me to know you heard every word. I love you both forever. I'll miss you both forever. The *entire* day. Your magnum opus.

To Imani and Derah: Thank you for being my sisters, my first phone call, my constants, my best friends.

To Crispin and Cuomo: the furriest and best writing partners a girl could ask for.

To Cindy Uh and the entire team at CAA: Thank you. Cindy, thank you so much for believing in this book every single step of the way, including in the moments I thought it should just be an op-ed or possibly a long email. I would never have finished this without you.

To Emi Ikkanda and the entire team at Penguin Random House: Thank you. Emi, you have made this book and this experience so much better than I could imagine.

Thank you to a number of amazing colleagues who helped me in so many ways while I was writing this book, including Afua Atta-Mensah, Laura Brounstein, Rebecca Cokley, Rachana Desai

ACKNOWLEDGMENTS

Martin, Ruth McFarlane, Nancy Northup, Gautam Raghavan, Dorian Warren, and so, so many others.

To every single friend who saw me through this process, offering love, faith, excitement, and forgiveness when I had to cancel plans, thank you. Truly. The fact that there is not enough space to thank everyone who has supported me in writing this book is the luck of my life.

An extra special thanks to *my* people. The ones who heard portions of this book as a text message or voice memos and responded with support, help, love, encouragement, reality checks, a place to write (thank you and love you always and forever, Julian), and laughter; especially Ashland, Danielle, Jacob, Jamie, Jenny (both of you!), Joe, Jorge, Mary Jo, Mili, MJ, Rachel, Roger, and TyrOne.

To Secretary Castro, Senator Warren, Congressman Castro, and everyone who lent me parts of your story to help tell this one.

To all the writers I read when I wondered if I could write a book, thank you for being so good and such an inspiration.

To every editor who ever published my work, encouraged my work, and made me feel like I could do this. Thank you forever.

And to every person who asked me what this book is about and when I said "authenticity," their eyes glazed over, but when I said more, those same eyes lit up. I hope you feel seen, loved, and like you can tell your own story now. The real one.

NOTES

Chapter 1: The Observation Effect

10. **are underdiagnosed for OCD:** Monnica T. Williams, "The OCD-Racism Connection and Its Impact on People of Color," *Psychology Today*, September 13, 2020, https://www.psychologytoday.com/us/blog/culturally-speaking/202009/the-ocd-racism-connection-and-impact-people-color.

Chapter 2: Unreal

24. **I wrote for *Salon*:** Maya Rupert, "Best Essays of 2017: This 'Cool Black Girl' Is Gone," *Salon*, December 23, 2017, https://www.salon.com/2017/12/23/this-cool-black-girl-is-gone-2/.

Chapter 3: The Authenticity Paradox

43. **"the daily practice of letting go":** Brené Brown, *The Gifts of Imperfection: Let Go of Who You Think You're Supposed to Be and Embrace Who You Are* (Hazelden, 2010), 50.
44. **who we "truly are":** Allie Volpe, "Is It Possible to Be Fully Authentic?" *Vox*, August 13, 2014, https://www.vox.com/the-highlight/358203/authenticity-being-real-social-media-tips.
50. **essentialist authenticity and existential authenticity:** Jack Bauer, "Authenticity, Self-Actualizing, and Self-Authorship," in *The Transformative Self*:

NOTES

Personal Growth, Narrative Identity, and the Good Life (Oxford University Press, 2021), https://doi.org/10.1093/oso/9780199970742.003.0016, 494.

50. **Essentialist authenticity requires:** Ibid., 495–96.
50. **Existentialist authenticity requires:** Ibid., 497–98.
54. **"the term for something":** "Word of the Year 2023," Wordplay, Merriam-Webster, https://www.merriam-webster.com/wordplay/word-of-the-year-2023.

Chapter 4: Code-Switched

60. **"debuting a Southern accent":** "Critics Accuse Harris of Using 'Fake' Accent During Atlanta Rally," Fox News, July 31, 2024, https://www.foxnews.com/video/6359683802112.
60. **employed a blaccent when speaking:** Trump War Room (@TrumpWarRoom), X, August 20, 2024, https://x.com/TrumpWarRoom?ref_src=twsrc%5Etfw%7Ctwcamp%5Etweetembed%7Ctwterm%5E1830736381590806994%7Ctwgr%5E56eab8e6b118fe01d2b89f7689f1d0dfb2e6aa5f%7Ctwcon%5Es1_&ref_url=https%3A%2F%2Fnewrepublic.com%2Fpost%2F185545%2Fmaga-attack-kamala-harris-accent.
60. **predominantly Black crowds:** "Breaking: Kamala Harris Unveils a New Accent at the Black Caucus Dinner," End Wokeness (@EndWokeness), X, September 14, 2024, https://x.com/EndWokeness/status/1835124216049357258.
60. **"happened to turn Black":** Eric Bradner and Aaron Pellish, "Donald Trump Falsely Suggests Kamala Harris 'Happened to Turn Black,'" CNN, July 31, 2024, https://www.cnn.com/2024/07/31/politics/donald-trump-kamala-harris-black-nabj/index.html.
61. **Harris was code-switching:** John McWhorter, "Harris Gonna Code Switch," *New York Times*, August 15, 2024, https://www.nytimes.com/2024/08/15/opinion/harris-code-switch.html.
62. **"blatant pandering":** Eric Abbenante (@EricAbbenante), X, August 1, 2024, https://x.com/EricAbbenante/status/1818964905476890708.
62. **this is, therefore, inauthentic:** Ashley Stevens (@The_Acumen), X, September 3, 2024, https://x.com/The_Acumen/status/1831154467519046133.

NOTES

62. **"brothas and sistas":** End Wokeness (@EndWokeness), X, September 14, 2024, https://x.com/EndWokeness/status/1835124216049357258.
62. **"we gon' win":** "Kamala Harris Ridiculed for 'Fake' Southern Accent," @dailymail, https://youtube.com/shorts/NVauEKRNDTg?si=kRYA2qKobsSFLXv_.
63. **"linguistic mirroring":** Janet Barrow, "In Review of Code-Switching, the Linguistic Practice That Both Becomes and Betrays Us," ALTA, https://altalang.com/beyond-words/what-is-code-switching-in-language/.
63. **"the chameleon effect":** Michael Harriot, "Was Kamala Harris Code-Switching or Pandering? We Asked an Expect," The Grio, September 6, 2024, https://thegrio.com/2024/09/06/was-kamala-harris-code-switching-or-pandering-we-asked-an-expert/.
64. **"[I]n order for code-switching to be in effect":** Ibid.
67. **an almost identical experience:** Michelle Obama, *Becoming* (Crown, 2018).
71. **the authentic her is the one they have already seen:** Ashley Stevens (@The_Acumen), X, https://X.com/The_Acumen/status/1831154467519046133.
71. **According to research, white people:** Courtney L. McCluney, "White People Prefer for Black People to Codeswitch at Work," *Forbes*, August 23, 2021, https://www.forbes.com/sites/courtneymccluney/2021/08/23/white-people-prefer-for-black-people-to-codeswitch-at-work/.
71. **"Black rhetorical traditions":** Associated Press, "McCain, Obama and Their Uneven Gifts of Gab," July 24, 2008, NBC News, https://www.nbcnews.com/id/wbna25829795.
71. **"He doesn't sound black":** Ibid.
72. **white people are particularly bad at:** Justin P. Friesen et al., "Perceiving Happiness in an Intergroup Context: The Role of Race and Attention to the Eyes in Differentiating Between True and False Smiles," *Journal of Personality and Social Psychology: Attitudes and Social Cognition* 116, no. 3 (March 2019): 375–95, https://www.apa.org/pubs/journals/releases/psp-pspa000.139.pd.
72. **but they could on white faces:** Ibid.

NOTES

Chapter 7: Black Girl Next Door

128. **the constant knowledge that they are being observed:** Caralena Peterson, "The Effortless Perfection Myth Explores the Pressures and Anxieties Young Women Face," *Teen Vogue*, September 26, 2022, https://www.teenvogue.com/story/effortless-perfection-myth.

128. **"who live with a mental illness":** Deep Shukla, "Why Mental Healthcare Is Less Accessible to Marginalized Communities," Medical News Today, April 20, 2022, https://www.medicalnewstoday.com/articles/why-mental-healthcare-is-less-accessible-to-marginalized-communities#Structural-racism.

129. **"mental toughness":** Ibid.

129. **"pursuing an image versus developing an identity":** Caralena Peterson, "The Effortless Perfection Myth Explores the Pressures and Anxieties Young Women Face," *Teen Vogue*, September 26, 2022, https://www.teenvogue.com/story/effortless-perfection-myth.

Chapter 8: Goldilocks

131. **According to research:** Christopher Ingraham, "Three-Quarters of Whites Don't Have Any Non-White Friends," *Washington Post*, August 25, 2014, https://www.washingtonpost.com/news/wonk/wp/2014/08/25/three-quarters-of-whites-dont-have-any-non-white-friends/.

133. **considerably less money:** Adrian Lee, "Q&A: Cristela Alonzo on the Magic and Diversity of TV," *Maclean's*, November 13, 2015, https://macleans.ca/culture/television/qa-cristela-alonzo-on-the-magic-and-diversity-of-tv/.

133. **"Why are we focusing":** Ibid.

134. **"not all Latino families are like that":** Greg Cwik, "*Cristela* Creator Writes Poignant Letter About Her Show," *Vulture*, April 18, 2015, https://www.vulture.com/2015/04/cristela-creator-writes-poignant-letter.html.

135. **"rep sweats":** Elisabeth Donnelly, "'You Get the Rep Sweats': Why *Fresh Off the Boat* Is So Important to Asian Americans," *Flavorwire*, February 5, 2015, https://www.flavorwire.com/503143/you-get-the-rep-sweats-why-fresh-off-the-boat-matters-to-asian-americans.

NOTES

135. **whether Constance Wu adopting a Taiwanese accent:** Hillary Crosley Coker, "Haters Gonna Hate: An Interview with *Fresh Off the Boat*'s Constance Wu," *Jezebel*, February 20, 2015, https://www.jezebel.com/haters-gonna-hate-an-interview-with-fresh-off-the-boat-1686663249.

135. **perceived by many as authentic:** KaeLyn, "*Fresh Off the Boat* Balances Stereotype and Authenticity in a Very Gay Episode," *Autostraddle*, April 1, 2015, https://www.autostraddle.com/fresh-off-the-boat-balances-stereotype-and-authenticity-in-a-very-gay-episode-284096/.

135. **Tyler Perry has faced:** Sesali Bowen, "Yes, Tyler Perry Is Still Obsessed with Unstable Black Women," *Refinery29*, April 2, 2018, https://www.refinery29.com/en-us/2018/04/195330/acrimony-review-tyler-perry-black-women.

136. **exploiting the pain of Black women:** Cassie da Costa, "Tyler Perry Built a Movie Empire by Selling Out Black Women," *Daily Beast*, January 18, 2020, https://www.thedailybeast.com/how-a-fall-from-grace-and-tyler-perry-movies-punish-black-womens-desires.

136. **at the expense of Black people:** Steve Rose, "Tyler Perry: Creator of a Racial Stereotype or the Greatest Indie Film-maker Ever?" *Guardian*, November 12, 2018, https://www.theguardian.com/film/2018/nov/12/tyler-perry-madea-creator-of-a-racial-stereotype-or-the-greatest-indie-film-maker-ever.

136. **"highbrow negroes":** Lester Fabian Brathwaite, "Tyler Perry Blasts 'Highbrow' Critics of His Movies: 'Get Out of Here with That Bulls—'," *Entertainment Weekly*, July 24, 2024, https://ew.com/tyler-perry-blasts-highbrow-critics-of-his-movies-8683311.

137. **ridicule their own heritage and racial identity:** Sakeina Syed, "On *Velma*, Mindy Kaling, and Whether Brown Girls Can Ever Like Ourselves on TV," *Teen Vogue*, January 23, 2023, https://www.teenvogue.com/story/velma-mindy-kaling-whether-brown-girls-can-ever-like-ourselves-on-tv-op-ed.

137. **especially white male romantic interests:** Izzy Ampil, "The Mindy Kaling Backlash Has Lost All Nuance," *BuzzFeed News*, January 18, 2023, https://www.buzzfeednews.com/article/izzyampil/mindy-kaling-backlash-velma-mindy-project-never-have-i-ever.

139. **shuttered and commitments left unfulfilled:** Winston Cho and Alex

NOTES

Weprin, "DEI Is Disappearing in Hollywood. Was It Ever Really Here?," *The Hollywood Reporter*," March 6, 2025, https://www.hollywoodreporter.com/business/business-news/dei-hollywood-trump-1236155842/.

139. **walk back those commitments:** Gene Maddaus, Brent Lang, and Angelique Jackson, "Hollywood Ditches DEI to Avoid Donald Trump's Wrath," *Variety*, March 4, 2025, https://variety.com/2025/film/news/hollywood-drops-dei-programs-donald-trump-disney-paramount-amazon-1236327202/.

146. **his offer to be rescinded:** Michael Sebastian, "Hasan Minhaj Explains Himself," *Esquire*, September 25, 2024, https://www.esquire.com/entertainment/tv/a62302036/hasan-minhaj-interview-2024/.

Chapter 9: For the Future

148. **senator at twenty-nine years old:** "Vice President Joe Biden," The White House: President Barack Obama, https://obamawhitehouse.archives.gov/realitycheck/node/110.

149. **"When we talk about authenticity":** Gilad Edelman, "Authenticity Just Means Faking It Well," *Atlantic*, April 25, 2019, https://www.theatlantic.com/ideas/archive/2019/04/what-makes-candidate-authentic/587857/.

149. **"'confronts observers'":** Ibid.

150. **While he ramped up media:** Michael M. Grynbaum and Santul Nerkar, "Trump's Media Blitz: Talk Radio, a Video Game Celebrity and Elon Musk," *New York Times*, August 17, 2024, https://www.nytimes.com/2024/08/17/business/media/trump-media-strategy.html.

152. **authenticity in the race:** Tara Golshan, "The 2020 Authenticity Primary," *Vox*, March 25, 2019, https://www.vox.com/2019/3/25/18263768/2020-democrats-presidential-primary-authentic-beto-harris.

153. **"The ability to interact":** Ibid.

159. **struggle with alcohol:** Suzanne Gamboa, "Julián Castro, with a New Memoir, Is Sounding Like a Presidential Candidate," NBC News, October 18, 2018, https://www.nbcnews.com/news/latino/julian-castro-sounding-presidential-candidate-he-opens-new-book-n921616.

NOTES

160. **"brazen":** Sean Sullivan and Vanessa Williams, "Stacey Abrams's Public Push for Veep Slot Complicates Biden's Search," *Washington Post*, May 15, 2020, https://www.washingtonpost.com/politics/stacey-abramss-public-push-for-veep-slot-complicates-bidens-search/2020/05/15/aeda76e0-950c-11ea-82b4-c8db161ff6e5_story.html.

160. **"aggressive":** Edward-Isaac Dovere, "Stacey Abrams's Remarkable Campaign for Vice President," *Atlantic*, April 24, 2020, https://www.theatlantic.com/politics/archive/2020/04/stacey-abrams-biden-vice-president/610441/.

160. **edit before speaking:** Charles M. Blow, "Julián Castro and the Cordial Candidacy, *New York Times*, December 16, 2018, https://www.nytimes.com/2018/12/16/opinion/julian-castro-democrat-2020.html.

164. **"just because they look like me":** Julián Castro, "Julián Castro on the Campaign Trail," *Latino Rebels Radio*, hosted by Julio Ricardo Varela, April 30, 2019, podcast, 23:01, https://www.iheart.com/podcast/270-latino-rebels-radio-28471110/episode/231-julian-castro-on-the-campaign-30907721/.

165. **was called phony:** Michael Grunwald, "Is Cory Booker for Real?" *Politico Magazine*, February 1, 2019, https://www.politico.com/magazine/story/2019/02/01/cory-booker-president-2020-profile-newark-projects-224539/.

166. **capacity to serve another term:** Ron Elving, "Biden, Turning 80, Faces an Age-Old Question: How Old Is Too Old To Be President?" NPR, November 20, 2022, https://www.npr.org/2022/11/20/1137756874/biden-turns-80-birthday-age.

166. **concerns about Biden's age:** Marc Caputo and Natasha Korecki, "It's Not Just Trump Questioning Biden's Age. Democrats Are, Too," *Politico*, June 13, 2019, https://www.politico.com/story/2019/06/13/joe-biden-age-trump-2020-1361782.

167. **"what you just said two minutes ago?":** Suzanne Gamboa, "Julián Castro Accused Joe Biden of 'Forgetting.' Did He Go Too Far?" NBC News, September 13, 2019, https://www.nbcnews.com/news/latino/juli-n-castro-accused-joe-biden-forgetting-did-he-go-n1054061.

167. **taking "a cheap shot":** Christopher Cadelago, "The Two Minutes When Castro Questioned Biden's Memory," *Politico*, September 13, 2019, https://

NOTES

www.politico.com/story/2019/09/13/castro-questioned-bidens-memory-1494495.

167. **He was called "too aggressive":** Tess Bonn, "Young Turks Founder Calls Castro-Biden Exchange a 'Tad Too Aggressive,'" *The Hill*, September 13, 2019, https://thehill.com/hilltv/rising/461272-young-turks-founder-calls-castro-biden-exchange-a-tad-too-aggressive/.

167. **"that type of criticism":** Suzanne Gamboa, "Julián Castro Accused Joe Biden of 'Forgetting.' Did He Go Too Far?" NBC News, September 13, 2019, https://www.nbcnews.com/news/latino/juli-n-castro-accused-joe-biden-forgetting-did-he-go-n1054061.

167–168. **the Democratic party *should* have a primary:** Astead W. Herndon, "The Democrat Saying What Others Won't," *The Run-Up* (*New York Times* podcast), June 15, 2023, https://www.nytimes.com/2023/06/15/podcasts/julian-castro-joe-biden-democrats.html.

Chapter 10: For the Culture

170. **first time during the campaign:** Joshua Jamerson, "Women Have Most of Top Roles in Campaigns for Leading 2020 Democrats," *Wall Street Journal*, May 24, 2019, https://www.wsj.com/articles/women-have-most-of-top-roles-in-campaigns-for-leading-2020-democrats-11558690201.

170. **mainstream political lexicon:** Alex Thompson, "2020 Democrats Are Dramatically Changing the Way They Talk About Race," *Politico*, November 19, 2018, https://www.politico.com/story/2018/11/19/democrats-2020-race-identity-politics-strategy-1000.49.

170. **legacy of white supremacy:** Vann R. Newkirk II, "The Racial Wealth Gap Could Become a 2020 Litmus Test," *Atlantic*, January 16, 2019, https://www.theatlantic.com/politics/archive/2019/01/new-litmus-test-2020-racial-wealth-gap/579823.

170. **hate violence:** P. R. Lockhart, "Amy Klobuchar Releases Plan to Fight Hate Crimes in Wake of El Paso Shooting," *Vox*, August 8, 2019, https://www.vox.com/policy-and-politics/2019/8/8/20791801/amy-klobuchar-hate-crimes-platform-2020-primary.

170. **supported reparations:** P. R. Lockhart, "The 2020 Democratic Primary De-

NOTES

bate Over Reparations, Explained," *Vox*, June 19, 2019, https://www.vox.com/policy-and-politics/2019/3/11/18246741/reparations-democrats-2020-inequality-warren-harris-castro.

172. **meant for us:** Don Terry, "A Delicate Balancing Act for the Black Agenda," *New York Times*, March 19, 2010, https://www.nytimes.com/2010/03/19/us/19cncagenda.html.

172. **primary win in South Carolina:** Neil Conan, host, *Talk of the Nation*, "Barack Obama and the African-American Vote," NPR, January 31, 2008, https://www.npr.org/2008/01/31/18576275/barack-obama-and-the-african-american-vote.

173. **Black voters were more disenchanted:** Audie Cornish, *All Things Considered*, "For Some Black Voters, 2012 Is a Different Story," NPR, September 5, 2012, https://www.npr.org/2012/09/05/160607546/for-some-black-voters-2012-is-a-different-story.

174. **sexism and racism she faced:** Steve Peoples, "Joe Biden Blames Kamala Harris' Loss on Sexism and Racism and Rejects Concerns About His Age," The Associated Press, May 8, 2025, https://apnews.com/article/biden-view-president-trump-abc-interview-kamala-harris-0e7c4aba0b021e40540dcc68872ff0d1.

Chapter 11: Just, Only, Too

190. **"skin color over qualifications":** "Stephen Breyer's Loss to the Supreme Court," *Wall Street Journal*, January 26, 2022, https://www.wsj.com/articles/stephen-breyers-loss-to-the-supreme-court-retirement-11643238845.

190. **"offensive":** Andrew Zhang, "Ted Cruz Calls Biden's Vow to Nominate First Black Woman to U.S. Supreme Court 'Offensive,'" *Texas Tribune*, February 1, 2022, https://www.texastribune.org/2022/02/01/ted-cruz-biden-supreme-court/.

190. **"a quota":** Emily Wagster Pettus, "Wicker: Black Woman Supreme Court Nominee Would Be 'Quota,'" *Mississippi Free Press*, February 1, 2022, https://www.mississippifreepress.org/wicker-black-woman-supreme-court-nominee-would-be-quota/.

190. **several Republicans declaring:** Julia Ingram and Alexander Hunter, "Some

NOTES

Republicans Attack Kamala Harris as 'DEI Hire.' Here's What That Means," CBS News, July 26, 2024, https://www.cbsnews.com/news/republicans-attack-kamala-harris-dei-hire/.

190. **DEI pick:** Tim Burchett (@RepTimBurchett), X, July 22, 2024, https://x.com/RepTimBurchett/status/1815388894722248845.

190. **make them look racist:** Olivia Beavers and Jordain Carney, "House GOP Leaders Urge Members: Stop Making Race Comments About Harris," *Politico*, July, 23, 2024, https://www.politico.com/news/2024/07/23/gop-race-comments-harris-00170735.

191. **all her options would be white men:** Ashley Parker and Dylan Wells, "Why Everyone Assumes Kamala Harris Has to Pick a White Man as VP," *Washington Post*, July 25, 2024, https://www.washingtonpost.com/politics/2024/07/25/harris-white-man-vice-president/.

191. **memes this prompted were hilarious:** Ibid.

Chapter 12: Come As You Aren't

205. **As Mike Robbins:** Henna Inam, "Bring Your Whole Self to Work," *Forbes*, May 10, 2018, https://www.forbes.com/sites/hennainam/2018/05/10/bring-your-whole-self-to-work/.

206–207. **in her TEDxSeattle talk:** Jodi-Ann Burey, "Why You Should Not Bring Your Authentic Self to Work," TEDxSeattle Talk, 2020, 15:41, https://tedxseattle.com/talks/jodi-ann-burey-why-you-should-not-bring-your-authentic-self-to-work/.

207. **defined in most workplaces as whiteness:** Fatema Elbakoury, "The Perils of Professionalism and Diversity," *Odyssey*, June 27, 2016, https://www.theodysseyonline.com/the-perils-of-professionalism.

208. **"Black Twitter is not a place":** Tressie McMillan Cottom, "Black Twitter Is Not a Place. It's a Practice," *New York Times*, May 3, 2022, https://www.nytimes.com/2022/05/03/opinion/the-real-twitter-is-not-for-sale.html?searchResultPosition=3.

211. **"Be Your Authentic Self at Work":** Ludmila Leiva, "Be Your Authentic Self at Work—But Only If You're White," *Refinery29*, August 27, 2018, https://www

NOTES

.refinery29.com/en-us/how-to-be-authentic-self-at-work-people-of-color.

Conclusion: Who I Think I Am

217. **recounted the date in the *Salon* essay:** Maya Rupert, "Best Essays of 2017: This 'Cool Black Girl' Is Gone," *Salon*, December 23, 2017, https://www.salon.com/2017/12/23/this-cool-black-girl-is-gone-2/.

ABOUT THE AUTHOR

MAYA RUPERT is a political strategist and the third Black woman in history to run a presidential campaign. She is the former senior adviser to the president at the Center for Reproductive Rights. She hosts the podcast *When We Win*, an NAACP Image Award nominee. A nationally respected voice on progressive politics and the Democratic party, she has appeared on national television and radio stations, including MSNBC, CNN, and NPR. Her writing has appeared in publications including *The New York Times* and *The Atlantic*. After Rupert received her JD from UC Berkeley, she clerked for the Honorable Eric L. Clay of the Sixth Circuit Court of Appeals. She lives in Washington, DC, with her cats.